Buddha, Socrates, and Us

ALSO BY STEPHEN BATCHELOR

Alone with Others

The Tibet Guide

The Faith to Doubt

The Awakening of the West

Buddhism without Beliefs

Verses from the Center

Living with the Devil

Confession of a Buddhist Atheist

After Buddhism

Secular Buddhism

The Art of Solitude

Buddha, Socrates, and Us

Ethical Living in Uncertain Times

STEPHEN BATCHELOR

Yale UNIVERSITY PRESS

New Haven and London

Published with assistance from the foundation established in memory of Philip Hamilton McMillan of the Class of 1894, Yale College.

Copyright © 2025 by Stephen Batchelor.
All rights reserved.
This book may not be reproduced, in whole or in part, including illustrations, in any form (beyond that copying permitted by Sections 107 and 108 of the U.S. Copyright Law and except by reviewers for the public press), without written permission from the publishers.

Yale University Press books may be purchased in quantity for educational, business, or promotional use. For information, please email sales.press@yale.edu (U.S. office) or sales@yaleup.co.uk (U.K. office).

Set in Minion Pro type by Motto Publishing Services.
Printed in the United States of America.

Library of Congress Control Number: 2024952446
ISBN 978-0-300-27549-0 (hardcover)

A catalogue record for this book is available from the British Library.

Authorized Representative in the EU: Easy Access System Europe, Mustamäe tee 50, 10621 Tallinn, Estonia, gpsr.requests@easproject.com

10 9 8 7 6 5 4 3 2 1

In memory of Kenneth McLeish
(1940–1997)

Life is short, live like your head is on fire.

—GOTAMA

Contents

Prologue: In Search of a Voice 1

Part I: Agency

1. Life as Practice 9
2. The Wisest Man in Greece 21
3. Fraternal Twins 30
4. Diotima's Middle Way 37

Part II: Contingency

5. An Unbearable Silence 47
6. The Socrates Show 57
7. Whose Buddha? Whose Socrates? 64
8. Convenient Fictions 74

Part III: Uncertainty

9. The Quest for Certainty 83
10. The Tragedy of Being Human 95
11. A Religion Is Born 102
12. Nāgasena or Nāgārjuna? 109

Part IV: Creativity

13. Refining Gold 119
14. The Truth of Comedy 126

15. Ataraxia 132
16. A Dialogical Self 140

Part V: Impossible Questions

17. The Foolish and the Wise 153
18. Only Tragedy Can Save the City 163
19. The Great Matter of Birth and Death 172
20. What Is This Thing? 179

Part VI: Starting All Over Again

21. A Cartography of Care 189
22. Silencing Socrates 196
23. A Revaluation of All Values 204
24. For Love of the World 216

Part VII: A Worldly Eightfold Path

25. The Parable of the Snake 227
26. Death by Mortar and Pestle 233
27. Contemplative Life 238
28. Active Life 247

Part VIII: Entering the Stream

29. Lucid Confidence 261
30. An Ethics of Uncertainty 270

Afterword 285

Dramatis Personae 289
Notes 301
Bibliography 315
Acknowledgments 323
Index 327

Buddha, Socrates, and Us

Prologue
In Search of a Voice

You can still stroll through the once bustling agora of Athens, the marketplace where Socrates spent his days bothering people like an insistent gadfly. The street plan is preserved but the buildings now lie in ruins. And if you take the winding upper path from the intact Temple of Hephaestus to the reconstructed Stoa of Attalos, you will suddenly see a life-size, standing bronze statue of Socrates himself set against the backdrop of the Acropolis. As you come closer, another life-sized figure comes into view beside him. Expecting this to be a statue of Plato, I was surprised to find myself face-to-face with Confucius.

Confucius and Socrates: An Encounter is the work of the contemporary Chinese sculptor Wu Weishan, unveiled in 2021 to launch "The Greece-China Year of Culture and Tourism." In a press interview, the artist explained how he saw the two thinkers "talking about the global pandemic, like how human beings can conquer the virus crisis!" He went on to regret the absence of WeChat in antiquity, which would have greatly facilitated their discussions.[1]

In a video address at the unveiling of the work, the Greek prime minister Kyriakos Mitsotakis failed to come up with a suitably inspiring quote from Confucius. He cited instead a saying of the Daoist sage Laozi: "A journey of a thousand miles starts with a single step." He then misquoted Socrates as having declared, "The most valuable acquisition is a steady friend." This is the twenty-seventh chief maxim of the philosopher Epicurus, written a century after Socrates's death.[2]

Yet, as I will argue throughout this book, a more fitting interlocutor for Socrates to discuss the urgent questions of our times would have been Gotama, the Buddha. Unlike Confucius, who died a decade or so before the philosopher was born, Gotama and Socrates were contemporaries. They were active at the same time, during the second half of the fifth century BCE. According to current scholarly dating, Gotama was born in Kapilavatthu in northeast India around 480 and died around 400 BCE.[3] Socrates was born in Athens ten years later, around 470, and died in the year 399 BCE. In both traditions, the two men are said to have died at the suspiciously round-numbered ages of eighty and seventy, respectively. The only date that can be settled with any certainty is that of Socrates's death.

Socrates spent nearly all his life inside the city of Athens, while Gotama wandered far and wide throughout the towns and countryside of northeast India. Separated by the vast Persian Empire, which extended from the edges of Europe to modern Pakistan, and then another seven hundred miles across the Gangetic plains as far as present-day Nepal, they would have had no knowledge of each other's existence. Yet both addressed in strikingly similar ways the core questions of how to lead a good, just, and dignified life in an unstable world.

Gotama and Socrates alike insisted on the primacy of ethics. Moved by compassion, they encouraged others to engage in critical self-evaluation rather than simply following the traditional beliefs and cultural habits of their forefathers.

They sought to awaken people from their existential slumber, to help them think for themselves and become autonomous moral agents. Neither of them wrote anything. All we know of what they did and said comes down to us from their followers—Plato and Xenophon, in the case of Socrates, and the monastic compilers of the early Buddhist canon, in the case of Gotama.

Gotama and Socrates lived during turbulent, violent, and deeply uncertain times. In China, India, Palestine, and Greece alike philosophers and religious teachers emerged during this period to explore viable ways of responding to the novel situations in which people found themselves. The philosopher Karl Jaspers coined the term "axial age" to describe this fervent and creative moment in human history.[4] Just as Gotama imagined the rebuilding of an ancient city governed by the principles of the dharma, so Plato's Socrates dreamed of a republic ruled by an enlightened elite who, in many ways, resembled an order of Buddhist monastics.

Our current age of anxiety is no longer confined to specific cities, regions, or cultures but extends across the entire surface of the earth. Perhaps we have already entered a second axial age. We might still be inspired by the great figures of European and Asian antiquity, but to respond to the needs of a highly diverse global community may require the courage to reexamine our ancestral beliefs in order to think outside the confines of our comfort zones. Above all, I believe, the challenges we face require the imagination to encompass the world in a single embrace, release the grip of oppositional thinking, and come to rest in the creative uncertainty needed to ask ourselves the deepest questions afresh.

Through exploring the impact of Socrates, Gotama, and their followers, I seek to provide a Socratic portrait of Gotama and a Buddhist portrait of Socrates, as well as a Greek perspective on Buddhism and a Buddhist perspective on Greek philosophical practice. In the chapters that follow I will offer a reading of the surviving texts of the philosophers and playwrights of Greek antiquity informed by my Buddhist education and orientation. Bouncing these different personalities and ideas off each other will hopefully render them all more three-dimensional and ambiguous, revealing facets of them that might otherwise remain hidden.

Born, raised, and schooled in Britain, I internalized a worldview whose roots lay in ancient Greece and Rome. My initial impressions of Buddhism and the Buddha were inevitably configured by the historical perspectives of my culture. I struggled to convince myself of traditional Buddhist beliefs, such as reincarnation, heavens and hells, and the workings of karma. I came to realize that it would be just as futile to force Buddhism into the categories of scientific rationalism as to interpret Western philosophy solely through the lens of Buddhist ideas. I want to make Buddhist and Greek thought more than merely compatible. I am seeking a new language, a synthesis that would transcend the binary of East/West, Greek/Buddhist altogether. Yet to find that voice, I first have to come to terms with the Greek and the Buddhist inside me.

This is the question that lies at the heart of my book: how can a life of rigorous ethical commitment be compatible with a perspective founded on the radically contingent, impermanent, and uncertain nature of human experience? Such is the challenge presented to humankind by Socrates and Gotama alike. This is where Gotama's refusal to address metaphysical questions encounters Socrates's admission that he knows nothing. Both men advocated leading a good life governed by reason and evidence, yet neither appeared to posit an ultimate reality in which the "good" can be ontologically secured. While keenly aware of the fickle and conflicted nature of the human mind, Gotama and Socrates sought to inspire and awaken in their followers a resolve to flourish as autonomous agents in a tragicomic and unreliable world.

An ethics founded on uncertainty is, by definition, something you cannot be certain about. Rather than a closed system of ideas and values, I treat it as an ongoing, open-ended dialogue with oneself and others, thereby acknowledging not only our uncertainty about the world we live in but the uncertainty of how to respond appropriately to the suffering and needs of that world. Being a work-in-progress, such an ethical life has no absolutes to rely upon and no final authority, divine or otherwise, to appeal to. It entails both humility and courage, risk and resolve, doubt and confidence. All I can do here is to offer a series of pointers that might help us articulate how such an ethics might be practiced and further refined.

Above all, I want to highlight Gotama's and Socrates's continuing ability to speak to the condition of the world in which we live today. Plato's dialogues, the plays of Aristophanes and Euripides, and the discourses of the Pali Canon alike return us to the distant world of the fifth century BCE only to discover that human beings faced many of the same dilemmas and crises that confront us now. Violence, tyranny, and injustice threatened peace, democracy, and justice then just as they do in the twenty-first century. And as we confront the long-term consequences of human-created climate change, how can we create communities sufficiently resilient not only to survive but to survive with their core values intact?

I have come to understand Gotama's dharma as primarily an ethical practice that can help us engage with the personal and collective suffering of our world and, in so doing, make us more fully rounded human beings. Throughout its history Buddhism has creatively adapted itself to changing circumstances through its interactions with cultures as diverse as those of India, China, Tibet, and Japan. In encountering Western civilization, it faces another set of challenges, which will likely lead to further mutations and innovations. By offering a Stoic reading of Gotama's discourse *On Not-Self*, for example, I will suggest how Buddhists could develop a robust, dialogical conception of the self rather than persist in denying its existence or comparing it to an illusion. And through drawing on Aristotle's distinction between the contemplative life (*bios theōrētikos*) and the active life (*bios politikos*), I will offer a Greek-inspired, secular iteration of Gotama's eightfold path, one which begins with mindfulness and culminates in finding one's own voice.[5]

As the title suggests, *Buddha, Socrates, and Us* is composed of three main narrative threads. The first thread recounts my own philosophical journey through Buddhism; the second thread imagines what a hypothetical Buddhist in Athens would have witnessed during the lifetime of Socrates; and the third thread provides the context needed to ask how Buddhist and Greek philosophy might address the existential concerns facing us today. I interweave these threads chapter by chapter, braiding them together to tell a multifaceted story, ranging over centuries and continents, animated by a cast of characters ancient and modern. Whether or not I succeed in finding a voice that speaks to the needs of our uncertain times is for the reader to judge.

I
Agency

1
Life as Practice

As I came of age at the end of the 1960s, I resolved never to lead the life of suffocating conformity that characterized my parents' generation. I detested the British middle-class existence of petty ambition, consumerism, and self-satisfaction whose sole purpose seemed to be the maintenance of the class-riven status quo. My blind, unfocused rage was fueled by the countercultural rebellion of the times, and it was further intensified by my deep insecurities as a child growing up without a father, a religion, or a church. I yearned for a life that was not merely to be endured but in some unfathomable way would be shaped and realized by my own deepest aspirations. My role models were writers, actors, artists, poets, musicians, philosophers, and mystics.

In autumn 1971 I bought two Buddhist books from Watkins, an esoteric bookshop in central London. These were the *Jewel Ornament of Liberation* by the Tibetan lama Gampopa and *The Way of Zen* by the British philosopher Alan Watts. I was a long-haired eighteen-year-old, who had just left grammar school after failing my final exams. Instead of starting a degree course in photography in London, I now had an empty year ahead of me before I would have to consider returning to the ignominy of further education. I was curious about Buddhism but knew nothing about it. I chose the two books on the strength of their cover art, much as I would have chosen an imported album of the latest American rock music. On returning to the suburb of Watford where I lived, I opened the *Jewel Ornament of Liberation* at random and started reading about the Vaibāṣika view of atoms:

> Atoms by nature are spherical, undivided and singular. A mass of them is an object (of perception) such as colour-form and so on. When massed together there are intervals between each atom. They appear to be in one place like a yak's tail in the pasture.[1]

This and what followed bewildered and intimidated me like the physics I had disliked studying at school. I placed the book on a shelf and did not look at it again. During my lunch breaks from the asbestos factory where I worked as a cleaner to earn enough money to escape Watford, I struggled to read *The Way of Zen*, which I found equally baffling.

I was frustrated by my inability to make sense of religious or philosophical language. My great-grandfather had been a Methodist minister, but my grandfather had abandoned religion altogether. Raised in a secular environment, I never attended a church service and was exempted from "Scripture" lessons at school. Nor was I taught anything about humanism or philosophy. Drawn to the forbidden and unknown, I was curious about Christianity, but my occasional encounters with representatives of the Church of England did not inspire me to look further. Orange-robed devotees chanting Hare Krishna on Oxford Street and the Beatles' much-reported sojourn in India with the Maharishi opened my eyes to traditions that seemed far richer in possibilities than the Christianity or Judaism of middle-class Britain. Crucially, they seemed to offer you something to do rather than merely believe in.

During my final year at Watford Grammar School, the dramatic society staged a performance of *Oedipus the Tyrant* by the Greek tragedian Sophocles. For days afterwards I was troubled by the image of the gangly, orange-haired boy called Bob Hanks, who played the role of Oedipus, clutching his face with blood-stained hands. That this image of Hanks's blinded, despairing face remains imprinted on my mind today suggests that it showed me something about being human that the rest of my education had failed to impart.

I left Watford in February 1972 and spent six months traveling overland through Europe, the Middle East, Iran, Afghanistan, and Pakistan to India. After crossing the Indian border in late August, I took a bus to Dharamsala, the capital-in-exile of the Dalai Lama in the state of Himachal Pradesh. I immediately enrolled in a class on Buddhism at the newly built Library of Tibetan Works and Archives. The teacher was Geshe Ngawang Dhargyey, a rotund, energetic, fifty-one-year-old lama in burgundy robes with a Cheshire Cat smile.

With the help of two young Tibetan translators, Geshe Dhargyey patiently explained to us the basics of Buddhism through a body of teachings known as the "Stages of the Path" (*Lam-rim*), which described in detail the steps a deluded, suffering person needed to follow to become a fully enlightened buddha. I was struck by how everything we were taught was also something we were challenged to do. These ideas were designed to be examined, tested, and applied in the context of my own mental and emotional life.

One of the first *Lam-rim* texts we studied was the *Jewel Ornament of Liberation*, the very same book by Gampopa that I had unwittingly bought in London the year before. I was disappointed that neither Gampopa's book nor Geshe Dhargyey's classes taught us how to visualize mandalas or meditate on emptiness. The *Lam-rim* offered a course in practical ethics. Geshe Dhargyey explained how without an ethical framework, the path to awakening would have no purpose or sense. We were instructed to reflect repeatedly on the potential and value of human life, the inevitability of death, and the need to rely on a qualified teacher. For without making a conscious choice to commit oneself to an ethical way of life, people tend to follow unquestioningly the prompts of their biological, social, cultural, religious, and psychological conditioning. From a Buddhist perspective, an interest in the dharma only begins to stir when you wake up to your finitude, mortality, and frailty and start to take your existential condition seriously.

For Gampopa and Geshe Dhargyey, the stages of this path to awakening were divided into three phases, corresponding to the capacities of three ethical types, known as the three "persons": the lesser person, the middling person, and the great person. The lesser of the three persons described in the *Lam-rim* recognizes that to devote oneself solely to the pleasures and rewards of this life is not enough to realize one's full potential as a human being. One then commits oneself to leading a moral life on earth as the means to secure a higher rebirth after death, either as a human being or as a god in one of the many Buddhist heavens.

By looking deeper into her existential dilemma, however, the middling person realizes that no matter where she is reborn, even as a long-lived god in heaven, she will still be trapped in the vicious circle of repeated birth and death, propelled from one realm to the next by the force of her moral and immoral acts. Disillusioned by the prospect of endless rebirth, such a person aspires to be liberated from samsara to thereby attain nirvana, where rebirth is ended and one suffers no more. This goal is reached through a rigorous training in morals, meditation, and philosophy. Such a final nirvana, Geshe Dhargyey explained, was the goal of Hinayana Buddhism, the path Gotama, the historical Buddha, taught his less gifted disciples, who were concerned with their personal spiritual welfare alone.

Empathy is what distinguishes the great person from the other two. He or she recognizes that all sentient beings are just like oneself in not wanting to suffer and wanting to be happy. Abandoning self-interest, the person aspires to become a bodhisattva: one motivated to attain the complete awakening of a buddha. One takes a vow to continue being reborn until all other beings are freed from samsara. This vow is the gateway to Mahayana Buddhism, the "great vehicle." Geshe Dhargyey believed that such an altruistic resolve to attain enlightenment for the sake of others was the highest ethical condition to which a human being could aspire.

Ethos, in Greek, means "character." Each of these three persons embodies a set of guiding motives and beliefs, which constitutes their broad ethical type. While morality requires adhering to the moral codes and precepts of one's religion or culture, the practice of ethics means to live up to the vision of the kind of person you aspire to be, thereby forming your character. This tripartite model, which I was being taught, presented the formation of character within an ethical hierarchy. One was required to pass through the "lesser" and "middling" stages on the way to becoming a "great" person. It was clear to the eager students at the Library that we were not expected to settle for being a lesser or middling person—let alone someone who merely sought to lead a fulfilling life on this earth. We became hell-bent on becoming bodhisattvas, working through countless lifetimes to achieve the altruistic goals of the Mahayana.

In addition to daily classes with Geshe Dhargyey, I started exploring the English-language books on Buddhism written by scholars and Western converts that were available at the Library. I was puzzled how these authors employed many of the same concepts and terms as Geshe Dhargyey but did not organize or treat them in the same way. They emphasized the Four Noble Truths and the Noble Eightfold Path as the foundational doctrines of Buddhism. These were also mentioned by Geshe Dhargyey but presented as teachings of Hinayana Buddhism, which had been superseded by the doctrines and practices of the Mahayana.

I was both wary of and drawn to these works in my own tongue. In common with my fellow students, I tended to dismiss their authors as well-intentioned scholars who, unlike us, had not had the good fortune to encounter a living tradition of the dharma, which had been preserved unchanged for centuries in Tibet. At the same time, I came across passages in these writings that seized my attention far more forcibly than Gampopa's detailed descriptions of the eighteen Buddhist hells, for example. In particular, I was struck by two parables—those of the Raft and the Arrow—that were presented in several of these books as defining features of Gotama's message.[2] Not only did Gampopa or Geshe Dhargyey not mention them, these parables struck a different note to what they taught.

The Parable of the Raft tells the story of a person who has set out on a journey and arrives at the bank of a wide river. Since there is no boat to take him across, he fashions a raft from whatever branches and reeds happen to be lying around and manages to paddle over to the far shore. But instead of leaving the sodden raft behind, the person lifts it onto his shoulders and continues his journey burdened by this unnecessary load. Comparing the raft to his teachings, Gotama points out that it would be foolish to continue clinging to something that has served its purpose. Just as one would let go of that raft, one should also let go of Buddhist doctrines and continue one's journey through life unencumbered by them.

This parable emphasizes autonomy, resourcefulness, and self-sufficiency. It encourages each person to fashion a practice suited to the constraints, challenges, and needs of their specific life situations. In showing the absurdity of stubbornly holding on to a sodden raft, it recognizes the provisional and pragmatic nature of the dharma. Buddhist teachings are a means to an end, not ends in themselves. All that matters is whether they successfully address the situation at hand. As soon as a doctrine or practice has served its purpose, it can be respectfully laid aside.

Parables speak to the imagination. In presenting brief, dramatic human stories situated in recognizable settings, a parable evokes what it is like to encounter and resolve an existential conflict. Through identifying with the character in the story, the listener or reader can picture herself facing the same dilemma. She is thereby enabled to ponder the deeper ethical or philosophical issues the parable seeks to address. By speaking in pictures, the parable reveals the multifaceted, temporal, and interpersonal quality of human situations. You only have to hear a parable once to understand it. And once understood, you do not easily forget either the story or its moral. It stays with you. Yet you find it difficult to explain adequately in words what you have understood. As time goes by, you discover how parables have an uncanny ability to keep casting fresh light on your life, no matter how much you and your world have changed.

Without being baptized or confirmed, not having read

more than a few passages in the Bible or received any instruction in Christian doctrine, Jesus's teaching came to me through his parables that are everywhere embedded in the cultural fabric of the West. From my childhood on, the parables of the Good Samaritan, the Prodigal Son, the Sower, the Mustard Seed, the Moat and the Beam, the Woman Taken in Adultery, and many others imprinted themselves on my ethical imagination. They continue to inform some of my deepest moral intuitions, my core sense of what is acceptable and unacceptable to say and do. They live on as sources of both moral guilt and rectitude. I am not a Christian, but I have been shaped by Christian culture.

As part of the liberal, experimental culture of the 1960s, Watford Grammar School introduced a weekly class for its sixth-formers called "Means and Ends." This was intended to complement the standard curriculum with an opportunity to reflect on larger ethical questions of meaning, value, and purpose. It was here, at the age of seventeen, that I was first exposed to Western philosophy. The only thing I remember being taught in this class was Plato's Allegory of the Cave.

Book VII of *The Republic* opens with Socrates describing a group of people who have lived chained together since childhood in a cave, facing a wall. Their heads are fixed in place so they cannot turn around. Behind them the cave ascends steeply to an opening through which rays of sunlight penetrate the darkness. Between the opening and the prisoners is a raised walkway along which objects and figures pass, their shadows being projected onto the wall in front. Since this is all those imprisoned in the cave have ever seen, they assume that these shadowy images are the only reality there is. Inhabiting this dark cavernous world is, for Plato, a metaphor for leading an unenlightened life on earth.

The philosopher is compared to a prisoner who breaks

free from his chains, climbs up the steep ascent to the opening, and escapes from the cave. He finds himself dazzled by the light of day. As his eyes become accustomed to the sun he beholds the glory of a world bathed in its light. When he returns to share the truth of what he has discovered with his fellow cave-dwellers, none of them believe him. They continue staring at the flickering shadows on the wall as though that was all there could ever be. For Plato, the fate of most human beings is to pass their entire lives in such a diminished state of existence. Only the philosopher is able to rise above this condition and wake up to the true nature of reality.

The Allegory of the Cave gave me a thrilling vision of a more exalted consciousness. It provided a metaphorical framework for interpreting my experiences with psychedelic drugs. Before I left England, I had been given a copy of Ram Dass's influential book *Be Here Now,* which charted the author's journey from LSD to Indian mysticism. Psychedelics, it seemed, briefly opened the "doors of perception" to the world outside Plato's Cave, and religions like Hinduism, Buddhism, and Daoism offered detailed maps and practical disciplines that gave one lasting access to this world.

Both the Parable of the Raft and the Allegory of the Cave describe an intolerable situation in which one is trapped by circumstance. Do you remain where you are, or do you risk breaking free to embark on a journey into the unknown? The Raft and the Cave lay out the parameters that frame your ethical decision but provide no guidelines to help you make that choice. Before you can act, you need to comprehend the entirety of the complex dilemma in which you find yourself. Your choice is existential. Your response will define you as a person. Everything is at stake. This is no abstract moral exercise about what would be the "right" or "wrong" thing to do.

Such formative ethical situations are often ambiguous.

A raft, like a religion, can be both a help and a hindrance. It can save your life only to become a deadweight that prevents you from living. Its worth is determined by how you make use of it rather than what it is in itself. The Allegory of the Cave can be both an inspiration and a warning. It may inspire you to cast off the shackles of suburban London and head off to India to study Tibetan Buddhism. But it warns you that on returning home no one might be interested in hearing about what you have discovered. Both stories highlight the value and danger of pursuing your own path in life.

The other Buddhist parable that left a deep impression on me was that of the Arrow. This parable tells of a man who has been wounded by a poisoned arrow. But he refuses to let his friends fetch a doctor until he knows everything that can be known about the person who fired it, the kind of bow he employed, even what birds provided the feathers used for the arrow's fletching. While all this information is still being gathered, the man would die. Likewise, continued Gotama, if someone refuses to practice the dharma until he is told whether the universe is finite or infinite, eternal or not eternal, whether mind and body are the same or different, and whether the sage exists after death or not, then he too would die long before finding answers to such questions. For this reason, Gotama declared nothing about such things. His teaching was solely concerned with removing the "arrow" of reactivity to enable the person to lead a flourishing life.

The parable highlights the therapeutic and anti-metaphysical nature of the dharma. Today we might add to this list questions about free will and determinism, and about the existence or nonexistence of God. For Gotama awakening had nothing to do with solving such imponderable questions. The dharma was concerned with ethics—how we should live—rather than metaphysics, ontology, or epistemology, which are concerned with how things really are. From this perspective the ignorance the dharma sought to dispel was not so much confusion about the true nature of reality, but confusion about how to act appropriately in response to the suffering of the world.

A student once asked Geshe Dhargyey why the Buddha had refused to say anything on these topics. Geshe-la grinned and explained that while such questions were not answered in the teachings of Hinayana Buddhism, the Mahayana tradition had answers for them all: the universe is infinite, not finite; but it will end when all beings have been freed from samsara; mind and body are two distinct entities; and a sage will continue to exist in the world after his death as long as there are sentient beings to save.

Why, of all the many questions posed to Geshe Dhargyey, does this one still stand out in my memory? I recall nodding in assent to what he said while at the same time feeling in my gut that something was not quite right. At the time I was unable to put my finger on what was amiss, but it planted a seed of doubt in my mind that would sprout and grow over the coming years. This was the first time my faith in Tibetan Buddhism wavered and my curiosity about the early Buddhist tradition grew. I realized, with a sense of guilt, that I trusted the poetic and imaginative authority of these parables far more than the personal authority of the teacher whom I was encouraged to revere as a buddha.

For Gampopa and Geshe Dhargyey, the Buddha was enlightened because, like Plato's philosopher, he had arrived at a direct, nonconceptual understanding of reality itself, whose true nature was concealed from ordinary mortals by their ignorance. The superiority of the Mahayana lay in its having a comprehensive and definitive understanding of all relative and ultimate truths. Since Gotama was considered to be omniscient, he could not have been ignorant of the answers to these questions. His decision to remain silent about such matters would therefore have been a skillful means to instruct his less intelligent disciples. The Hinayana, therefore, was an inferior vehicle not only because it failed to teach the highest ethical goal but because it failed to disclose everything Gotama actually knew.

As I understand it now, Gotama remained silent on these matters because holding opinions about them was an obstacle to practicing the dharma. They were metaphysical distractions that diverted one's attention away from how to lead a mindful, compassionate, and caring life. Gotama was a skeptical ethicist rather than an omniscient quasi-deity. His concern was to embrace the tragic human condition; let go of the reactive patterns of greed, hate, and opinionatedness; and respond to life from a nonreactive perspective. He encouraged people to engage with imagination and care the challenges that confronted them day-to-day.

Being pierced by the poisoned arrow of reactivity paralyzes you. It prevents you from making appropriate ethical judgments. It inhibits you from leading a sane and fulfilling existence. Metaphysical beliefs—including those of Buddhism—can anesthetize you to the suffering of life. The parables of the Raft and the Arrow suggest that the aim of the dharma is not to achieve the eternal peace of nirvana, the traditional goal of Buddhism, but to flourish as a fallible and mortal human in response to the suffering and tragedy of this world.

2

The Wisest Man in Greece

I passed through Athens on my overland journey to India in 1972, but have no recollection of anything I saw or did there. I must have climbed up the Acropolis and contemplated the remains of the Parthenon, but my memories seem to have merged inseparably with the ubiquitous images of those iconic sites throughout our culture. I did not return to the city again until fifty-one years later, when I flew into Athens in search of Socrates in 2023. I had come to contemplate Greece through Buddhist eyes, hoping such a perspective might shed light on the philosopher and the world he inhabited. In addition to Athens, I would travel through the Peloponnese to see Delphi, Elis, Olympia, Corinth, and other ancient sites that would have been familiar to Socrates and his circle two and a half thousand years ago. I had recently made similar journeys to India to follow in the footsteps of Gotama. This too felt like a pilgrimage.

Ancient Athens lies in ruins, its most precious artifacts preserved in museums. Yet the natural landscape remains largely unchanged. The bright blue sky, the hills in and around the city, the cool spring breezes blowing off the Aegean, the pine trees and grasses, the tortoises stumbling across the dusty ground would all have been familiar to Socrates and Plato—albeit without the incessant rumble and roar of motorized traffic in the background.

Hardly any trace of Socrates is visible in Athens today. Unlike Pythagoras, he appears on no T-shirts, unlike Hippocrates he is rarely depicted on fridge magnets, even "Socrates's Prison," a rock-cut chamber near the Pnyx, the open-air site of the democratic assemblies, is unlikely to have been where he was held before being obliged to drink hemlock. For a Socratic souvenir, all you will find is a cheap plaster bust of an expressionless, bearded man arranged on the shelves of gift shops throughout the city, alongside Aphrodite, discus throwers, Zeus, and the Parthenon. In Athens today "the wisest man in Greece" has been reduced to a minor player in the lucrative tourist industry.

Back in the fifth century BCE, Socrates was flabbergasted to learn that the Oracle of Apollo at Delphi had declared there to be no one in Greece wiser than he. "I am very conscious," he said to himself, "that I am not wise at all."[1] At the same time, his faith in the Oracle obliged him to accept that the god could not be lying. He was left with a conundrum: how can a man be both wise and not wise at the same time? Or as Aristotle might have framed it many decades later, how can something be both A and not-A? The grammar of human language dictates that only one of these claims can be true. Yet it is here, in this excluded middle, that we arrive at the heart of Socratic philosophy: to never stop questioning, to consider all answers as tentative or ambiguous, to accept that the quest for truth might be endless. For only as long as you are questioning do you remain suspended in uncertainty, without which a philosophical life is impossible.

Socrates came from a working-class family of stone masons. Crito, a wealthy neighbor and friend, recognized his brilliance at a young age and provided for his education.[2] As an adult Socrates came to abandon the natural philosophy of his day, which sought to understand the phenomena of the world through careful observation and analysis, rejected the clever logic and arguments of professional intellectuals known as Sophists, and turned his attention exclusively to ethics. For Socrates, the only questions worth pursuing were those that helped you achieve excellence through becoming a good person.

Socrates was a street philosopher. He challenged people from all strata of society, educated or not, to address the core questions of what it means to be human. He was not an aloof scholar who only taught the privileged youth of Athens in the rarified atmosphere of an academy. This strange man was a well-known character around the city: eccentric, provocative, unsettling, fascinating, ugly, scary.

Like all male Athenian citizens of fighting age, Socrates was also duty bound to take up arms to defend his city. He needed to keep himself physically fit in gymnasia and be ready for battle as soon as he was called up by the democratic assembly. In 431 BCE, when he was in his late thirties, Athens became embroiled with Sparta in the Peloponnesian War that would flare up intermittently over the next twenty-seven years. In the autumn of 424 BCE, Sparta's ally Boeotia routed the Athenian army at the land battle of Delium. Of the seven thousand foot soldiers who had marched from Athens to Delium, around one thousand were killed in hand-to-hand fighting or hacked down during the chaotic retreat.[3]

Protected by a helmet and body armor, made either of metal or hardened layers of glued linen, clutching a concave bronze shield, and wielding the spear and sword of a hoplite, Socrates fought as part of the infantry in this battle. Now a seasoned soldier in his mid-forties, long familiar with bloodshed and killing, he would have been just another anonymous figure in one of the serried ranks of soldiers, who fought as a single, brutal mass. Had he been felled by the blow of a sword or spear or trampled to death by the Theban cavalry, which broke through the Athenian lines, then Plato and Xenophon, who were only children at the time, would not have been able to immortalize him. Yet at the yearly City Dionysia, the great spring festival to the god Dionysus, which took place in Athens only a few months after this battle, Socrates would be lampooned as a philosophical clown in two of the three comedies staged at the festival that year.

On each day of this three-day festival, a comedy as well as a tetralogy of three tragedies and a satyr play would be performed in the amphitheater on the southern slopes of the Acropolis. Two of the three comedies selected to be performed in competition that spring—*Beard*, by the now forgotten poet Ameipsias, and *Clouds*, by the young rising star Aristophanes—presented Socrates as the butt of their jokes. Only a few lines of *Beard* have survived. The longest fragment reads: "You have come to us, Socrates, the best of a small number of men, and the vainest by far. Well, at least you are hardy. Where could we get you a decent coat?"[4] Ameipsias shows Socrates as a proud, robust, and eccentric man living in poverty, who evoked mixed feelings of incomprehension, pity, ridicule, and grudging admiration. We have no idea how the playwright turned these impressions to comic effect or even what the play was about. *Clouds*, by contrast, is one of eleven comedies of Aristophanes to have come down to us intact.

Clouds is a scurrilous send-up of pampered aristocrats and pompous intellectuals, who feed off each other's sense of entitlement and self-importance. The elderly Strepsiades, its anti-hero, has learned of a place called the Thinkery, where the best minds of Athens gather under the guidance of Socrates to conduct research into the nature of reality and devise ingenious logical arguments to bamboozle others. They are also atheists, who have replaced the gods with clouds, which drift onto the stage as a chorus of women. The old man implores them to make him the smartest speaker in Greece so he can outwit his creditors. It all comes to nothing. The creditors do not for a moment swallow Strepsiades's meaningless blather and hasten to the law courts to file a suit against him. The old man bemoans his stupidity in having entrusted himself to Socrates and blames the clouds for misleading him. A flaming torch in hand, he is raised onto the roof of the Thinkery by the mechanical crane and sets the place alight.

The Socrates depicted in *Clouds* bears as much resemblance to Socrates the stonemason's son as Monty Python's Brian bears to Jesus of Nazareth the carpenter's son. The Socrates of Aristophanes's comedy represents the complete reversal of everything that Socrates in Athens stood for. The actual Socrates was neither a proto-scientist nor a Sophist, neither an atheist nor a materialist. Most of those in the audience would have understood this just as most cinemagoers in the twentieth century would have been aware that Brian was not Jesus. Therein lay the key to the play's and movie's comic effect: to take a well-known and respected character and turn him into an absurd double. But the subtleties of the comedian's art can be lost on those with axes to grind. Just as furious Christians denounced Monty Python's film for blasphemy and sought to have it banned, so a quarter of a century later angry democrats in Athens would cite Aristophanes's *Clouds* as evidence for prosecuting Socrates.

Although it failed to win the competition for best comedy at the Dionysian festival that spring, *Clouds* is today considered a masterpiece of Greek theater. Not only does it contain the earliest mention of Socrates in Greek literature, it is also the first known comedy to parody professional intellectuals. And little has changed in how potty professors and mad scientists, their heads still firmly lodged in the clouds, have been depicted ever since Aristophanes's play was premiered in Athens two and a half thousand years ago.

As the festival drew to a close, the question on the lips of many non-Athenians present was "Who *is* this man Socrates?" In response, the actual Socrates silently rose from his seat.[5] Before them stood a stocky, bearded man in his mid-forties, barefoot, wearing a simple woolen cloak. With protruding eyes, a snub nose, thick lips, and possibly balding, he was the antithesis of the Greek ideal of male beauty. A familiar figure to Athenians, Socrates passed much of each day talking and arguing with all and sundry in the marketplace. And for many that day he would have been recognized as a war veteran, having served with distinction in the disastrous battle of Delium a few months earlier.

Socrates's student Alcibiades was also present at Delium. His account of the rout is recorded in Plato's *Drinking Party* (*Symposium*), which describes a banquet supposedly attended by seven friends, including Socrates and Aristophanes, eight years after the battle. After eating, they continued sipping wine and took turns to deliver speeches about love (*eros*). Late at night, after Socrates had delivered his speech and Aristophanes was trying to make himself heard above the applause, an inebriated Alcibiades swept into the room. At the time one of the city's most admired military leaders and orators, the handsome and flamboyant Alcibiades proceeded to enthusiastically praise Socrates.[6]

In recalling his teacher's exemplary conduct in the battle of Delium, Alcibiades turned to Aristophanes and quoted to him a passage from *Clouds*. "I couldn't get your words out of my mind," he said to the playwright: "'With swaggering gait and roving eye . . .'"[7] Alcibiades was struck by the way Socrates *embodied* his philosophy. For even while being hunted down by soldiers intent on killing him, he carried himself in the same calm, circumspect, and ironic way as he did in daily life. What impressed him was Socrates's utter fearlessness. Such a figure was the antithesis of the philosophical clown depicted in *Clouds*. This was someone you simply did not mess with. Alcibiades had quoted the only line in Aristophanes's play that had any bearing on what Socrates might actually have been like.

Alcibiades had already witnessed Socrates at war during the siege of Potidaea, one of the first campaigns of the Peloponnesian War, during which Socrates had saved the young nobleman's life. The two of them had shared the same tent, allowing Alcibiades to observe Socrates at close hand. He recalled how early one morning Socrates started pondering a philosophical problem. He went outside and stood immobile trying to resolve it, remaining deep in contemplation all day. As night fell, some of the soldiers brought their bedding outdoors, curious to see how long he would continue. He didn't move until the sun rose the following morning.

For Alcibiades, Socrates was totally unique. "There is a parallel for everyone," he went on, "—everyone else, that is." In contrast to the Sophists lampooned in *Clouds*, Socrates employed the ordinary, everyday language of blacksmiths and cobblers for his philosophy. Rather than develop metaphysical theories or make scientific claims about the natural world, he kept returning to the only thing that mattered for him: how to lead a good life. Socrates's exclusive concern was ethics.

Socrates may have been physically ugly and contemptuous of convention but the example he set and the words he uttered were irresistible. He both enraptured and terrified Alcibiades. "He is the only man in the world," reflected the young aristocrat, "who has made me feel shame."[8] For as long as he was with his mentor, Alcibiades readily assented to everything Socrates said, but as soon as he found himself alone again, he reverted to his pompous, self-serving ways. He admitted that he spent much of his life doing his best to avoid Socrates. At times he wished him dead, only to realize that Socrates's death would make him even more miserable. "I can't live with him," he confessed, "and I can't live without him."[9]

Socrates made his students acutely aware of their inner contradictions. He achieved this not only by what he said but by the example of how he lived. He appeared completely indifferent to the things most people craved, such as beauty, wealth, and fame. On seeing items displayed for sale in a market, he would remark, "Just look at how many things I can do without!"[10] He refused any payment for his teaching and appeared to have no other source of income. His wealthy admirers may have invited him to sumptuous dinner parties, but essentially Socrates was a beggar. "He considers all possessions," declared Alcibiades, "beneath contempt, and that's exactly how he considers all of us as well. In public, his whole life is one big game—a game of irony."[11] For Alcibiades, Socrates's life was a self-conscious performance played out on the great stage of Athens.

While seeking to lead an impeccably ethical existence, Socrates claimed not to know anything about the nature of truth, goodness, or virtue. At the end of a dialogue on the cardinal Greek virtue of justice in the first book of Plato's *Republic,* Socrates concluded:

> The result of the whole discussion has been that I know nothing at all. For I know not what justice is, and therefore I am not likely to know whether it

is or is not a virtue, nor can I say whether the just man is happy or unhappy.[12]

Socratic dialogues often end in such a state of perplexity (*aporia*), leaving the participants suspended midway between "is" and "isn't," uncertain of what to think or do. Many found this infuriating. Yet enacting an ethical life founded on radical uncertainty lay at the heart of Socrates's philosophical practice. How to achieve this remains, to this day, the great conundrum and challenge of the Socratic way of life.

3
Fraternal Twins

Towards the end of their lives, both Socrates and Gotama witnessed the military conquest of their homelands, followed by a period of bloody revenge and score settling. Five years before the philosopher's trial, Athens had been soundly defeated by Sparta and her allies, concluding the Peloponnesian War that had raged on and off for the previous twenty-seven years. For Athens this marked the end of its political supremacy in the Aegean and its golden age of high culture. In Gotama's case, his homeland of Sakiya was invaded by King Vidudabha of Kosala about a year before his death. Possibly to punish Sakiya for duplicity in its political dealings with Kosala, Vidudabha launched a brutal, genocidal attack. Gotama may initially have sought to intervene to prevent the carnage, but his words fell on deaf ears.

Not long before they died, both Socrates and Gotama were denounced to a democratic assembly. For Socrates, this was a people's court of 501 male citizens of Athens, a majority of whom voted to sentence the philosopher to death. Gotama, meanwhile, was denounced by his former attendant and disciple Sunakkhatta to the citizens' assembly of Vesali, capital of the largest surviving republic at Gotama's time, honored today as the first democracy in the Indian subcontinent. The assembly of Vesali was said to have had been composed of seven thousand members, whereas the assembly of Athens that gathered on the Pnyx had six thousand, from which the courts and councils were chosen. Sunakkhatta accused Gotama of being just a clever intellectual, what the Greeks would have called a Sophist, whose teachings were "hammered out by reasoning, following his own line of inquiry as it occurs to him."[1] Despite his closeness to Gotama, Sunakkhatta dismissed him as a fraud, devoid of any genuine spiritual attainments or wisdom. This public humiliation by a long-standing disciple marked the end of Gotama's prominence as a teacher in Vesali. Socrates died four or five weeks after being sentenced to death, and Gotama probably died within a year or so of being denounced by Sunakkhatta.

Both Socrates and Gotama died from ingesting something they knew to be poisonous. In the case of Socrates, this was the hemlock he had been ordered to drink by the court that found him guilty of introducing new gods to the city and corrupting the young. In the case of Gotama, it was probably a pork stew or broth offered by his host, Cunda the Smith, in a mango grove near the town of Pava (modern Fazilnagar in Uttar Pradesh). Gotama instructed Cunda to serve the pork dish to him alone and then bury the leftovers in a pit to prevent anyone else from eating it. He collapsed shortly afterwards with severe attacks of rectal bleeding and died a few days later.[2]

By the end of their lives, both Gotama and Socrates had fallen out of favor with the communities that had once held them in esteem. Regimes were now installed in Athens, Savatthi, and Rajagaha for whom these wise men of former times were perceived as troublemakers. Their powerful supporters— the aristocrats Alcibiades and Critias in the case of Socrates, the kings Pasenadi and Bimbisara in the case of Gotama—had all been killed in the preceding months and years. Both men ended their days surrounded by a few loyal friends, relatives, and admirers: Gotama in a sal grove outside Kusinara, Socrates in a prison cell in Athens.

Both Socrates and Gotama appear to us in the records as fully formed individuals, who appear to have sprung out of nowhere. One has little sense of how they evolved into the kind of persons they became. Socrates mentions during his trial how as a young man he had studied naturalistic philosophy with Archelaus, a follower of Anaxagoras, and Gotama describes his training in meditative absorption with two otherwise unknown teachers, Alara Kalama and Udaka Ramaputta. All this reveals is that the two men mastered certain forms of philosophy and contemplative practice esteemed at their time before rejecting them. The dialectical skill displayed in the dialogues of both Socrates and Gotama shows that they must have spent considerable time discussing and debating ideas with others. Then at some point in their mid-thirties both assumed a sage-like authority to actively challenge the assumptions and fixed views of the time and thereby give birth to something entirely new.

Both Socrates and Gotama renounced involvement in the political life of their societies, lived in poverty, wore a single, threadbare robe, walked barefoot, refused to accept money for their teaching, and wrote nothing. In Gotama's case, this lifestyle was common to all those who had left the household life to become wandering mendicants. It was nothing unusual. For Socrates to adopt such a way of life in Athens was exceptional and provocative, inviting not only mockery by comic playwrights such as Aristophanes but fury from Xanthippe, his long-suffering wife. And while writing was largely unknown in India at Gotama's time, the Greeks of the same period were avid scribblers, scratching their thoughts onto wax tablets, which would then be written up in ink on papyrus by slaves. But Socrates wrote nothing.

What unites them most deeply, I believe, is how both men advocated and enacted an ethics of uncertainty. They shared a passionate resolve to lead a virtuous life that did not rest on metaphysical commitments. They led a life of questioning and self-examination without positing any absolute truths. With reasoning and by example they sought to convince their interlocutors to become autonomous ethical agents, liberated from unthinking adherence to the norms of their societies and traditions to embark on a life of authenticity. They sought to arouse people from a state of sleepwalking to one of flourishing and fulfilment.

Two principles informed Gotama's perspective on ethics. He encouraged his disciples to let go of binary habits of mind, reinforced by the grammar of language, that insist that things must be either one thing or another—either A or not-A. We are prone, for example, to believe that we must either exist as something solid and permanent, or not really exist at all. Gotama regarded both alternatives as dead ends, as paths that go nowhere, and sought instead to create a middle way between them. At the same time, he recognized how the relinquishing of such certainties and opinions creates a space of still, quiet attention better suited to making appropriate ethical judgments and choices. To practice Gotama's ethics of uncertainty required maintaining an open, questioning mind, which embraced life as mysterious, fluid, processual, and indeterminate. Such a perspective allowed a freedom from the absolutizing tendencies of thought, thereby enabling original, creative solutions to ethical and other dilemmas.

Socrates's perspective likewise recognized the centrality in ethics of maintaining an open, questioning mind. In what are considered the earliest dialogues of Plato, we find Socrates inviting his interlocutors to offer definitions of the classical Greek virtues of wisdom, courage, justice, moderation, and reverence in order to arrive at an understanding of what they are and, by implication, what they are not. Although the person being questioned initially assumes that he knows perfectly well what courage or justice is, as the investigation unfolds, every attempt at definition is shown to be inadequate or inconsistent and has to be rejected. It is not as though Socrates enjoyed entangling his debate partner in conceptual knots before finally revealing the "right" answer. Socrates cannot define what these virtues are either. There does not appear to be a right answer. The dialogue ends without reaching a conclusion, with both parties suspended in an *aporia* of unknowing, uncertainty, and doubt.

An adequate definition of either Buddhist or Greek virtues will perhaps forever elude us, but this does not mean that we are incapable of leading a good and ethical life. For we intuitively know the virtues through the way they are enacted in our own and others' behavior. We recognize wisdom and compassion, courage and justice as soon as we witness them embodied in the words and deeds of a real or fictional person. To the extent that we can use the terms "wisdom" or "courage" intelligibly in the language game called English, we know perfectly well what they are. But as soon as we try to seize hold of them with a definition, they slip like water through our fingers.

By contrast, both Plato's Theory of Forms and Buddhist analyses of mental states in the scholarly Abhidharma literature insist that virtues *can* be finally pinned down either by exact definitions or by gaining mystical insight into their true nature. Just as Plato turns Socrates into the mouthpiece for his own doctrines in the later dialogues, so do the writers of the Abhidharma insist that their definitions were taught by Gotama himself. The followers of Socrates and Gotama alike seemed ill at ease with the aporetic or empty nature of things and chose instead to provide definitive answers to questions about which Socrates and Gotama preferred to remain silent.

The same shift from uncertainty to certainty is evident in how both men's views on the afterlife were developed by their followers. When addressing the Kalama people, Gotama maintained that practicing his dharma will be of benefit irrespective of whether life continues after death in another realm or whether there exists a karmic law of cause and effect.[3] Yet on another occasion, he famously described how on the night of his enlightenment he recalled in detail all of his past lives.[4] Similarly, in the defense speech at his trial, Socrates maintained that he had no idea whether after death there is simply nothing or the soul relocates elsewhere.[5] But in the account of his last days given in the *Phaedo*, he described in greater detail than any discourse in the Pali Canon how the immortal soul proceeds from one life to the next.[6] In both cases, uncertainty is replaced by dogmatic claims to truth. While reincarnation became an indispensable doctrine for both Buddhism and Platonism, it seems that neither Gotama nor Socrates was fully committed to it.[7]

Fraternal (nonidentical or dizygotic) twins are born at the same time to the same parents but, unlike identical twins, emerge from different ova fertilized by different sperm. Like all siblings they share around 50 percent of their DNA. Comparing Socrates and Gotama to such twins recognizes how they came into the world at the same time, shared a number of key characteristics, but in other respects were quite different. The two men were united by their common commitment to ethics but separated by their attitudes to sex and violence. In common with the Indian ascetic traditions of his time, Gotama renounced all civic duties and domestic responsibilities to pursue the life of a homeless wanderer. In doing so, he embraced celibacy and nonviolence as necessary foundations for a life fully committed to wisdom and liberation. Although Socrates eschewed (with a couple of exceptions) a role in the political life of Athens, he rarely left the city of his birth and remained committed to his duties as a citizen, both as a soldier and a father of children. He defended himself against the charges of which he was accused at the end of his life, but honored the laws of the city, accepted the court's guilty verdict, and ignored his friends' entreaties to flee Athens to save his skin.

Two and a half millennia later, the lives of these "fraternal twins" continue to intrigue, inspire, and challenge us. I find myself drawn as much to the unworldliness of Gotama as I am to the worldliness of Socrates. Yet rather than seeing this as a binary choice—to follow either the example of Gotama or the example of Socrates—perhaps what our time calls for is a middle way *between* the unworldliness of one and the worldliness of the other.

4
Diotima's Middle Way

It would be as inconceivable to imagine Gotama taking up a shield, sword, and spear to fight as a hoplite as it would to imagine Socrates establishing an order of nuns. Gotama's commitment to nonviolence was explicit in the first monastic vow: not to take the life of another human being under any circumstances. Socrates, by contrast, had a sacred obligation to protect with his life the city that had nurtured and cared for him. He accepted his duty as a male citizen of Athens to be available and fit for military service at all times, and he regarded courage as a virtue most fully realized by the soldier on the battlefield. The idea that one needed to renounce all forms of violence to lead an ethical life may never have crossed his mind.

Unlike the figure of Gotama presented in the Pali Canon, Plato's Socrates did not consider himself a teacher who offered a systematic body of views and doctrines. In his defense speech as recorded by Plato he insisted that he had no students or disciples. Yes, groups of young men followed him around Athens to listen to him interrogate people, but that was their choice not his. And although Plato used Socrates as a mouthpiece for his metaphysical doctrines, such as in the Allegory of the Cave, it seems that Socrates held none of these views himself. Socrates saw himself as a gadfly sent by a god to wake up the slumbering souls of Athens. He sought to expose the confusion and inconsistencies in people's opinions and get them to think clearly for themselves. Unlike Gotama, he appeared to offer no organized system of philosophical ideas, no training in meditation or spiritual exercises, no step-by-step path to follow, and no body of full-time professionals to support each other in their practice.

If the refusal to fight as a soldier in defense of the city would have been abhorrent to an Athenian citizen at Socrates's time, the Buddhist practice of celibacy would have been simply bewildering. The notion that wholehearted dedication to a life of the mind entailed refraining from sexual intercourse would have been incomprehensible. For the Greeks, sex was just part of what it meant to be human. They enjoyed and joked about all varieties of it openly and without embarrassment. Rather than being a hindrance to philosophical understanding, a loving erotic relationship with a young male student was regarded as a fine and noble means to cultivate the soul of one's beloved boy. At the same time, the Greeks warned against abusing one's authority as a teacher simply to gratify one's physical lusts. One of the few details we have of Socrates's youth is that he had such a relationship with his teacher, the natural philosopher Archelaus. Consistent with his claim that he had no students, there is no record of Socrates ever taking a boy as his beloved.

While Socrates studied with women, Gotama did not. And while Gotama taught women, Socrates did not. We find clear evidence in the earliest texts that Gotama welcomed women into his order from the outset of his teaching career. During this period of social upheaval in northeast India, it was not only men who left home to become wandering mendicants and philosophers. Women too left behind their domestic duties, renounced marriage and childbearing, shaved their heads, and donned a simple robe to embark on a life of the mind. Since other renunciant groups of the time accepted women into their communities, this was not unique to Buddhists. Gotama regarded women as capable of achieving exactly the same degree of insight, liberation, and spiritual fulfilment as men. A text in the Pali Canon called the *Therīgāthā* (*Verses of the Women Elders*) is the oldest example in any religious tradition of a canonical work composed exclusively by women reflecting on issues that matter to women.

In Socrates's Athens, by contrast, women were confined to their homes and obliged to wear veils if they ventured outdoors. They received no education and were responsible solely for raising children and managing the household of servants and slaves. The only exceptions were those chosen at a young age to serve as priestesses and the occasional noblewoman who succeeded in gaining the respect of men through her own intellectual brilliance. Nowhere in Plato's dialogues or the conversations recorded by Xenophon do we find Socrates subjecting a woman to his relentless questioning and testing. All his interlocutors are men. During his final days in prison, he coldly dismisses his wife and other women from the cell because their weeping and wailing disturbs the silence needed for a dignified philosophical death.

Of the dozens of characters portrayed in Plato's dialogues only two are women: Aspasia, the common-law wife of the great Athenian statesman Pericles, and Diotima, a priestess from Mantinea, a town in the Peloponnese southwest of Athens. Both women are presented as teachers of Socrates, who treat their student sternly, admonishing him when necessary. In Plato's *Menexenus*, Socrates mentions to his friend Menexenus how he was currently studying oratory with Aspasia and had recently committed to memory a funeral oration she had composed. At Menexenus's urging he then proceeds to recite the oration, which takes up the rest of the dialogue. In conclusion, Menexenus exclaims, "Your Aspasia is indeed lucky if, woman though she be, she can compose speeches like that one!"[1] Why Socrates was studying oratory in the first place is not explained.

Little is known about the priestess Diotima except that she was a wise woman whom Socrates describes as teaching him the art of love (*eros*). When Socrates's turn comes to say something about love in Plato's *Drinking Party,* instead of presenting his own views, he shares with the company an exchange on the topic that he once had with Diotima.

Socrates recalls how he had told Diotima that love is "a great god and belongs to beautiful things."[2] In good Socratic fashion, she then turned his own argument against him to demonstrate that love is not beautiful at all. "Is it ugly, then?" retorted Socrates. "Watch your tongue!" she snapped. "Do you really think that if a thing is not beautiful, it has to be ugly? Or if a thing's not wise, it's ignorant? Or haven't you found out yet that there's something *between* wisdom and ignorance?"[3] Diotima is attacking Socrates's (and our) unreflective commitment to binary thinking, which assumes that something must either be or not be beautiful, wise, good, etc. In doing so, she reveals to him the possibility of a middle way *between* such poles. When Socrates asks her to clarify what lies between wisdom and ignorance, she explains:

> It's judging things correctly without being able to give a reason. Surely you see that this is not the same as knowing—for how could knowledge be unreasoning? And it's not ignorance either—for how could what hits the truth be ignorance?[4]

When it comes to making appropriate judgments, Diotima recognizes how human beings rely on a range of cognitive, emotional, and intuitive skills. For her, judgment is not a discrete mental act that can be neatly contained by binary terms, such as "rational" or "irrational," "knowledgeable" or "ignorant." This is particularly true of ethical judgments, which may call for a swift evaluation of conflicting elements within an urgent and unprecedented situation. Diotima's middle way is not a narrow path that succeeds in steering a course between conflicting poles but a spacious, nonreactive perspective that embraces the complexity of a situation without being paralyzed by it. The aim is to negotiate the ambiguities and contradictions of life by the light of one's own intuition rather than uncritically follow the standards of commonly accepted moral norms to guide one.

Diotima then proceeds to attack Socrates's assertion that love is a great god. For how could love, which, by definition, longs for good and beautiful things, be a god? If, as the Greeks believed, a god already dwells in happiness and beauty, there would be nothing for that being to long for. Unable to accept that love could be merely human, Socrates presses Diotima to explain what it is. Again, she insists that love lies *in between* gods and men, mortals and immortals. Being neither one nor the other, it operates as an intermediary between them. "Being in the middle of the two," she continues, love "rounds out the whole and binds fast the all to the all."[5]

Might this and other such exchanges with Diotima have pivoted Socrates away from the naturalistic philosophy of his teacher Archelaus, which sought to ascertain what things *are,* towards a philosophy focused on uncertainty and ethics, which strove to understand what one ought to *do?* For Diotima, love of wisdom was a quasi-erotic, Dionysian longing for the ecstasy and release of wisdom. In loving what is beautiful, *eros* might first be drawn to beautiful boys, but if pursued to its logical conclusion, it will culminate in loving the most beautiful thing of all: wisdom. Yet such love, fired with yearning, will forever remain in a liminal zone between ignorance and wisdom. This very in-betweenness, however, may be precisely the condition under which humans are optimally able to flourish.

Diotima appears to have awoken Socrates to the contingent, fluid, ambiguous, and indeterminate condition of living processes. Such a world of uncertainty and tragedy is the only world for which we can *care*. Here alone can an ethical life grounded in love unfold. She revealed to Socrates what Gotama and his followers would have called the middle way.

Just as Diotima criticized Socrates for assuming that if something is not beautiful it must be ugly, so would she have criticized him for assuming if something is not certain it must be uncertain. As Descartes would later come to discover, the one thing he could not doubt was the indisputable fact that he was doubting. The only thing of which he was certain was his own uncertainty. In refusing to split experience into binary opposites, Diotima understood how these opposites are inextricably bound up with each other. What appear to be entirely separate states (beauty vs. ugliness, knowledge vs. ignorance, certainty vs. uncertainty) are simply two poles of a spectrum, along which incremental gradations merge into each other like the colors of a rainbow. Much if not most of our lives take place in the fuzzy mid-zone *between* these poles.

Deep down, what matters to me most is that I am an agent, whose choices, words, and acts can make a difference both to the quality of my own life and to that of the community, society, and world I share with others. Without this fundamental conviction in my own agency, I would be unable to imagine myself or act as an ethical being. I would be incapable of making or acting upon resolutions that would go against the biological, social, political, and religious conditioning of my upbringing.

By giving primacy to ethics (what ought to be done) over metaphysics (what is the case) neither Gotama nor Socrates showed the slightest interest in whether or not human beings possess free will. The issue simply does not arise either in the dialogues of Plato or the discourses of the Pali Canon. For the starting point of both fraternal twins was not to ascertain the nature of truth but to address the question of how to respond appropriately to the ethical demands presented by the suffering of the situation at hand. For Gotama, what matters is not whether life "is" suffering, but how to embrace suffering; not whether craving "causes" suffering, but how to let go of craving. And Socrates, perhaps as a result of his conversations with Diotima, abandoned his previous interest in natural philosophy to focus on the only thing that came to matter for him: how to lead a good life in a contingent and unpredictable world.

II
Contingency

5
An Unbearable Silence

My journey through Buddhism has involved as much chance as choice. Very little was planned. In retrospect, it seems no more than a series of accidents and random encounters, one leading haphazardly to the next, as I wandered around Asia and Europe from one teacher, monastery, and community to another, adopting ideas and pursuing passions as I went. As a creature who craves order and meaning, I have constructed this journey in my memory and writings as a tidy narrative where each step follows logically from the one before as I headed unerringly towards my goal. But this is largely a fiction. In fact, I simply followed my nose, more or less keeping to the path I had chosen but with no idea of where it would lead me.

Looking back, I realize how everything I experienced or learned on this journey need not have happened at all. None of it, I believe, was fated or preordained. Had my parents not separated when I was three, I would have grown up in Toronto rather than Watford. Had I not failed my high school art exam, I would have enrolled at the Regent Street Polytechnic to train as a photographer. Had my grandfather, who had vehemently rejected religion, not left me a modest fund for my further education, I would have been unable to use it to pay for my indoctrination into Tibetan Buddhism. The list of possible paths I could have taken is endless. Yet I suffer from the ironclad conviction that the one I ended up taking was not contingent at all but somehow inevitable. Because I can only know my life as it has actually happened, I feel in my bones that that was how it *had* to be.

Gotama's primary concern was not about how the world *is*, but how the world *could be*. He had embarked on his vocation as a teacher by declaring that he had found a middle way. To tread the middle way is a constant balancing act as one seeks skillfully to steer a course through the shifting, unpredictable, and perilous landscape of a highly contingent world. As the philosopher Robert Ellis has observed, the middle way should be thought of as "a principle of judgment, focusing on how we respond to our experience rather than claims about how things finally are."[1] In avoiding absolutes, the practice of the middle way embodies an ethics of uncertainty and risk. For as I weave my way through life, I keep finding myself in situations which call for a response, but for which I lack the ideological or religious convictions that would tell me what to do. Yet, as an ethical agent, I cannot not act.

Vaccha was a wandering monk, clad in a simple robe with a begging bowl slung over one shoulder, who walked across the Gangetic plain at the same time as Gotama. Several dialogues between the two men are found in the Pali Canon. The *Connected Discourses on the Undeclared* records the following encounter:

> VACCHA: Mr Gotama, is there a self?
> *Silence.*
> VACCHA: Mr Gotama, is there not a self?
> *Silence.*
> Vaccha got up from his seat and went away.[2]

An Unbearable Silence

Why did Vaccha leave? Did he conclude that Gotama did not know the answer to these questions? Did he think Gotama was making fun of him? Or did he find the silence unbearable?

To lead the kind of examined life that Gotama proposes threatens to undermine many instinctive and comforting certainties. To heed his silence requires acknowledging the depths of your own ignorance. In refusing to say "yes" or "no," Gotama leaves the questions hanging. He holds no view about either the existence or nonexistence of the self. His silence invites Vaccha to stay with the questions rather than reach for an answer. He confronts Vaccha with the oddity and poignancy of being a self-aware creature who can become a question for him- or herself.

A longer encounter between Gotama and a young court chaplain called Kaccāna illuminates this exchange with Vaccha.[3] Dispatched by King Pajjota of Avantī, Kaccāna and seven companions had walked six hundred miles from their home in the ancient city of Ujjeni (modern Ujjain) to northeast India. Their mission was to persuade Gotama to visit Ujjeni.

As they came to know each other, Kaccāna asked Gotama to explain what he meant by a "true perspective," which traditionally is the first limb of the eightfold path or middle way. "Most people," responded Gotama, "are attached to the binary of 'is' and 'is not.'"[4] He then went on to show how those with a true perspective no longer orient themselves to the world in this binary fashion. When Vaccha had asked Gotama whether the self existed or not, the very same "is" and "is not" were the terms he used. Like most of us, Vaccha and Kaccāna took for granted the binaries built into the grammar of human languages. It seems obvious to us language users—like Hamlet in his famous soliloquy—that we must either "be" someone or "not be" someone. Aristotle would have agreed: a third option (an excluded middle) is inconceivable.

Gotama invited his interlocutors to take a closer, more

holistic look at the world around them. There they will discover myriad living things, constantly arising and ceasing within complex webs of relationships. Closely observe a seed. Watch it sprout, grow into a stem, then turn into a flower, which, having spread its seed, wilts and dies. You witness a seamless process of changing phenomena, which is porous and fluid with no clear-cut beginnings or ends. "Is" and "is not" split experience up in a way that facilitates human communication but is alien to the natural world. The neat dividing lines of thought and language are not discernible in the fuzzy fabric of life.

Gotama's perspective is full of perplexity, surprise, curiosity, and wonder. As soon as you suspend the habit of seeing yourself and things through the binary categories of "right" and "wrong," "yes" and "no," or "is" and "is not," you are left in a state of questioning and unknowing. To cultivate this perspective means letting go of entrenched opinions and embracing uncertainty. You find yourself confronted with the ambiguity and complexity of dilemmas in life to which you are nonetheless called upon as a moral agent to respond.

"Kaccāna," continued Gotama, "most people are bound to their prejudices and habits." Whereas those who live from this perspective

> do not get caught up in the habits, fixations, prejudices, or biases of the mind. They are not fixated on "my self." They have no doubt that when someone is suffering, she is suffering, and when she stops suffering, her suffering is no more. What they know is independent of others.[5]

Attachment to the binary of "is" and "is not" lies at the root of the preoccupation with "me" as well as the indifference one feels for those outside the charmed circle of "mine." It provides an ontological foundation for the certainties in which we become emotionally invested. The perspective of which Gotama speaks demands a break from this deeply familiar way of inhabiting the world. It calls for a heartfelt revolution away from *being* to *suffering,* from *ontos* to *pathos,* from ontology to a new kind of pathology and therapy. Turning one's attention from *what is* to *what suffers* is where the practice of an ethics of uncertainty begins.

By relinquishing "prejudices and habits," you find yourself alone. Unable to rely on the confirmation and support of those with whom you once shared such views, you may feel like a stranger in the world. To become "independent of others" means achieving autonomy, to be able to make your own ethical judgments in the light of the specific needs of the given situation. Those who enter the stream of the eightfold path are said to have let go of attachment to moral rules. Such rules may hold societies and religious communities together, but they are also prejudices and habits instilled in people's minds. The skeptical ethicist treats each moral dilemma she encounters as specific to the situation at hand. Abstract precepts or moral thought experiments provide no more than a broad template to guide her response. Having weighed up as best she can what the most caring response would be, she takes the risk of acting yet without any consoling certainty that it is the right thing to do.

Gotama concludes:

> "Everything is," Kaccāna, is the first dead end. "Everything is not" is the second dead end. The sage reveals the dharma from a middle that avoids dead ends.

A dead end is a path that goes nowhere. Views such as eternalism ("I am an immortal soul") or nihilism ("I am just a random collection of atoms that will disintegrate at death") are seductive because they seem to offer answers to life's big questions. To cling to such views may console you, but they risk paralyzing you. Gotama does not reject such views because they are wrong but because they prevent one from being fully alive.

"The sage," declared Gotama to the monk Anurādha, "is not apprehended as real and actual here in this very life."[6] He cannot be pinned down or defined. He is one who has broken free from the dead ends of dogmatic certainty and embraced the radical contingency of life. Being independent of others, he no longer needs to dissimulate or pretend. There is no one he has to impress. He responds to life situations with imagination, creativity, and care. Centered and balanced, he treads a wide and open middle way. From such a sensibility does Gotama reveal the dharma, sometimes in acts, sometimes with words, sometimes through silence.

On understanding what Gotama meant by a true perspective, Kaccāna is said to have gained insight into the dharma. As was the case in the early days of Gotama's teaching, he was accepted into the monastic order with the simple exhortation "Come join us!"

It is not known how long Kaccāna stayed in northeast India as a member of Gotama's community. In the end, Gotama turned down King Pajjota's invitation to Ujjeni, and instructed Kaccāna to teach and establish a community there in his stead. Nothing much came of it. King Pajjota—known as "Pajjota the Terrible"—may have taken Gotama's refusal as a snub and withdrawn his support from Kaccāna. Whatever the reasons, Kaccāna failed to attract many followers. He spent much of his time alone at the Osprey's Haunt, a hermitage perched on a steep mountain slope above a town called Kuraraghara.

Many years later, when his benefactor and student Soṇa Kuṭikaṇṇa asked to become a monk, Kaccāna tried his best to dissuade him.[7] It took Kaccāna three years of "difficulty and trouble" to convene the requisite number of monks to perform the ordination. Not long after Soṇa was ordained, Kaccāna gave him permission to go to Jeta's Grove in Sāvatthī, the headquarters of the movement, so he could meet and study with Gotama himself. On reaching Jeta's Grove, Gotama asked the new arrival to speak some words of dharma. Soṇa recited from memory the *Chapter of Eights,* a collection of texts built around a core of four eight-verse poems, in all likelihood composed by his teacher Kaccāna.

The *Chapter of Eights* offers a sustained reflection on the peril of being trapped in fixed views that deny and obscure the contingency of life. Reflecting perhaps on his own experience of isolation, Kaccāna's first poem, *The Cell,* opens:

> The creature concealed inside its cell—
> a man sunk in dark passions
> is a long, long way from solitude.[8]

True solitude has nothing to do with sitting cross-legged with eyes closed for long hours in a hermitage or cave. Solitude is a way of being in the world emptied of habitual fixations, prejudices, and biases. This silence of the mind's compulsive chatter is the stillness of nirvana itself. Yet in our eagerness always to be right, we hasten through life from one opinion to the next like "monkeys who let go of one branch only to seize another."[9]

The stranglehold of opinion impedes human flourishing. Once in its grip you are cast into a barren land, where nothing can grow. The sage treads a middle path, where he neither "takes up *nor* discards any view." He accepts the conclusions of those who are experts in their respective fields but treats them as provisional. "Not passionate, not dispassionate, he doesn't posit anything as 'ultimate.'"[10]

Kaccāna regards attachment to opinions and views as the origin of human conflict. When convinced that you are right, you will consider anyone who disagrees with you to be wrong. From here you are only a step away from enflaming the binary split of "is" and "is not" with moral indignation. History provides ample examples of how trivial differences can escalate into vendettas and wars. "One who dwells in 'ultimate' views," says Kaccāna, "will declare all other views 'inferior' (*hina*)—he has not overcome disputes."[11] The sage, however, has both the courage to let go of opinions and the tolerance to endure the silence of their absence.

In *On True Perspective,* Gotama's disciple Sāriputta presents another dimension to this way of being in the world. "When practitioners," says Sāriputta, "understand evil and the roots of evil, good and the roots of good, then they possess a true perspective."[12] To let go of fixed opinions allows one to dwell in a nonreactive space where previously unimagined ways of responding to the suffering of oneself and others can emerge. Such a perspective optimizes one's capacity to make ethical judgments and choices. It grants the freedom, courage, and clarity to risk thinking, speaking, and acting differently from how one has been conditioned.

One of the pithiest summaries of Gotama's dharma is found in an early collection of verses known as the *Dhammapada:* "Do not perform evil, do what is good, and purify the soul—that is the advice of awakened ones."[13] If we understand "purifying the soul" to mean liberating one's mind from reactive opinions, then it would correspond to freeing oneself from attachment to the binary of "is" and "is not," which serves as the ontological foundation for dogmatic views and beliefs. When this perspective is combined with the injunctions to avoid evil and do good, the verse provides a succinct definition of an ethics of uncertainty.

Kaccāna was renowned not only for his sharp intelligence but also for his physical beauty. The *Dhammapada Commentary*, a potpourri of extra-canonical and canonical fragments loosely tied to the verses of the *Dhammapada,* includes a tale involving a wealthy young man called Soreyya.[14]

One morning, Soreyya and a friend were driving in a carriage to a bathing place. On the way, they chanced to see Kaccāna arranging his robes prior to entering the town on his daily almsround. At the sight of Kaccāna's naked torso, Soreyya thought, "Oh, that this monk might be my wife!" Immediately, Soreyya was transformed into a woman. Filled with shame, she fled the scene and attached herself to a caravan heading for Taxila, the capital of Gandhāra, the easternmost province of the Persian Empire in the far northwest of the Indian subcontinent. On reaching the city, this "jewel of a woman" was presented to an unmarried merchant as a prospective wife. They were married and Soreyyā gave birth to two sons. Having already fathered two sons when she was a man, she thus became both a father and a mother.

It being biologically impossible for a person who has transitioned from a man to a woman to bear children, this story is not to be taken literally. By employing the tone, cadences, and structure of a fable, the narrator is freed to address taboo topics such as homoeroticism and gender ambivalence that are otherwise ignored in Buddhist literature. In constructing the story around Kaccāna, the narrative also offers a symbolic illustration of his philosophy. A gender-fluid person is a living example of an excluded middle, a person who eludes the binary categories of male and female, who cannot be reduced to "being" or "not being" a man or a woman. Soreyya's sudden gender transition and flight to Taxila demonstrates how the uncertainty and fluidity of personal identity can also be a struggle involving feelings of guilt and shame. The story would have enabled those troubled by their sexual identity to feel acknowledged and, to some extent, understood.

This tale shows how marginalized people, who did not fit into the normative identities of their culture, could have found acceptance and companionship in the single-sex renunciant communities emerging in India at this period. They may also have been naturally drawn to a philosophy that questioned some of the binary categories that excluded them, while valuing paradox, fluidity, and uncertainty. Rather than prompting a queer person to walk away, Gotama's silence might have come as a welcome relief. The familiar experience of social and psychological isolation could likewise have rendered the prospect of being a solitary contemplative less daunting, even attractive.

As happens in fables, Soreyyā's former bathing companion found himself one fine day in Taxila. He recognized the woman that Soreyyā now was and suggested she ask forgiveness from Kaccāna, who was staying nearby. If Kaccāna had failed to establish much of a following in his homeland, it is not inconceivable that he would have ended up in distant Taxila. As soon as Kaccāna pardoned Soreyyā for having lusted after his body, she was transformed back into a man. Weary of the household life, Soreyya entrusted the two sons to the care of their father, received monastic vows from Kaccāna, and eventually became a liberated saint.

6

The Socrates Show

It is possible, though unlikely, that a follower of Gotama could have been present in Athens during the lifetime of Socrates. Let us imagine an intelligent and curious young man, who spent fifteen years, from around 445 to 430 BCE, as part of Gotama's community during the early years of his teaching career in north-east India. For some reason—trade, study, service, marriage—he then traveled by caravan along the North Road from Sāvatthī to Taxila. Had he been heeding Gotama's injunction "to go forth into the world for the benefit of the many," he might even have been a missionary. For a few more years he moved farther westward along the efficient network of roads in Persia until reaching the Greek colony of Ionia in Asia Minor, from where he crossed the Aegean by ship to Athens, arriving in the spring of 423 BCE, just as Aristophanes's comedy *Clouds* was being premiered at the City Dionysia. At this point he would have been around forty years old. Had he lived another twenty-four years, he would have been about seventy when Socrates, a man of his own age, was executed.

This thought experiment allows us to imagine what it would have been like for someone grounded in early Buddhist thought and practice to witness the events that unfolded in Athens during the last quarter of the fifth century BCE. Adopting this perspective allows me to provide a Buddhistic portrait of Socrates and his world by highlighting those features of life in ancient Athens that would have likely stood out for such an observer. As such a hypothetical Buddhist in Athens, my starting point would be to consider how the Greeks addressed the preeminent Buddhist concern with suffering.

Suffering was not a theme of great interest to Greek thinkers. It is discussed only once in the collected works of Plato.[1] Yet it is the principal focus of the poets who wrote the great Greek tragedies: Aeschylus, Sophocles, and Euripides. In another variant of the Delphic Oracle's answer to the question "Who is the wisest person in Greece?" she purportedly replied, "Wise is Sophocles, wiser Euripides, of all men Socrates is wisest."[2] By comparing Socrates to the two most renowned tragedians of his day suggests that Socratic wisdom was considered closer to the wisdom of poets than philosophers. Since these tragedians were concerned with how to lead a good life in a world fraught with suffering, theirs was an ethical wisdom. The Oracle appeared to be saying that when it came to ethics the wisdom of Socrates outshone even that of the tragic poets.

Much of what we know today about the thinkers of ancient Greece is found in a single volume called *Lives of the Eminent Philosophers* by Diogenes Laertius, a man about whom we know nothing. Drawing on a wide range of classical works, many of which are now lost, Diogenes Laertius was interested as much in the lives of the philosophers as their ideas. After naming Socrates's parents and his birthplace in Athens, the very first thing he tells us about the philosopher is that "he was thought to have collaborated with Euripides."[3] Several ancient sources attest that Socrates worked with the celebrated tragedian. The comic poet Telecleides says that "Socrates provided the kindling" for some of Euripides's plays and "patched up" others, implying that he served as an inspiration and editor for Euripides's tragedies. Another fragment of Telecleides describes the two men as "bolted together"—close friends who shared an intimate philosophical, ethical, and artistic complicity.[4] And in his comedy *Frogs,* Aristophanes has the chorus accuse Euripides of "stylishly sitting beside Socrates, blabbering away."[5]

In his earliest surviving comedy, *The Archanians,* Aristophanes caricatures Euripides as dwelling in a state of Socratic aporia, suspended between binary opposites in a state of creative uncertainty. The play's protagonist goes to Euripides's house in search of some stage props, knocks on the door, and asks the servant whether his master is at home. The servant replies that the playwright "is in, but not in." When asked how this is possible, the servant replies, "His mind's outside collecting verses, so his mind's not in, but the man himself is inside working on tragedies." Euripides is wheeled out seated on a high couch. "I have to act as if I'm a beggar today," explains the protagonist in a similarly aporetic vein, "and be who I am, yet not be so."[6] Both playwright and protagonist are shown as inhabiting an excluded middle that escapes the logic of "is" and "isn't."

Very little is known about Euripides. The poet was born on the island of Salamis just off the coast of Piraeus around 480 BCE, thus making him the same age as Gotama. Since Aristophanes ridicules him in *Law and Order Women* as the "son of a vegetable-selling bitch," he may have had lowly origins like Socrates, the son of a stonemason and midwife.[7] For Aristotle, Euripides was "the most tragic of the poets," who presented human beings as they *were* in contrast to Sophocles who presented them as they *should be*.[8] Inspired perhaps by Socrates's involvement with ordinary citizens in the agora, Euripides departed from the convention of grandiose but two-dimensional heroes and heroines and sought to depict people realistically, warts and all. His plays became so popular that Athenian prisoners of war in Sicily were said to have gained extra rations or even freedom by reciting lines from them to their captors.

At the same City Dionysia that saw the first performance of *Clouds*, Euripides's tragedy *Suppliant Women* was presented in competition for the prize in tragedy. *Suppliant Women* is a protracted howl of anguish. The play tells of seven mourning women from Argos, whose sons have been killed in a battle against Thebes. Despite their tearful supplications, the Thebans have refused to return the bodies of the dead: the gravest of insults that serves as a recurrent theme in Attic tragedy. Adrastus, the vanquished king of Argos, appeals to Theseus, king of Athens, to come to their aid. Theseus attacks the city and forces the Thebans to hand over the corpses. The dead are then cremated with due solemnity and ritual at the Attic town of Eleutherae.

When performed at the City Dionysia that spring, *Suppliant Women* would have provided an allegorical framework for the audience to come to terms with the defeat of Athens some months earlier at Delium, where Socrates had fought as a hoplite. With a few scratches of his stylus on a wax tablet, Euripides magically transformed Athens from the vanquished combatant of Delium into the wise impartial mediator of other people's conflicts, embodied in *Suppliant Women* by the mythic Athenian king Theseus. This is theater as civic therapy. Theseus is the Philosopher King, Athens's best possible version of herself, the lone voice of calm and reason amidst the despair and confusion of defeat. He takes this opportunity to reflect on the nature of civic society. "Adrastus," he declares, "there are three classes of citizens."

The rich are worthless as they are always lusting after more; the poor are dangerous because they despise the rich out of envy and are tricked by the tongues of crooked leaders. Of the three, only those in the middle save the community, guarding as they do the law and order of the city.[9]

These reflections have nothing to do with the political arrangements of the mythic world of the play, ruled by make-believe monarchs. Theseus is addressing concerns about the future of democracy in the city-state of Athens, its self-confidence badly shaken. He tacitly reminds the spectators of their duty as an enlightened middle class to ensure the security and survival of the city and its democratic institutions.

At the same time, Euripides wants his audience to recognize how, as democrats, they bear responsibility for the campaign and its disastrous outcome. Then, as now, democratic regimes planning invasions of foreign countries sought to justify their actions in the name of democracy. The Athenians may well have convinced themselves that the invasion of a neighboring country would be for the good of its inhabitants, thereby allowing them to present their military intervention as a defense of democracy rather than a self-interested land grab. But in the wake of their crushing defeat at Delium, it might well have seemed that the democratic system of government itself had failed them.

Imagine for a moment looking down on Athens from the sky. About a quarter of a million people, half of them slaves, are packed into a city enclosed by thick, high walls. Beyond the walls lie the villages and farmland of Attica, periodically invaded by their enemies in the Peloponnesian War, which drove thousands of terrified people into the city for safety. For while the powerful navy of Athens controlled the sea, its foes controlled the land. To secure access to the port of Piraeus on the coast, the Athenians built two walls, each four miles in length, between which ran a road wide enough for two chariots to pass. This was their lifeline. No matter how many foreign militias were raiding the countryside, foodstuffs and other goods could be brought into the city by ship. One might picture Athens as a womb which nurtured a fetus whose long umbilical cord stretched along this walled corridor to the sea. As a result, the city became a hothouse of political and juridical wrangling, a pressure cooker for philosophy, theater and art, and a petri dish for not infrequent pandemics.

Athens was steadily hemorrhaging the lives of its male citizens. "Life is a misfortune," declared the defeated Adrastus in the play, echoing the current woes of many spectators. Theseus disagrees. He tells Adrastus how he has often discussed the question of suffering with others and his opinion has never changed. He insists that the opposite is true, that "there is more good fortune than bad in our lives."[10] Despite all the war and pain, he recognizes how it is a wonder to be alive at all. He encourages Adrastus to reflect on how extraordinary it is to think and speak, to inhabit a world that satisfies our basic needs, to interact with strangers for our mutual benefit. Indeed, it may be at times of greatest grief, when directly confronted with death and loss, that philosophical wonder seizes us most urgently. Rather than drown in self-indulgent misery, Theseus suggests, open your eyes and allow yourself to be astonished again.

The City Dionysia of 423 was in some respects "The Socrates Show." Of the three comedies in competition, the controversial philosopher was the subject of two of them: *Beard* and *Clouds*. And not only was Socrates a veteran of the military campaign allegorized in *Suppliant Women,* as Euripides's collaborator he could well have played a role in the gestation and delivery of the play itself. When he stood up from his seat in the amphitheater in response to the question "Who *is* this man, Socrates?" was it to acknowledge the city's acclaim? Or was it to silently reflect back to his audience the very question of what it means to be human?

"I am not in any sense a wise man," Socrates declared to the mathematician Theaetetus in Plato's dialogue of the same name. "I cannot claim as the child of my own soul any discovery worth the name of wisdom. But with those who associate with me it is different."[11] Socrates thought of himself as a midwife who watched over the pregnancy of men's souls. His role was to facilitate wisdom in others by providing the supportive conditions for it to emerge. Men too, he claimed, suffered excruciating labor pains, which he sought both to induce and allay by his art of relentlessly testing and probing their minds. He may have assisted in delivering their offspring, but he would take neither credit nor blame for the results. All he could do was help people "discover within themselves a multitude of beautiful things, which they bring forth into the light." He insisted that their child was the product of their own creative genius and had nothing to do with what they may have learned from him.

Was this how Socrates collaborated with Euripides? Was *Suppliant Women* a child of Euripides's imagination, skillfully helped into the world by Socrates's maieutic art? Did Socrates's probing comments and questions enable Euripides's intuitions to achieve their final shape and form? Was Socrates's role in the process to clear away the confusion in Euripides's mind to reveal an empty but fertile space of possibility where the playwright could deepen and develop his vision?

7
Whose Buddha? Whose Socrates?

We can say with some confidence that Socrates attended the first performance of Aristophanes's *Clouds* at the Dionysian theater on the slopes of the Acropolis in Athens during the spring equinox of 323 BCE. All we can say about Gotama is that during the same equinox he would probably have been somewhere in an area the size of Pennsylvania in the northeastern part of the Indian subcontinent. And while we can read the first known account of Socrates in the text of Aristophanes's comedy as it was likely performed at the time, the first brief accounts of Gotama and his teaching do not appear until one hundred and fifty years after his death in chiseled rock edicts erected in different parts of India by the Buddhist emperor Aśoka.

Scholars of early Buddhism can only dream of having access to the kind of source materials available to those who study ancient Greece. Seven tragedies of Sophocles, eighteen tragedies of Euripides, and eleven comedies of Aristophanes have come down to us virtually intact from the fifth century BCE. In addition, we have the contemporary historical writings of Herodotus and Thucydides; the dialogues of Plato; the histories, military texts, biographies, and memoirs of Xenophon; and hundreds of textual fragments and stone inscriptions. At the Parthenon and other archaeological sites, we can still see the remains of buildings Socrates would have known, and we have museums packed with statues, friezes, vases, and all manner of everyday implements and jewelry, some of which Socrates and his circle may have once held in their hands. All that survives from Gotama's time in northeast India are pottery shards, a few punch-marked coins, glass beads, some rusted iron tools, and a number of tiny bone relics.

The sheer volume of artifacts from ancient Athens allows us to build up a picture of Socrates with far greater granularity than we can ever hope for with Gotama. The busts of Socrates and his Athenian contemporaries, whether Greek originals or Roman copies, provide at least some idea of how these people looked. With Gotama and his disciples we have no idea of their appearance at all. Compared to the vivid accounts of Socrates, Gotama comes across in the earliest texts as an iconic figure worthy of veneration but almost entirely devoid of those telling quirks of character that allow a personality to emerge. Whether it is Gotama or one of the senior disciples giving a discourse in the Pali Canon, the speakers serve as more or less interchangeable mouthpieces for disseminating Buddhist doctrine.

Gotama was born and spent much of his life on the vast, flat alluvial plain formed over millions of years by sediment deposited by rivers, which ran from the Himalayas all the way down to the Ganges. This extraordinarily fertile land generated the wealth which by Gotama's time was enabling cities to be built and kingdoms to be formed. But since neither stone nor kiln-fired bricks were available as building materials, nothing remains of any structures or edifices from the period. The timber, thatch, and sun-baked bricks from which they were made have returned to dust and left no trace. And there was no paper or any other material available that could withstand the seasonal extremes of rain and heat to serve as a durable basis for recording written information. Gotama's was an oral culture that passed its learning from one generation to the next through systematic techniques of memorization. All we know of Gotama's world is found in texts that were preserved in the memories of monastics for four hundred years before being committed to writing on palm leaves in Sri Lanka in the first century BCE.

Such canonical Buddhist texts are the only source we have from which to form a picture of Gotama. Although no single event described in the canon can be dated with certainty, across the wide spectrum of episodes recounted in the discourses some have a greater claim to historical truth than others. The final year or so of Gotama's life, for example, follows a discernible chronology, can be tracked geographically, and narrates its unfolding tragedy with great pathos. The same is true regarding what happened as the community struggled to come to terms with his death in the following months. In these discourses, the principal actors—Gotama, Ānanda, and Kassapa—spring briefly but vividly to life as figures in a drama rather than faceless monks declaiming eternal Buddhist truths.

In contrast to the extreme paucity of information about Gotama, for Socrates we have not only Plato's dialogues from which to construe a picture of the philosopher but also Xenophon's shorter *Conversations of Socrates*. Xenophon was an Athenian nobleman and soldier, a contemporary of Plato, and a member of Socrates's circle until he was exiled from Athens in his mid- to late twenties a couple of years before Socrates's trial and death. He never returned to Athens and died in Corinth.

Socrates is said to have first encountered the handsome

young Xenophon in a narrow lane in Athens. He blocked the way with his staff, then asked him where he could purchase various goods in the market. After Xenophon had told him, Socrates inquired, "And where do men become good and honourable?" Xenophon was speechless. Socrates said, "Follow me then, and learn."[1] In addition to his memoir of his teacher, Xenophon wrote a version of Socrates's defense speech at his trial, an account of a dinner party at which Socrates was present, where—as in Plato's *Drinking Party*—each guest took turns in talking about love (*eros*), and a Socratic dialogue that discusses the management of country estates.

After knowing Socrates solely through the works of Plato, my first reading of Xenophon came like a visceral blow. Plato and Xenophon are clearly talking about the same person, but it does not seem like the same person at all. Scholars have identified more than thirty details about Socrates corroborated by Plato and Xenophon alike, but that fails to dispel the disconcerting impression that these two versions of Socrates do not match. Like identical twins, they might look the same but have very different personalities.

The difference between Plato's Socrates and Xenophon's Socrates lies in the difference between Plato and Xenophon. It is as though Socrates serves as a theatrical mask or persona through which others took turns to speak. While Plato was a towering literary and philosophical genius, Xenophon was a plain-speaking, morally earnest military officer and country gentleman. While Plato's texts sparkle with wit and brilliance, Xenophon's tend to be labored and dull.

As a soldier and farmer Xenophon may have been more concerned with how the virtues are *enacted* in the world rather than what the virtues *are*. In Plato's *Defense Speech* Socrates denies that he is a teacher who recruits students and shows them a path. Xenophon takes issue with such accounts that present Socrates as "excellent at setting people on the road to goodness, [but] incapable of leading them to their goal."[2] For Xenophon, Socrates taught his students how to become good people "by obviously *being* such a person" himself.[3] Socrates inspired his followers to cultivate their own minds and characters by witnessing how he had cultivated his. He taught them ethics by *showing* them an ethical life as well as telling them about it.

The conversations recorded by Xenophon also reveal a Socrates who eagerly instructed his interlocutors how to behave. Instead of a midwife, who helps others give birth to their own insights, this Socrates is a strict teacher, who lays down the law with humorless efficiency. Xenophon recalls how Socrates "encouraged his associates to practice self-discipline with regard to food and drink and sex and sleep and heat and cold and physical exertion."[4] Through his teachings, Socrates made his students "abstain from irreverent and wrong and discreditable actions not only in public but in private."[5] Socrates insisted on unwavering veneration of the gods since the gods are always aware of our thoughts and actions. We even find Socrates lecturing his eldest son, Lamprocles, on the correct way to treat his famously foul-tempered mother Xanthippe.[6]

Through Xenophon we encounter a Socrates who in many ways is closer to Gotama as he appears in the Pali discourses than to the Socrates portrayed by Plato. Xenophon's Socrates is unambiguously a teacher who has dedicated himself, like Gotama, to inform, educate, and discipline his followers just as a general (e.g., Xenophon) might have trained his soldiers. In addition to examining their minds, the followers of both Socrates and Gotama are encouraged to lead a life of renunciation and rigorous training with like-minded friends. For Xenophon, "the company of good men"—a *sangha*—is in itself "a training in virtue."[7] When he says of teachers that "they show their pupils how they themselves practise what they preach, and lead them on by reasoned argument," Xenophon could just as well have been talking of Gotama. And when he adds that Socrates "made it clear to his companions that he was a truly good man, and excelled in discussing ethical questions and all human problems," this too would have been a fitting description of Gotama.[8]

The Socrates who barred Xenophon's way with a staff to persuade the bright young man to follow him suggests that the philosopher may have been forming a community of some kind. Perhaps we get a glimpse of that community from Theseus's speech in *Suppliant Women*, where he identifies a third class of citizens in Athens, whose role is to safeguard the city. Did Socrates recruit Xenophon and others as a vanguard of philosophers who, under his tutelage, would carve out a middle ground between the powerful and the weak? This not only makes one think of Gotama's community of monastics who seek to embody a middle way, but it reminds us of the "guardians" that Plato, decades later, would describe in his *Republic* as the philosophical elite who wisely rule his ideal city.

I had hoped that Plato's and Xenophon's independent accounts of Socrates would bring Socrates into sharper focus. A flat two-dimensional image, I imagined, would suddenly acquire a third dimension that would render Socrates more lifelike. Instead, it is Plato and Xenophon who become more lifelike, and Socrates disappears into the gap that opens up between them. For there are as many Socrateses as there are pairs of eyes through which to behold him and imaginations to construe him. Plato's and Xenophon's different portrayals of the philosopher make him recede further into the distance until the "real" Socrates vanishes altogether. As a result, Socrates has become for me less distinct, less lifelike, and more of an enigma.

Since we only have one version of Gotama—that of the early discourses and monastic training texts—we are spared the Plato/Xenophon dilemma. This allows us to maintain an innocence about Gotama. The same person, more or less, appears in all the primary sources we consult. Like a formal studio portrait, he is fixed forever in the same posture with the same gaze. He may not have a particularly distinctive or engaging personality, but at least the portrayal of him is consistent. This is reassuring, especially for those who wish to revere Gotama as the Buddha: an exemplar of unchanging human perfection.

But *whose* Gotama is presented to us in these early Buddhist texts? It may be the only version of Gotama that has come down to us, but it is still *somebody's* version. Gotama is depicted as he is because somebody, or a community of somebodies, wanted him represented in a way that accorded with *their* desires and interests to maintain a consistent image of him and his teachings. Presumably, this is how all orthodoxies are formed. Yet the canonical discourses themselves tell of a monk called Purana, who, after Gotama's death, refused to submit to the consensus agreed on by the senior monastics as to what Gotama taught.[9] Purana's Gotama has not come down to us. We are just left with the tantalizing hint that the official account of Gotama was not the only version circulating among his followers.

A more poignant example of the struggle within the early community after Gotama's death is provided by the canonical accounts of the dispute that arose between Ānanda, Gotama's faithful attendant and nephew, and the stern ascetic and former brahmin Kassapa (usually known as Mahākassapa). In a poem included among the *Verses of the Elders,* Ānanda bemoans that he has nothing in common with such newcomers and compares himself to a fledgling bird abandoned in a nest just as the devastating monsoon rains are about to fall.[10] After years of working closely with Gotama, Ānanda leaves us with an image of desolation and despair.

Ānanda's very human Gotama can still be glimpsed here and there in the discourses, but this version of Gotama has otherwise been airbrushed out of the picture. Instead, the Gotama of the early texts is largely Kassapa's Gotama. Having gained control of the monastic community in the weeks and months after Gotama's death, Kassapa organized a council in Rajagaha to lay down the foundations of what would become Buddhist orthodoxy. It was here that the process of compiling and organizing the discourses and monastic training texts began.

Since the compilers and redactors of the canon were exclusively monastics, the choices of which discourses to include would inevitably have been influenced by their shared monastic perspective on the dharma. These discourses make it abundantly clear that if you seek to embark on the eightfold path to attain Nirvana, you have to become a monastic. For the ultimate goal of the path—arahantship—is a state that can *only* be attained by men and women who have renounced the world and committed themselves to poverty and celibacy. The Gotama who is presented as holding these views is the ascetics' Gotama.

The canonical texts say little about the kind of lives led by Gotama's non-monastic followers. The secular world filters through to us incidentally in the descriptions of the settings of Gotama's discourses, in the rules that describe what monastics should avoid, in the analogies and allegories used to illustrate the teachings, and in the occasional sketches of kings, ministers, merchants, doctors, farmers, artisans, and others. At times, Gotama praises the attainments of his men and women "lay" followers, but in the five volumes of the Pali

Canon he devotes only one complete discourse (*To Sigālaka*) to addressing the issues of household life.[11]

Had the task of remembering Gotama's teachings been assumed by a guild of goldsmiths, we would have a very different picture of who this man was and what he taught. We would also acquire a great deal of information about the lives, working conditions, and concerns of goldsmiths. But no goldsmiths' Gotama, or any kind of householders' Gotama, has ever reached us.

"Absence of evidence," as the saying goes, "is not evidence of absence." Just because a human society leaves few traces of its existence does not mean that that society was primitive, uncultured, and barbaric. But this is often the assumption we moderns make. The people who produced, more than twenty thousand years ago, the sublime art found in prehistoric caves still tend to be represented as "cavemen" with matted hair and feral eyes who only communicate by gestures and grunts. Yet the very fact that we can still be deeply moved by their art suggests that they were probably just like you and me.

A world made entirely of degradable materials that were endlessly recycled may not leave any marks in the archaeological record, but a prosperous, highly organized, and complex society could nonetheless have flourished there.[12] Nor need a culture that did not write anything down be tainted with the negative connotations we associate with illiteracy. Whether it be Vedic hymns or Homer's epic poems, such literature was preserved for centuries without pen ever touching paper. Elegant architecture, carefully designed parks and gardens, elaborate theatrical and musical productions are all possible without a single dressed stone or written document being involved. We know that the householders of Gotama's time enjoyed theatrical performances for the simple reason that monks and nuns were forbidden to attend them. But we have no idea what those plays were about, how well or badly they were written, in what sort of settings they were presented, or what kind of music, if any, accompanied them.

I find it hard to imagine how the originality, complexity, subtlety, and precision that characterize the ideas and arguments in the earliest Buddhist texts would not somehow be reflected in the aesthetics of the textiles, craftwork, and buildings of the cultures where these texts were composed. That two and a half millennia later we too can be engaged by the very same ideas implies how those initially inspired by them were no different from us in their interests, longings, intelligence, and sensibilities.

8
Convenient Fictions

The first studies of "history"—in the sense we understand the term today—were composed by two Greeks of the fifth century BCE, Herodotus and Thucydides. Herodotus was the older of the two and may have inspired Thucydides, but little is known about the lives of either man. Both sought to provide evidence on which to establish the actual causes and circumstances of the events they described without any appeal to myth, divine intervention, or rumor. "My business is to record what people say," wrote Herodotus, "but I am by no means bound to believe it."[1]

While there were no figures comparable to Herodotus or Thucydides in India, the texts of the Pali Canon nonetheless open a window onto a distinctively human world, populated by imperfect men and women going about their daily and often messy business in identifiable locations in northeast India, rather than the mythic interactions between men and gods as found in epics such as the *Mahābhārata* and the *Rāmāyaṇa*. The Pali discourses are the first examples in Indian literature where the contingent, tragic human world takes center stage. Gods still occasionally appear in a supporting role, but they are marginalized and at times even ridiculed. The account of the last year or so of Gotama's life in the early Buddhist canon may be the first Indian text with a reasonable claim to historical truth.

Yet even a historian as exacting in his method as Thucydides had to make choices as to what to include and what to exclude in his writings. History is not just an inventory or list of everything that happened on a particular occasion, but an interpretation that renders that occasion meaningful for the writer and his readers within a broader narrative. However objective the historian aspires to be, what he writes will still be a perspective on the events he describes, which will be determined by numerous factors such as political motives, gender, and class biases, many of which he may not even be conscious. By and large, the stories that have come down to us did so because they served the vested interests of powerful groups who sought their version of events to prevail in the collective memories of their community, state, religion, or political faction.

The dominant political power that cast its shadow over both Greece and India during the lifetimes of Gotama and Socrates was the Achaemenid Empire of Persia, founded in 550 BCE by Cyrus the Great, which expanded into the greatest empire the world had ever known. According to Herodotus, the Achaemenid emperor Darius the Great employed a Greek sailor called Scylax of Caryanda to determine the course of the Indus River and scout the surrounding territories in preparation for the Persian invasion and occupation of Gandhara that took place in 516 BCE. This is the earliest account of a European traveling to the Indian subcontinent. Given his mission, it seems unlikely that Scylax ventured farther east to where Gotama was born, lived, and died.

Scholars have argued that Gotama's Sakiyan ancestors may have migrated to their homeland in northeast India via

Persia from Central Asia.[2] Rather than being descendants of the Aryan tribes that began migrating to India in approximately 2000 BCE, the Sakiyans could have been Scythians, nomadic pastoralists from the Eurasian Steppes, who started arriving in India around a thousand or so years after the Aryans. It is claimed that Gotama's clan name "Sakiya" derives from the Sanskrit "Śaka" and Iranian "Saka," which are how the Scythians are known in those languages. Gotama's ancestral Scythian origins may help explain elements in his teaching that are not found in the preexisting Indian religions of his time but bear similarities to Zoroastrian ideas that could have been acquired during the Scythians' migration through Persia.

The Zoroastrian ethical concept of deeds performed by "body, voice, and mind," for example, appears throughout early Buddhist literature, but such a tripartite division of the human being is absent in other early Indian texts. Gotama's understanding of action (*karma*) as "intention" (*cetana*) recognizes how agency originates in thoughts and decisions made in the mind. In this way, Buddhist ethics acquires its distinctively personal and psychological character. Just as Socrates sought to make people think for themselves rather than blindly follow established convention in their behavior, so Gotama emphasized how ethics originates in assuming personal responsibility for the choices we make that determine what we say and do in response to life's dilemmas.

Zoroastrian ethics is founded on a vision of the world in which the principles of good and evil are in a constant struggle with each other. When Ahura Mazda (God) created the world, it immediately split into two: with the forces of darkness and deception on one side, and the forces of light and truth on the other. This binary perspective provided a backdrop against which humans could start to make sense of and come to terms with their own ethical struggles between the impulse to do good and the temptation to succumb to evil. The dark forces of evil were eventually personified in the figure of Ahriman, who came to serve as the prototype for Satan in the monotheistic religions of Judaism, Christianity, and Islam and the figure of Mara in Buddhism. Just as Satan tempts Jesus to "command this stone that it be made bread," so Mara suggests to Gotama that "he need only to resolve that the Himalaya should become gold, and it would become gold."[3]

The discourses of the Pali Canon contain numerous dialogues between Buddha and Mara, which provide an archetypal framework for depicting the struggle to make ethical judgments. If Gotama had Scythian ancestors who migrated to India through Persia, the struggle between Mara (darkness and deception) and Buddha (light and truth) may well reflect the influence of a Zoroastrian worldview. In terms of the Buddhist doctrine of an ethics of mind, the tricksterish figure of Mara serves as a potent psychological metaphor for understanding the complexity and uncertainty that often bedevil making ethical choices in the solitude of our own thoughts and feelings.

Curiously, there is no word in Pali for "Persia." Yet since Taxila, the capital of Gandhara, the easternmost region of the Persian Empire, is known to the compilers of the Pali Canon, the failure to mention Persia cannot be due to its distant location. It is hard to imagine that the future rulers of the lands where Gotama was active would have been ignorant of such a vast, powerful, and potentially threatening empire to the west, to which they were connected by a major trade route. It may have been that Persia was perceived as a sleeping giant whose name should not be mentioned for fear of arousing him from his slumber.

Greece (Yona), however, *is* mentioned in Pali literature

despite being so much farther away from India than Persia. It occurs only once, in a canonical discourse delivered by Gotama to a young brahmin called Assalāyana. Assalāyana has been pressured by his friends to challenge Gotama's rejection of the fourfold caste system, which brahmins believe to be divinely sanctioned. "Mr Gotama," announces Assalāyana, "we brahmins declare that we are the noblest and fairest skinned caste among men. We alone are the sons and heirs of God (Brahmā). What do you say to that?" Gotama replies: "What do you think, Assalāyana? Have you not heard that in Greece and Kamboja and other outland countries there are only two castes, masters and slaves, and that masters become slaves and slaves become masters?" Assalāyana says that he has. "Then," continues Gotama, "on the strength of what argument or with the support of what authority do brahmins make such claims?"[4] For Gotama, facts on the ground have greater authority in settling such matters than theological beliefs.

"Yona," the word used for Greece, is the Pali version of "Ionia," a Greek colony in Asia Minor, now on the west coast of Turkey, across the Aegean from Athens. Ionia served as the cradle for Greek civilization and philosophy: the pre-Socratic thinkers Thales, Heraclitus, and Pythagoras were born there, as was Hippocrates, a contemporary of Socrates and the founder of modern medicine. It lost its independence to Cyrus the Great, who conquered it in 547 BCE and incorporated it into the Persian Empire. For Persians and Indians alike, Ionia came to stand for Greece as a whole. Gotama's observation about masters becoming slaves and slaves becoming masters was an entirely accurate description of Greece at his time. Yet apart from this one brief glimpse into the Greek world, the Pali Canon offers no further information about Ionia or its customs.

To employ the example of Greece in a religious debate in

north India in the fifth century BCE meant that Gotama and Assalāyana must have known something about it. This implies that educated Indians of the time had a broader sense of the world beyond their frontiers than we might imagine. Even though a huge Persian army under Xerxes had sacked Athens around the time of Gotama's birth, the Greeks had fought back and defeated them. With the help of Athens, Ionia too recovered its freedom from Persia. Like those who once would have been unable to locate Ukraine on a map but now celebrate that country for its courageous defiance of Russia, Indians of Gotama's time may have lionized distant Greece for simply having stood up to the mighty Persians and won.

Once we start assembling and making sense of these scattered bits of information that survive from fifth century BCE Greece, Persia, and India, it becomes clear that what is asserted about the origins of Western philosophy and early Buddhism is built upon selected fragments configured by historians to form a credible story. Most of what actually happened during that distant century is forever lost to us. Even the most indisputable historical facts emerge from a background of obscurity.

To understand the contingency of history can bring us closer to the heart of Gotama's dharma. In the discourse *On the Simile of the Elephant's Footprint* Gotama is quoted as saying, "One who sees contingency sees the dharma; and one who sees the dharma sees contingency."[5] In its pithiest formulation, contingency simply means "when this is, that comes to be; with the arising of this, that arises."[6] Through providing explanations of what happened in the past, historians offer insight into the workings of contingency. To "see" the dharma is to recognize the contingent nature of life itself. This serves to undermine attachment to beliefs in an absolute, noncontingent reality (like Brahman or God) that underpins the phenomenal world or a self who remains unchanged amidst the whirling chaos all around it. To "see" contingency is to recognize how as ethical beings we have the freedom and agency to create another future through our own thoughts, words, and acts.

Seen from this perspective, history enables us to see how Buddhism itself arose contingently from a matrix of prior causes and conditions. The idea of Buddhism as something existing in and of itself breaks down to reveal a complex, fluid, interactive, and ever-mutating process, which is more akin to a living organism than an unchanging body of beliefs and practices. As our historical consciousness becomes more acute, it refines our awareness of the contingent and tentative nature of ourselves and the world. We come to recognize how things did not have to be the way they are but could have turned out otherwise. In this sense, thinking historically becomes a practice of the dharma.

III
Uncertainty

9
The Quest for Certainty

In 1975, I left India for a small Tibetan monastery near Zurich, Switzerland, to train in Buddhist doctrine and philosophy under the guidance of my teacher Geshe Tamdrin Rabten. I was a twenty-two-year-old, red-robed, shaven-headed novice monk. Some months earlier, Geshe Rabten had been appointed as abbot of this monastery and the Dalai Lama's religious representative in Europe. To complete these studies traditionally took around fifteen years. I had been assured that such a course in logic, dialectics, and epistemology would provide me with rational certainty about the core tenets of Buddhism. I was convinced that this was my vocation. Nothing—poverty, celibacy, my mother's horror at my decision, near-zero prospects of a career or pension—would stand in the way.

Tamdrin Rabten was born in 1920 in the Tehor district of the eastern Tibetan province of Kham, now part of Sichuan in China. He grew up on his family's farm, working in the fields, riding horses, and tending livestock. He had little education. At the age of eighteen, against his father's wishes, he made his way on horseback to Sera Monastery in Lhasa to become a monk. With no material support from his family, he wore rags stitched together with wire and suffered malnutrition. Only when appointed as tutor to a young reincarnate lama did his fortunes change and he acquired the nickname "Fat Rabten."

In 1959, aged thirty-nine, Rabten fled Tibet for India in the wake of the failed uprising against Chinese rule. After several years in a former British prison camp, which had been converted into a monastery for exiled Tibetan monks in the jungle of Bengal, he passed his final exams to become a *geshe* (doctor of divinity). In 1964 he was appointed as a philosophical advisor to the Dalai Lama. He settled in a small stone shack in the hills above Dharamsala, where he spent most of his time meditating on emptiness.

Of all the Tibetan lamas I met, Geshe Rabten was the one with whom I felt the greatest affinity. He was a short, stocky, dark-skinned man with the gait of a truck driver and an abrupt, wry laugh. His eyes peered from the depths of his face with a resigned weariness tempered by flashes of irony. He would sway back and forth as he taught, gently snapping his fingers in front of him, intoning the words as if to the rhythm of a music he alone could hear. He was a stern man, who spoke his own mind and did not suffer fools. As my Tibetan improved, I began to serve as his translator. I enjoyed the intimacy we shared as I channeled his curt, well-formed sentences while seeking to capture in English the cadences of his Tibetan. I became familiar not just with the content of what he said but with how he had internalized and embodied the dharma and made it his own.

Geshe Rabten took his monastic vows more seriously than many other lamas I knew. If a woman visited him in his room, he would ensure he was not alone and that the door was left open. Afraid of the karmic consequences of imparting practices to those unprepared to receive them, he refused to give us the bodhisattva vows, let alone any tantric empowerments. "If I did," he said, "I would go to hell." Instead he would send us to another lama, one who did not share his reservations. He was strict with himself but tolerant of and kind towards those around him. He was a moral person but he did not moralize. There was something raw, honest, and genuine about him that moved me deeply.

As a monk in Sera Monastery, Geshe Rabten would often spend all night debating with his classmates. His training in dialectics involved mastering the basic logical moves of language through repetitive, formal exercises, synchronized with bodily gestures and movements. In the winter months, he recalled how his hands would become sore from the clapping, would crack on both sides, and start to bleed. When sitting on the ground to answer questions, he would bury his body up to the waist in the dry sandy soil of the debating courtyard to absorb the last warmth from the day's sun. His sole concern was to think clearly and exploit his opponents' mistakes to win the debate with a firm handclap accompanied by a resounding "*Tsa!*"

Geshe Rabten was someone who had never read a novel, seen a play by Shakespeare, or listened to a symphony by Mozart. He had never heard of Plato or Aristotle. He knew nothing about evolution by natural selection or the general theory of relativity. He had little idea of any religious tradition apart from the Buddhism in which he had been raised and trained. He took it for granted that the earth was flat and was populated by a host of invisible deities and spirits, both benign and malefic. He believed without question in heaven and hell. Yet he was one of the sanest, most grounded, and integrated people I have ever met. He became my Socrates, the person who constantly challenged my sense of who I was and what I aspired to be. He was the man against whom I measured myself as an ethical being.

I had spent my final year in Dharamsala studying Śāntideva's *A Guide to the Bodhisattva's Way of Life,* a classic eighth-century work of the Centrist (Madhyamaka) school of Indian Buddhist thought. As a Centrist, Śāntideva maintained that emptiness was the ultimate truth of all things. For by carefully examining—whether through reasoning or meditative inquiry—who you really are or what a thing truly is, you will not arrive at any essential nature or self or substance that cannot be further analyzed ad infinitum. This is what it means for you or anything else to be "empty." In the language of the Gelug tradition, emptiness is the unfindability of any inherently existent self or thing. Geshe Rabten assured us that in studying and debating the key doctrines of Buddhist philosophy we could gain a conceptual, inferential understanding of emptiness, which would then serve as the basis for direct nonconceptual insight into emptiness through meditation.

Geshe Rabten taught us methodically without any evangelical fervor. He shared with us his passion for philosophical ideas and contemplative practices that had enriched his own life. The Nalanda tradition of textual study and debate, in which he had been educated in Sera Monastery, was founded on logic and critical reason rather than on unquestioning faith. The approach is summed up in a verse attributed to Gotama, which is frequently cited by Gelug lamas:

> Just as a goldsmith assays gold
> By rubbing, cutting and burning,
> So should you examine my words.
> Do not accept them out of faith in me.[1]

Here, it seemed, the values of the European Enlightenment converged with those of the Buddha's enlightenment. Reason rather than scriptural authority would be the basis for our studies. This was the spirit in which I would pursue my quest for ultimate truth.

Studying Buddhist logic with Geshe Rabten led me to understand how logic is the science of making sense. To study logic is to learn how language users make and fail to make sense to each other. Formal logic dissects everyday speech to show in technical terms how it works. Anyone who can engage in a rational conversation knows intuitively whether the other person is making sense or not. But unless you are a logician, you might find it hard to explain exactly how and why. Through the practice of formal debates with my classmates, I became more aware of the inner workings of thought and language. Training in logic was an exercise in critical thinking, designed to sharpen one's ability to analyze Buddhist doctrines. As a result, I became more interested in how human beings *think*. I started paying greater attention to the rhetorical strategies people employed to defend their beliefs and hold fast to their certainties.

For the first couple of years we studied the Sutrist (Sautrāntika) school of philosophy. This "Hinayana" form of Buddhism provided us with the basic concepts in Buddhist logic, epistemology, and soteriology. We were told that a clear grasp of these concepts was necessary for understanding how Buddhist thought had evolved in India before reaching its pinnacle in the Centrist understanding of emptiness.

Yet the Sutrist understanding of ultimate truth was in stark opposition to the doctrine of emptiness as expounded by such Centrists as Śāntideva. Day after day Geshe Rabten presented us with a coherent and intelligent way of thinking about the dharma that contradicted much of what I had been taught until then. I was intrigued and perplexed. For the Sutrists, ultimate truth had nothing to do with the emptiness of inherent existence or the absence of self. They defined an ultimate truth as something that exists independently of thought and language, and is capable of performing a function. Rather than the one ultimate truth of emptiness, there were a potentially infinite number of ultimate truths. The standard example given in the texts was a jug.

A jug is an object that exists in its own right, independently of people's ideas about it, and is able to perform a function, for example, to store liquids. You can see and touch a jug. Tap it with your knuckle and you hear the sound it makes. Moreover, a jug has utility, it serves a purpose, it is valued. Jugs are inseparable from human societies that manufacture and make use of them. For something to be ultimately true means it is capable of directly impacting human experience and producing an effect in the world we share with others.

As part of the continuous flux of the unfolding world of causes and effects, these ultimate truths are impermanent. They are constantly changing. A jug is the result of previous causes (the clay of which it was made and the potter who made it) as well as being able to cause future effects (to ferment wine or fill a hole in the road after being broken). Sutrists located ultimacy in the pouring forth of life itself. Ultimate truths are the unhidden things all around you that assail your senses: the yellowing leaves of autumn, the song of birds, the smell of incense, the taste of honey, the touch of a lover's hand. All the mental and emotional states that arise within us are ultimate truths as well. Ignorance is an ultimate truth, as is wisdom. Love is an ultimate truth, as is hate.

In June 1974, shortly after being ordained as a novice monk in Dharamsala, I attended a Vipassanā retreat with the Indian businessman and meditation teacher S. N. Goenka, which introduced me to the practice of mindfulness meditation. Sutrist philosophy was well adapted to this practice. In focusing attention on the breath, bodily sensations, and feelings, I experienced the raw, fluid immediacy of these ultimate facts of life. As the mind became still, the natural world became more vivid and poignant, charged with heightened value and meaning, radiant with beauty. I observed for myself the unfolding of life as the intricate warp and weft of conditions and consequences, whether in the arising of a thought that made me feel guilty or in the stirring of a breeze that sent a ripple through the grasses outside.

The Sutrists, as their name implies, were followers of the Buddha's *sūtras* or discourses. As a Hinayana school they would have studied a now lost Sanskrit equivalent of the Pali Canon, which today survives only in Chinese translation. The Sutrists appeared to have returned to the discourses attributed to Gotama to rethink the dharma afresh. Would this, I wondered, account for their finding ultimacy in the transient, poignant things of everyday life as revealed through the practice of mindfulness?

By the time Sutrism arrived in Tibet from India in the eleventh century it no longer made any reference to the early discourses of Gotama but had evolved into a school of thought that was primarily concerned with epistemology. The question of how we *know* things had come to exercise the brightest minds in medieval India. Hindus, Jains, and Buddhists alike sought to demonstrate the superiority of their knowledge by composing technical treatises on logic and epistemology and then testing their ideas in debate. In Sutrism, epistemology underpinned ontology. Sutrists maintained that a jug or a person *existed* because it could be "*known* by a valid mind." A valid mind (*pramāṇa*) was regarded as "infallible," which meant that it was "capable of inducing certainty." Such certainty could be acquired in two ways, either through logical inference (*anumāna*) or through direct sensory or contemplative perception (*pratyakṣa*).

The key difference between inference and direct perception is that the former is conceptual and the latter nonconceptual. While inference arrives at its conclusions by means of words and concepts, direct perception apprehends what appears without any words or concepts. Although inference can grant rational certainty, because it relies on concepts it is said to be "distorted" by the admixture of ideas and mental images. Only through contemplative training can one arrive at an understanding in which the distorting effect of conceptuality has been removed.

Since all Indian traditions of Buddhism regarded ignorance—a distorted and invalid form of knowing—as the fundamental cause of suffering, the primary goal of Buddhist practice was the eradication of ignorance through gaining undistorted, valid insights into the true nature of reality. At root, suffering—including birth, sickness, aging, and death—was understood to result from cognitive error. This was often summarized as mistaking what is foul to be beautiful, what is impermanent to be permanent, what is painful to be pleasant, and what is not-self to be self. To overcome suffering and attain Nirvana required correcting these basic errors. Since these kind of mistakes were innate—inherited from countless past lives—rather than merely learned in the course of this life, the corrective process required far more than just adopting the right Buddhist beliefs. To eliminate instinctive ignorance entailed knowing and seeing things correctly through sustained, nonconceptual, contemplative insight.

The Sutrist epistemology at the heart of Tibetan Buddhist monastic education offered us a detailed explanation of the cognitive steps needed to take one from ignorance to enlightenment. One first needed to doubt the validity of one's instinctive but erroneous perceptions of oneself and the world. Then one had to stop vacillating and replace doubt with faith in the justified beliefs about reality provided by Buddhism. Since these beliefs do not provide certainty, they need to be superseded by inferential understanding, based on sound reason and logic. For that inferential insight to be genuinely liberating, its conceptual element has to be dissolved through direct, contemplative perception acquired through prolonged meditation.

The Sutrists emphasized how this epistemological journey did not occur in an introspective vacuum but was embedded in and accompanied by an ongoing ethical practice, which consisted of four paths. These paths were already familiar to me from Gampopa's *Jewel Ornament of Liberation:*

1. The path of formation
2. The path of unification
3. The path of vision
4. The path of cultivation

Gampopa explained how these four paths entailed the cultivation of a total of thirty-two virtues, which were distributed among the four paths. They ranged from the four foundations of mindfulness, the four resolves and the four steps of creativity on the path of formation, the five strengths on the path of unification, the seven facets of awakening on the path of seeing, to the limbs of the eightfold path on the path of cultivation. The practice of these virtues provided the ethical ecosystem needed for the epistemological process to mature and reach completion.

The path of formation describes the foundational phase of one's practice where one gathers together those forces, skills, tools, resources, virtues, and perspectives needed to pursue the project of awakening. It is comparable to the German idea of *Bildung*, the process of lifelong learning whereby a person harmonizes her faculties of heart, mind, and imagination to achieve greater personal integration as well as the ability to lead a dignified, autonomous, and creative existence within society. The path of formation entails coming to terms with the challenge of being human. By assembling the existential skill set of mindfulness, resolve, and creativity one acquires the basic tools needed for a committed and responsive ethical life.

The second path is that of unification: the disciplined and focused inner practice enabled by and built upon the maturity achieved on the path of formation. It involves a keen awareness of one's psychological and emotional life, the inner strength to come to terms with the "wild elephant of the mind," and the refinement of the contemplative skills and insight needed to quieten and disentangle oneself from such turbulence. Unification is a remedy for the dispersive nature of reactivity, which scatters attention through the proliferation of thoughts and anxieties, thereby fragmenting one's inner cohesion. It entails achieving an inner harmony, which Gotama compared to that of a well-tuned lute.

While the path of formation served to confirm and reinforce one's faith and belief in the teachings of the dharma, the path of unification involved attaining a rational, inferential conviction in the truth of the dharma. As this understanding became less and less conceptual through meditation, one experienced moments of direct insight, which marked one's entry into the path of vision. Once you had stabilized your vision, you then needed to devote whatever time was needed to dissolve the residual habits of reactivity and conceptuality along the path of cultivation, which was achieved by dwelling in ever subtler levels of meditation. Finally, this culminated in a state of complete enlightenment, where suffering came to an end and there was nothing more to be learned or done.

Geshe Rabten used to joke that if enlightenment consisted simply in eradicating concepts and thoughts from your mind, then a cow sitting in a field chewing its cud would be a buddha. Although we would laugh at this parody of the popular idea of meditation as "emptying the mind," I was troubled by my suspicion that, despite the technical language and emphasis on logic, this was in fact how Buddhist philosophy conceived of the process of awakening. It may require years of rigorous contemplative discipline to reach the goal, but the end result was nonetheless a state of mind in which concepts and thoughts had been eradicated. How was this, I wondered, any different from the experience of a cow sitting in a field?

Geshe Rabten knew Sutrism inside out. This was the philosophy on which he had cut his teeth as a young monk in Sera Monastery. Yet it would never have occurred to him to consider himself a Sutrist. Tibetans took it for granted that the Hinayana school of Sutrism had long been superseded by the ethics of the bodhisattva and the Centrist philosophy of emptiness. Sutrism served as a useful didactic tool to prepare one for the study of Mahayana thought. But as a school of Buddhist philosophy in its own right, it had little more than antiquarian value.

In the course of my studies, I guiltily came to recognize that I was more sympathetic to many of the key tenets of Sutrism than to those of the Centrism regarded by Geshe Rabten as the apex of Buddhist thought. Perhaps because of my secular upbringing, a love of nature, and the practice of mindfulness, I found the idea of locating ultimate truth in the fleeting events of everyday existence appealing. Emptiness of inherent existence, by contrast, struck me as an intangible abstraction. I understood how the idea of emptiness was a valuable tool to help one become less rigid and fixed in one's views and more open to the contingency of life, but I failed to understand how it could become an object of direct contemplative experience.

Despite the clinical precision of the epistemic surgery described in the Sutrist textbooks we studied, I struggled to understand how such a step-by-step procedure could actually be carried out by a living, breathing human animal. Like the doctrine of emptiness, it was a compelling and well-reasoned theory but seemed more designed to meet the intellectual needs of monks in secluded monasteries than the earthly needs of men and women in the world. In the end, my studies led me to question how any of these transcendent, nonconceptual insights into emptiness or selflessness would enable me to be more caring and responsive. They seemed eerily disconnected from the ethical ecosystem of the four paths and thirty-two virtues that supposedly nurtured them. Rather than provide the consolations of certainty, my philosophical training only served to deepen my uncertainty and doubts.

10
The Tragedy of Being Human

In Ancient Greece the gods were everywhere. Brightly colored statues of deities lined the streets and stood proudly in the open spaces of the towns and cities of Attica. These beings were experienced as powerful forces with wills of their own that humans had to contend with throughout the course of their lives. Most days of the year were sacred to one or another of them. Festivals to honor them abounded. Yet these gods were just as subject to their whims, lusts, and hatreds as humans. Their inscrutable actions were believed to determine the fates of the men and women to whom they were largely indifferent. All one could do was offer the oblations, sacrifices, and prayers required to placate them. A small army of priests and priestesses conducted these rituals, and immense resources were poured into the construction of temples and sanctuaries.

As a visitor to Greece today, many of the most famous sites of antiquity that we see are the remnants of religious sanctuaries. We may now think of Olympia as the site of the first Olympic Games, but for the ancients it was the sanctuary of Zeus and his wife Hera, which also included a magnificent stadium. We may be drawn to visit the celebrated and intact theater at Epidaurus, only to discover that it is an appendage to the sanctuary of Asclepius, the god of healing. As you wander through their extensive ruins, you realize that these sanctuaries served as centers of devotion, supplication, and prayer. Apart from priests, priestesses, and their attendants, no one lived there. In Delphi, the sanctuary of Apollo and home to the Pythian Oracle, you will find a theater as well as a stadium built into the inhospitable slopes of Mount Parnassus. In Athens theatrical performances took place at the sanctuary of Dionysus, the god of theater and excess, who was contemptuous of pitiful human attempts to contain and dominate the overwhelming, chaotic potency of nature.

The polytheistic religions of Greek antiquity did not foster an aloof, spiritual practice that existed separately from the "mundane" business of theater and sport. For theater and sport were not considered mere entertainments but opportunities for displaying human excellence: physical excellence in the stadium, poetic excellence on the stage. The plays and games were presented to the gods as offerings of all that was best of humanity. Both athletes and playwrights competed fiercely with each other to win prizes and acclaim. *Arete*, the Greek word often translated as "virtue," means "excellence." By achieving your purpose, by becoming the best possible version of yourself, whether as a priest, a poet, or a discus thrower, was to achieve *arete*.

Seated on a stone bench at the amphitheater in Epidaurus with hundreds of strangers, peering at the stage far below to watch a tragedy by Aeschylus, Sophocles, or Euripides, would have been part of one's pilgrimage to the sanctuary of Asclepius. No longer within the familiar confines of one's home city, restored, purified, and inspired by devotions and prayers, one would now be invited to confront a world where terrible things happen.

By depicting unbearable suffering on the stage of a theater, played out in the struggles of mythic characters from a remote past, the tragedians established a distance that allowed spectators to contemplate their own anguish and the collective traumas of their world. The plays are tragic not only because of the pain suffered by the characters but because of the characters' hopeless entanglement in their own fates. At times the figures on stage are seen to reap the fruits of their own choices and acts; at times they are shown as mere playthings of divine forces beyond their control. In both cases, the audience is invited to reflect on the tragedy of being human. Like parables, these plays speak to the imagination. Once seen, their lessons are hard to forget. They throw into question what it means to be the kind of person you are. They leave you hanging, suspended in an aporia of ethical uncertainty, disturbed yet strangely uplifted.

The tragedies and comedies performed at religious festivals in these sanctuaries were opportunities for truth telling. The strictures of social convention were lifted, and the suffering and absurdity of human existence put on display for all to see.

Aeschylus's *Oresteia* trilogy was premiered at the City Dionysia in 458 BCE, where it won first prize. Euripides, then in his early twenties, was probably there; he presented his first play in the same competition three years later. Socrates, as a youngster, may also have been somewhere in the audience in the company of his friend Crito. The chorus of *Agamemnon*, the first play of the trilogy, explains how tragic drama serves as a vehicle for philosophy:

> Zeus puts us on the road
> to mindfulness, Zeus decrees
> we learn by suffering.
> In the heart is no sleep; there drips instead
> pain that remembers wounds. And to unwilling
> minds circumspection comes.[1]

Our hypothetical Buddhist observer in ancient Athens would have noticed how closely these lines echoed the logic of dharma practice. Zeus—God, nature, or simply contingency itself—impacts our minds and senses moment to moment, sweeping us along on the irrepressible current of life. Yet this sublime unfolding of experience also endows us with mindfulness: the capacity to notice, reflect on, and embrace suffering, which enables us to comprehend the human condition in such a way that wisdom finally dawns.

On April 4, 1968, Robert F. Kennedy, then campaigning for the Democratic nomination for president, gave a brief, impassioned speech in Indianapolis on the death of Dr. Martin Luther King, who had been assassinated earlier that day. "My favorite poet," he said to the traumatized audience of mainly African-Americans, "was Aeschylus." He then quoted from memory an earlier translation of these same lines from *Agamemnon*:

> In our sleep, pain which cannot forget falls drop by drop upon the heart until, in our despair, against our will, comes wisdom through the awful grace of God.

King's death moved Kennedy, a Catholic, to cite a pagan playwright to honor a Baptist minister. The words "awful grace of God" gave the lines a suitably Christian inflection just as the term "mindfulness" in the rendition quoted above by Sarah Ruden, a Quaker, imparts a more contemplative, Buddhist flavor to the text. Kennedy concluded with some words from the classicist Edith Hamilton: "Let us dedicate ourselves to what the Greeks wrote so many years ago: 'to tame the savageness of man and make gentle the life of this world.'" He was shot dead two months later.[2]

The Tragedy of Being Human

Aeschylus was fully aware that spectators were liable to be dazzled by the theatrical spectacle of his plays without being existentially engaged by the drama. "Everyone's ready," observes the chorus in *Agamemnon*, "to groan along with the misery. But the teeth of the pain don't sink into their own hearts."[3] These plays were meditations on what it means to be frail, fallible, and mortal. In seeing their own tendencies mirrored in the characters' actions, the audience was invited to consider whether under similar circumstances they would have behaved in the same way. Or would they have risen to the ethical challenge of the situation and responded with wisdom rather than anger, equanimity rather than despair, love rather than revenge?

The tragedies served to arouse empathy, pity, and compassion for others—including one's enemies. Aeschylus's *Persians,* the oldest surviving tragic drama, focuses on the military defeat suffered by Xerxes the Great, who invaded Greece in 480 BCE with a massive army and navy, with the goal of incorporating it into the Persian Empire. *Persians* is unique among the surviving tragedies in not being set in the mythic past but in recent history. It was first performed only eight years after the events it depicted, while Xerxes was still ruling Persia.

Persians is centered around the figure of Queen Atossa, mother of Xerxes, as she waits in Susa for her son to return from the war in Greece. All the characters, including Xerxes, are treated with utmost respect, their dignity and honor intact despite their humiliation. There is no hatred, resentment, bitterness, or revenge against these foreigners, whose army had recently sacked Athens and destroyed the iconic temples on the Acropolis, directly above the amphitheater where *Persians* was premiered. Those present at that performance would have been aware of the rubble and broken statuary still lying on the hilltop that rose steeply behind them. Many would have witnessed this destruction and been veterans of the war. Aeschylus himself fought in the naval battle of Salamis, where the outnumbered Greeks inflicted a crushing defeat on the Persians. Now the playwright invited his audience to empathize with the suffering of those who had laid waste their city.

In 415 BCE, forty years after the death of Aeschylus, Euripides's play *Trojan Women* was performed at the City Dionysia. Here the audience was presented with the suffering of the Trojans: the archetypal Greek foe. After a ten-year siege, as related by Homer in the *Iliad,* the Greeks have conquered Troy. All men of military age have been killed. As the city burns, the remaining women and children wait to be dispatched to Greece by sea as slaves. Yet rather than celebrating the Greeks' victory, Euripides focuses on the suffering of the vanquished. The Greek commanders are depicted as brutal, ruthless, and cold-hearted. There is no redemption for these proud women of Troy, no hope of recovering what they have lost. Their entire world has collapsed.

A few months before the first performance of *Trojan Women,* Athens had seized control of Melos, an island state in the Aegean that refused to ally itself with either side in the Peloponnesian War. In the summer of 416 BCE, Athens dispatched thirty-eight ships with more than three thousand troops to force Melos into submission. Athenian emissaries issued an ultimatum: either the Melians ally themselves with Athens or face annihilation. Ignoring the island's neutrality, they bluntly informed the Melians that, in the words of Thucydides, "The strong do what they can and the weak suffer what they must."[4] Melos rejected the ultimatum. Athens laid siege to the city. As winter closed in, the starving Melians surrendered. All men of military age were executed and the women and children sent into slavery.

This brutal act, extreme even by the standards of its

time, sent shockwaves through the Greek world. It would have been fresh in the minds of the audience at the first performance of *Trojan Women*. The comparison between the fate of the defeated Trojans and Melians was inescapable. In portraying the plight of the Trojan women with compassion, Euripides tacitly invited the audience to consider the similar fate of Melos and the callous behavior of the Athenians. When, in the play, the envoy announces to the women that the Greeks had "voted" to murder Astyanax, the child heir to the Trojan throne, the spectators would have been reminded of their own role in the democratically authorized seizure of Melos. Some of those present in the amphitheater may have participated in the bloodbath itself.

Today, seated on a shaded bench among the stone remains of the sanctuary of Dionysus in Athens, you can contemplate the vacant stage on which these dramas of Aeschylus and Euripides were performed numerous times over many centuries. You can see the surviving rows of empty stone seats—some cracked and broken, others intact with the names of their patrons still inscribed on them—where the prominent male citizens of the city would have contemplated their tragic human condition through the medium of drama. Behind the seats rises a grass slope, on which thousands of others would have sat in less comfort, and then the abrupt cliff wall of the Acropolis on top of which the Parthenon stands in all its ruined glory. It is hard to sense the religious awe that once infused this place, to imagine the terrible dilemmas with which the spectators struggled in their lives, to recall the wailing of the *aulus* and the beating of drums that accompanied these plays. Instead, the terrain is crisscrossed with concrete pathways and neatly printed signposts designed to manage the daily flow of thousands of tourists, who live in a world where politicians are no longer expected to quote Aeschylus.

11

A Religion Is Born

After Gotama's death, his monastic and non-monastic followers alike faced the challenge of how to survive as a community that continued to embody what he had taught. Crucial to this task was the preservation of his discourses. The process of memorizing what he taught was already underway during his lifetime, but we know neither which discourses had been memorized nor in what form. What seems certain, though, is that this body of knowledge would have been regarded as the most precious thing the community possessed and that every effort would be made to ensure its survival for future generations. Key to this endeavor would be the training of men and women in the art of memorization. Lacking plentiful Egyptian papyrus and slaves to serve as human writing machines, Gotama's followers had no choice but to inscribe his words in their own flesh, to lay them down again and again in the neural pathways of their brains.

In Plato's *Phaedrus,* Socrates claims that writing leads to forgetfulness, since it relies on conventionally agreed external signs rather than memories that have been internalized and made one's own. Writing, he says, allows people to acquire a great deal of information yet without necessarily understanding what it all means, giving them the illusion of being knowledgeable without really knowing anything.[1] Socrates compares a written text to a painting. A painted figure appears to be lifelike, but if you ask it anything, it remains immobile and mute. So too with written words: they may appear to be full of wisdom but are incapable of responding to questions. They repeat exactly the same thing forever. Once something is written down, it can circulate anywhere in the world and be perused by sympathetic and antagonistic readers alike. Indifferent to criticism, it is unable to defend itself. When asked by Phaedrus what the alternative might be, Socrates says:

> It is a discourse that is written down, *with knowledge,* in the soul of the listener; it can defend itself, and it knows for whom it should speak and for whom it should remain silent.[2]

A written text may preserve the words of a great sage but at the risk of those words remaining as dead as oranges preserved in marmalade. The only place for such words to come alive is in the mind of a sentient, breathing person. Such reasoning could explain why neither Socrates nor Gotama wrote anything and why they never stopped talking and debating with people.

Gotama's followers treated memorized texts as though they were precious bodies of recorded information to be preserved unchanged. By contrast, Socrates emphasized the need to understand what you remember. For how would memorizing something without knowing what it means be any different from a slave copying it onto a sheet of papyrus? This may have been the concern of Purana, the monk who refused to submit to the consensus agreed by Kassapa and other elder monks as to what Gotama taught. His main worry was that only one version of Gotama's teaching would then be preserved, while other versions would be lost forever. But he may also have worried that the endless repetition of a single body of information by people who did not necessarily understand what they had memorized could have a deadening effect on the vitality of the tradition.

This is a dilemma. On the one hand, I am indebted to the generations of men and women who spent long stretches of their lives memorizing and passing on the teachings of Gotama. Without their efforts, Buddhism might have disappeared without a trace and I would not be writing these words now. On the other hand, the sanctification of a canon of orthodox texts could have stifled the creativity needed for the tradition to adapt to changing circumstances. It might have seemed self-evident that to ensure the preservation of the dharma, the dharma had to remain unchanged. Henceforth, anyone who attempted to creatively modify or reform it could risk being accused of superiority conceit and charged with the inexpiable sin of inciting a schism in the community.

For Socrates, what mattered was the ability of memorized words, phrases, and citations to function as guidelines or prompts in your ethical life. In practice, most Buddhists would agree. The internalized values, precepts, and ideas of the dharma come to serve as an inner compass for helping you make better judgments in response to complex, unprecedented life situations.

The word for memory in Pali is *sati*, which today is routinely translated as "mindfulness." Gotama taught how the practice of mindfulness extends from paying close attention to your breath to bearing in mind the core values and ideas of the dharma. The fourth foundation of mindfulness involves recollecting the virtues rather than attending to physical sensations, feelings, or mind states occurring in the present moment. Instead of insisting that everyone memorize long, discursive texts, Gotama encouraged his followers to be mindful of the key clusters of virtues, such as the four foundations of mindfulness or the eightfold path, which would serve as aids to living well. Once inscribed in the soul of the practitioner, such virtues provide an ethical orientation that helps one respond with greater sensitivity and care to life itself. Memorization itself becomes a practice of mindfulness.

For the rulers, government officials, doctors, artisans, and merchants who followed Gotama's teachings, to remember and keep these virtues in mind would have lain at the heart of their dharma practice. They may have had neither time, inclination, nor need to memorize much more than the basic lists and a few treasured verses and quotes. They would have listened to discourses given by Gotama and others, which would have amplified and clarified their understanding of the dharma, but in practice it seems likely that their primary reference would have been an internalized cartography of its core ideas and values.

My guess is that this cartography would have been built around the thirty-two dimensions of awakening: the most extensive list of the virtues taught by Gotama. These virtues were divided into six clusters, which could then be correlated to the four paths (formation, unification, seeing, and cultivation), the four tasks that characterize these paths (embracing life, letting reactivity be, seeing reactivity stop, and cultivating a middle way), and the four immeasurable qualities that underpin them affectively (love, compassion, rejoicing, and equanimity). To facilitate memorization, the thirty-two virtues could have been imagined as the thirty-two physical marks of a "great person" or the thirty-two parts of one's own body. In this way, the core teachings would be preserved in one's memory for actualization in one's life. As a way of practicing the mindful recollection of dharma, such a model would have been particularly suited for householders in a preliterate society.

A curious sequence of short discourses in the Pali Canon provides us with the names of twenty-one householders, who, despite their active involvement in the world, attained the kind of liberation usually ascribed only to enlightened monastics (*arahant*). According to the text, each of these twenty-one men

> had found fulfilment in the true person [*tathāgata*], become a seer of the deathless, and lived their life from the perspective of the deathless.[3]

These men came from five different regions of north India, eight were merchants or bankers, four were rulers or government officials, and one was a doctor. They included Gotama's cousin Mahānāma, the ruler of Sakiya, and his personal physician, Jīvaka.[4] There are no women mentioned, which probably reflects the extent to which most women at this time, like their sisters in Athens, bore the primary burden of childcare and domestic duties from which wealthy, powerful, and educated men, such as those on this list, were exempt.

These twenty-one men resemble the sort of people who formed the circle around Socrates in Athens. Alcibiades, Xenophon, Crito, Critias, and the others were likewise engaged in the political, cultural, and social life of the city while having sufficient leisure to pursue a life of the mind under the inspiration and guidance of Socrates. One wonders how Gotama would be portrayed today had the primary record of his life and teaching come down to us through one of these twenty-one followers rather than Kassapa and other monastics.

Such praise of specific non-monastic individuals is highly

unusual among the canonical discourses. Yet these texts are likely to go back to Gotama's time for the simple reason that it is hard to see how it would have been in the interest of the monastics who were responsible for the canon to insert them at a later date. These occasional lightning flashes briefly illuminate the liberated nirvanic life of "ordinary" people at Gotama's time. As such they offer vivid examples of how the dharma might be fully lived in our secular world today. These men all achieved a level of insight, integrity, and freedom that allowed them to live from the perspective of the deathless (a synonym for nirvana) in the midst of the pressures and turmoil of civic life. They were thus fully engaged with the world yet from a standpoint which was disengaged from the world. Creating and sustaining a middle way that paradoxically lies between engagement and disengagement has perhaps always been the greatest challenge in the practice of the dharma.

Following what came to be known as the First Council at Rājagaha, Gotama's dharma evolved fairly rapidly into a renunciant Indian religion, whose ultimate goal was the complete liberation from and transcendence of the world and its inevitable suffering. It thus came to share the same goal as its principal rivals, the Jains and Brahmins, yet without positing any eternal consciousness that could enjoy such transcendent bliss and freedom. For Gotama, consciousness emerged out of a psycho-physical matrix of changing conditions and was thus utterly contingent and ephemeral.

Buddhists are still regarded in Hindu literature today as nihilists (*Nāstika*—literally: Is-not-ists). Since Buddhism regards not-being-born and not-dying (Nirvana) as preferable to being-born and dying (Samsara), it could also be accused of nihilism by modern secular critics. Bluntly stated, the final goal of the Buddhist religion is to stop living: to bring the cycle of birth, death, and rebirth to an end. But if the practice of the dharma is to tread a middle way between "is" and "is not," then how does a Buddhist who values not-being-born ("is not") above being-born ("is") avoid the pitfall of nihilism?

Let's put this more concretely. When looking into the eyes of a newborn baby am I, as a good Buddhist, to think that it would have been infinitely better had this child *not* been born? Would I be inclined to gently inform the mother that had she not succumbed to her base sexual appetites, not only would her child not have been conceived, it would have been spared the suffering of sickness, aging, death, and all the other tragedies of being human, while she would have been spared the toil and burden of motherhood and its lifelong worries? Like the French-Romanian philosopher and Buddhist sympathizer Emil Cioran, could I have ever written a book entitled *The Trouble with Being Born*? The answer to all these questions is an emphatic "no." Despite its suffering, I love life deeply and unconditionally. I am awed, overwhelmed, and profoundly moved that there is anything at all instead of just nothing.

12

Nāgasena or Nāgārjuna?

In 323 BCE, around seventy-five years after Gotama's death and the First Council at Rājagaha, Alexander the Great reached Taxila, the capital of Gandhara, the easternmost province of the defeated Persian Empire. Greek rule now extended all the way from Europe to northwest India. Alexander's soldiers refused to continue farther east into the subcontinent and forced their leader to retreat. Two years later, Alexander died in Babylon at the age of thirty-two. After his death the territories he had conquered were divided among his generals to create a vast Greek-speaking, Hellenistic cultural sphere, which flourished for nearly three centuries until Rome took over as the new superpower of the ancient world.

Buddhism flourished in Gandhara throughout the Hellenistic period. Yet the only record we have of an encounter between the two traditions is a Pali text called *The Questions of King Milinda,* which consists of a dialogue between a Buddhist monk called Nāgasena and the Indo-Greek king Milinda, who reigned for about thirty years during the second century BCE in northwest India.

Milinda is a well-established historical figure, regarded as the most powerful of Greek rulers after Alexander. In Plutarch's account of his death, we learn that Milinda's ashes were parceled out among his followers to be interred in burial mounds, just as Buddhist tradition recommends that those of a universal monarch's or a buddha's be distributed and enshrined.[1] We do not know whether Milinda formally converted to Buddhism, but he appears to have been sympathetic to Buddhist culture and ideas.

Of Nāgasena we know nothing; he is presented as a wise, learned, and saintly monk, much like the impossibly perfect *arahant*s of the Pali Canon. His answers to Milinda's questions give us a vivid, detailed glimpse into the doctrines of an early school of north Indian Buddhism three or four hundred years after Gotama died. "Nāgasena" may have been no more than a fictional device to enable a series of imaginary dialogues with a renowned king to explain the dharma to Greek-speaking people who, like modern Westerners, were intrigued by Buddhism but baffled by some of its key doctrines.

The Questions of King Milinda reads like a long list of FAQs that educated and curious Greeks would have likely raised about Gotama's teachings around the time of Christ. The Buddhist community implores Nāgasena to resolve the king's doubts and dispel his misunderstandings. Milinda then poses his questions to Nāgasena, who provides orthodox Buddhist answers, which the king deferentially accepts.

Nāgasena is clearly familiar with the discourses found in the early Buddhist canon, but his replies show that by his time Buddhism had adopted a more discursive, analytical approach to the dharma. Whereas Gotama never once denied the existence of the self in any of his discourses, Nāgasena explains and justifies at considerable length the scholarly Buddhist doctrine that there is no self. Like many people today, Milinda finds it hard to reconcile the idea of no-self with that of rebirth. Twice he poses the question "Who takes rebirth?"

Nāgasena or Nāgārjuna?

And twice Nāgasena comes up with ingenious but not entirely convincing answers.[2]

As a man thoroughly engaged in the affairs of the world, Milinda is heartened to learn from Nāgasena that at Gotama's time there were numerous householders "who realized the peaceful and uttermost goal of nirvana" while still enjoying the pleasures of the senses. But if nirvana can be realized while remaining active in the world, retorts the king, then why is it necessary to become a monk to attain it? Nāgasena appeals to the doctrine of rebirth to resolve the conundrum. Arahantship, he explains to Milinda, is only possible for householders if they have already mastered the rigorous disciplines of monastic training in previous lifetimes.[3] This theological sleight of hand allows Nāgasena to assure the king that he can attain nirvana as a householder while at the same time ensuring that he continue to hold monks and monastic discipline in the highest regard.

As Rome became the dominant power in Europe, the Greek communities in India became increasingly cut off from their homelands. By then, some families would have been settled on the subcontinent for several generations. No longer being seen as foreigners, these Greeks gradually became integrated into Indian society. A century before Milinda, the Buddhist emperor Aśoka had appointed a Greek as governor of the western Indian province of Aparanta, and sent a Greek monk called Dharmarakshita there as a Buddhist envoy. A first century BCE inscription at the Buddhist rock-cut temple of Karla in Maharashtra likewise lists three Greeks among its benefactors.

In the process of assimilation to India, many Greeks became Buddhists. Like Milinda, they too may have been divided between an allegiance to their Greek heritage and a fascination with Buddhist philosophy and practice. Their most lasting legacy to Buddhism was their contribution to the creation of the Buddha image. Until then, Gotama had not been represented in human form but symbolized by physical reminders of his absence: a stupa, an empty seat, a bodhi tree, or footprints. The surviving rock-cut Buddhist temples of India, such as those at Karla and Ajanta, provide well-preserved examples of this early aniconic style. Coming from a polytheistic culture with a rich iconographic tradition, it would have been natural for these Greek converts to seek an iconic form by which to represent Gotama.

The Greek Buddhists came to imagine Gotama as Apollo, the god of wisdom, law, and healing, and they represented him in statues and bas-reliefs as a lithe, sensitive, androgynous figure in flowing Greek robes. In contrast, they depicted bodhisattvas as swarthy, mustachioed warriors pursuing the path to enlightenment with military determination and zeal. By turning Gotama into a god, the sculptors of this Gandharan school of art helped trigger the proliferation and evolution of Buddhist iconography throughout Asia and so unwittingly played their part in turning the dharma into a world religion.

Buddhist thought, meanwhile, was steadily turning away from the study of Gotama's canonical discourses towards the more analytical and scholarly texts of the Abhidharma, which dispensed with narratives, personalities, and anecdotes to reveal the "essential" meaning of the dharma. Through precisely defining and categorizing the key terms used in the discourses, the Abhidharmists elaborated a complex, atomistic philosophy, which saw reality as composed of a finite number of irreducible elements—similar in some respects to Plato's essential forms or ideas (*eidos*). In the preamble to *The Questions of King Milinda*, we find Nāgasena deploring how his preceptor had "foolishly" taught him the Abhidharma rather than Gotama's own discourses, only to be reprimanded by another monk for holding such erroneous views. It soon became the norm for Buddhists to begin their studies by first mastering a commentarial system like that of the Abhidharma or Sutrism rather than reading Gotama's discourses. Many schools of Buddhism today dispense with studying his discourses altogether. The scholastic curriculum for Sera Monastery, where Geshe Rabten was trained, does not include a single discourse attributed to the Buddha.

Not long after *The Questions of King Milinda* appeared in northwest India among the Greeks, an enigmatic figure from south India called Nāgārjuna composed a polemical work entitled *Verses from the Center* that rejected the Abhidharma project and sought to restore Gotama's original vision of a middle way. While Nāgasena modeled himself on the great *arahant*s of the past, Nāgārjuna spoke with startling freshness in his own distinctive voice. This radical break with tradition initiated a new era where voices other than that of Gotama assumed equal authority to declaim the dharma rather than merely interpret it.

For Nāgārjuna, Gotama's core vision of contingency and emptiness had become dangerously compromised. In one of the earliest accounts of his awakening, Gotama spoke of how the dharma consisted of two principles: the lawful contingency that governed the unfolding of life itself and the nonreactive emptiness of mind that allowed the clarity and freedom to make appropriate judgments in response to it.[4] Nāgārjuna saw this mutually interdependent play of contingency and emptiness as the very dynamic of the middle way itself. Yet over time emptiness or nirvana became conceived as an unconditioned, absolute reality in contrast to the transient and contingent world. To misconceive emptiness in this way, declared Nāgārjuna, "injures the undiscerning like mishandling a snake or miscasting a spell."[5] Instead of being a liberating idea that frees one from reactivity, the idea of emptiness was turned into a dogmatic belief that reinforced reactivity. Rather than being a cure, the idea of emptiness became part of the sickness. Rather than dispelling illusions, it became the grandest spiritual illusion of all.

Nāgārjuna recognized how emptiness is not a sacred or mystical state to be realized by the diligent meditator. For Nāgārjuna emptiness is simply a "letting go of views." As an empty*ing* rather than an empti*ness*, it has to do with releasing the hold of habitual patterns of belief that keep one stuck and hinder one's flourishing. Such emptying requires the courage and audacity to drop cherished opinions and be awed again by the mystery of being alive each moment. To turn away from the world to imagine emptiness as a transcendent source of salvation is to miss the point entirely. "Believers in emptiness," Nāgārjuna wryly remarks, "are incurable."[6]

Nāgārjuna never identifies his doctrinal opponents by name, but initial readers of *Verses from the Center* would have immediately recognized the text as a sustained, comprehensive critique of the current state of Buddhism and an attack on some of their most cherished beliefs. But Nāgārjuna is not primarily concerned with refuting specific doctrinal views. He wants to alert his readers to the innate human tendencies of reification and reactivity that lead us to become attached to such views. For only then will people be able to take the necessary steps to overcome such habits and views alike.

Only one canonical discourse is mentioned in the twenty-seven chapters of Nāgārjuna's key work. This is *To Kaccāna*, found in the Pali Canon, where Gotama explains to the young priest Kaccāna how a true perspective on life is one that is no longer trapped in the binary of "is" and "isn't."[7] For Nāgārjuna, the practice of emptiness (or emptying) challenges one to steer a middle way between these two dead ends. Emptying is a practice of staying alive and alert to the possibilities of life, aware of how ethically constrictive fixed views can be, while remaining poised on the cusp of the present to respond with discernment, creativity, and care to whatever calls for your attention.

Nāgārjuna did not present a doctrine of emptiness, carefully laid out and argued point by point. He left that well-nigh impossible task to his followers in the Centrist school of philosophy, which would form in the centuries after his death. A poet as well as a philosopher, he disclosed emptiness and contingency as much in the rhythms, cadences, imagery, and metaphors of his language as in the subtlety of his reasoning. He shocked his readers with the disconcerting possibility that they could think and speak about Buddhism in a radically new way. Through reconfiguring the core ideas and values of the dharma and articulating them in his own voice, he showed what it was like to be rooted in a tradition without having always to defer to the authority of others.

Nāgārjuna was a disruptive figure. In seeking to recover what Gotama taught, his *Verses from the Center* broke with the conventions of Buddhist literature, questioned the authority of established tradition, and opened up a new imaginal space for other perspectives to be explored and different voices to be heard. While Nāgasena sought to explain the Buddhist dogmas of his day as convincingly as possible, Nāgārjuna sought to un-explain and deconstruct them. While Nāgasena strove for certainty, Nāgārjuna recognized how at the heart of contingency lay uncertainty.

"One who sees contingency," declared Nāgārjuna in the concluding verse of his chapter on awakening, "sees suffering, arising, ceasing and pathing."[8] These four primary facts of life—that we suffer, that reactivity arises yet also ceases, and that in its ceasing a path can unfold—underpin the four paths and tasks that constitute the logic and practice of awakening itself. Nāgārjuna's verse echoes and amplifies Gotama's statement that "one who sees contingency sees the dharma." Nāgārjuna recognizes how Gotama had no interest in gaining insight into an Absolute Truth but taught a dharma that allowed people to respond more effectively, creatively, and compassionately to the unpredictable contingencies of life. Nāgārjuna thus sought to dismantle the scholarly apparatus of the Abhidharma and other Buddhist dogmatic systems to recover the vital, nonreactive space of emptiness from which an ethics of uncertainty could emerge afresh.

Contingency and uncertainty are of comparable centrality in Attic tragedy. Yet rather than explain them as ideas or principles, Aeschylus, Sophocles, and Euripides revealed them in dramas performed by actors on a stage. At the conclusion of four of Euripides's sixteen surviving plays, the chorus repeats the same refrain:

> Zeus on Olympus keeps much in store;
> The gods accomplish many startling things.
> What we expect does not take place,
> And the god makes way for what we don't expect.
> *This* is what has happened here today.[9]

In polytheistic language, Euripides emphasizes how life unfolds in unpredictable and shocking ways because we mortals are incapable of grasping what the gods have in mind for us. In his first discourse, Gotama makes the same point in nontheistic language by recognizing how life inevitably involves encountering what we dislike, being separated from what we love, and not getting what we want. Whether we rationalize this as the will of gods or the ripening of karma, life just happens to us in ways over which we have little if any control.

IV
Creativity

13
Refining Gold

To embark on a path of human flourishing requires the creativity to imagine another way of living in this world. For Gotama, creativity was not a quality that some gifted people possessed and others did not; it was available to everyone. Creativity is the art of solving problems. It is the human capacity to think outside the box of what is tried and tested to imagine something new, whether in the sphere of politics, work, relationships, art, or philosophy. In seeking to do things differently, creativity is the very opposite of reactivity, which seeks to keep everything the same.

One evening Gotama arrived by himself in the city of Rājagaha and went in search of a place to stay overnight.[1] He ended up lodging in a potter's workshop with an eager young ascetic called Pukkhusāti. When Gotama asked him who was his teacher, Pukkhusāti explained that he considered himself a follower of an enlightened master called Gotama, whom he fervently hoped to meet one day. Instead of revealing who he was, Gotama sought out more information about this famous teacher. Only when they started talking the next morning did the truth, to Pukkhusāti's embarrassment, slowly emerge.

Gotama encouraged Pukkhusāti to cultivate an equanimity that would enable him to remain unshaken by the delights and disappointments of the world. He likened this equanimity to pure gold, which is both malleable and radiant. "Imagine a goldsmith," he suggested, "who has prepared a furnace, heated the crucible, then taken a piece of gold with his tongs and placed it inside the crucible. Sometimes he blows on it, sometimes he sprinkles water on it, and sometimes he just observes it. In this way the gold becomes refined, rid of impurities, malleable and radiant so that he can fashion from it whatever kind of ornament he likes."[2] Like pure gold in the hands of a master craftsman, this equanimity would enable Pukkhusāti to engage more creatively with the situations he encountered in life.

This encounter provides a rare glimpse of Gotama. He looks and behaves just like any other wandering monk in India of the time. He is content to camp in a workshop with whoever happens to be there. He does not project the charisma or authority of one who is used to being revered and obeyed. He is alone, unaccompanied by an attendant or disciples. He plays with Pukkhusāti by teasing out more information about "Gotama" instead of revealing his true identity. He enjoys his anonymity and has a sense of humor. He is kind and generous. He wants to dispel Pukkhusāti's embarrassment and confusion and show him another way to live.

For a homeless mendicant, Gotama knew a lot about gold. He described in detail the process of panning, refining, and working with the metal. He explained how you needed to separate the particles of gold from soil and gravel by rinsing the mix in a trough, then further washing it to remove the remaining fine grit, sand, and black dust. After that the gold needed to be placed in a melting pot above a fire, and the fire fanned until the gold was separated from its ore and properly smelted.[3] Since gold can also be mixed with iron, copper, tin, lead, and silver, these too needed to be removed.[4] The complex process of refining gold served Gotama as a metaphor for how to purify and train one's mind.

The equanimity Gotama encouraged Pukkhusāti to cultivate is a necessary but not sufficient cause for awakening. To be effective, equanimity needs to be integrated with collectedness and courage. "Were a goldsmith only to fan his fire," explained Gotama, "he would risk overheating the gold; were he only to sprinkle water on it, he would risk it getting too cool; and were he only to stand back and observe it, the gold would not reach the right consistency."[5] Through observation and training, a goldsmith knows intuitively how to work with his fire, tools, and materials to produce the kind of gold from which he can create whatever kind of ornament he has in mind, be it a bracelet, earrings, or a necklace. Likewise, practitioners of the dharma need to balance their collectedness, courage, and equanimity to be able to imagine and then become the kinds of persons they aspire to be.

In comparing the mind to gold and the practitioner to a goldsmith, Gotama encouraged his followers to cultivate imagination and creativity. Since the analogy refers to panning rather than mining gold, it suggests how the virtues one seeks to integrate are scattered through the landscape of one's experience and culture rather than concentrated in a single seam. They need to be patiently gathered together and further refined so that one's mind too becomes "malleable and radiant" and can then be turned to realizing one's goals.

Throughout history gold has been valued for its nonreactive properties. No matter how long it is exposed to the atmosphere, it neither oxidizes nor corrodes. Inert to all body chemistry, gold leaves the body unaltered after any amount of contact. It has no taste, is nontoxic and non-irritable. It thus serves as an eminently suitable metaphor for the nonreactive awareness in which Gotama urges people to dwell. Since in its pure state it is too soft to be turned either into a dental filling, electrical connector, or wedding ring, it needs to be alloyed with other metals to render it workable. Similarly, nirvanic awareness by itself is inert, incapable of responding to ethical challenges without being "alloyed" with other virtues such as mindfulness, discernment, and compassion.

"Just as a skilled potter," said Gotama, "can craft whatever kind of pottery vessel he likes, or as a skilled ivory carver can craft any kind of ivory work he likes, or as a skilled goldsmith can craft any kind of gold article he likes; in the same way—with his mind thus collected, purified, malleable, radiant, and steady—the practitioner directs and inclines it to forms of creativity."[6] The artisan first imagines how a raw material—a lump of clay, an elephant's tusk, or liquid gold—could be transformed into something functional and beautiful. He then applies his skills to manufacture such an article. There is something almost magical about this process.

The Hungarian novelist Sándor Márai described an artist as one "who can engrave an entire battle scene on a tiny piece of stone or paint a crowded city full of people, dogs and spires on a slip of ivory. Because an artist, and only an artist, can shatter the laws of space and time."[7] Gotama likewise described the creativity of the dharma practitioner as a kind of magic. "Having been one he becomes many; having been many he becomes one. He appears. He vanishes. He goes unimpeded through walls, ramparts, and mountains as if through space. He dives in and out of the earth as if it were water. He walks on water without sinking as if it were dry land. Sitting cross-legged he flies through the air like a winged bird. With his hand he touches and strokes even the sun and moon."[8] Once the mind is stabilized, radiant, and integrated, a new kind of freedom dawns. Previously unimagined possibilities open up as one's creativity is unleashed.

Gotama rejected the notion that magical powers such as walking through walls and flying in the sky were marks of spiritual attainment. He saw them as mere "conjuror's tricks" that benefited no one except the magician. The only genuine miracle, he said, was that of instruction, whereby a teacher inspired others through words, metaphors, and reasons to change the way they lived on earth.[9]

We are so familiar with works of art that the process of imagining and creating them no longer astonishes us. We have become immune to the magic of artistic creation. But imagine a traveling bard reciting *The Iliad* around a fire at night to a spellbound group of farmers, conjuring up through mere words, oratory, and gestures a thousand ships dispatched to Troy and the mighty battles that ensued. Or imagine marks and pigments traced on the walls of a cave that come vividly to life as mammoths, horses, and deer when illuminated by flickering torchlight. Or recall those early cinemagoers who ran terrified from the theater on seeing a train come hurtling towards them from where the screen used to be.

Gotama understood creativity as a capacity that could be cultivated by aspiration, perseverance, intuition, and experimentation. A potter, for example, first aspires to create a work that so far only exists in her imagination. She then requires the perseverance to commit herself to doing whatever is necessary to bring it into being. She needs to let go of her conceptual preferences and trust her aesthetic intuitions for guidance in creating the work. And she has to keep on experimenting. For it is only through making pots that fall short of her ideal that she arrives, often by serendipity, at the kind of pot she intuitively knows to be "right." The practitioner likewise makes a sustained effort to become the kind of person she aspires to be. She too has to trust the intuitions of her heart and soul to guide her along the path. And she needs to keep experimenting with different approaches and practices to discover what works for her.[10]

For Gotama, creativity was not restricted to making art or reshaping one's character but extended to imagining another kind of society. He compared himself to a man who had wandered into a forest and stumbled across an old path that led to the ruins of a city. On returning home the man appealed to the local ruler to rebuild this city, so that it would once more become prosperous, beautiful, and filled with people. Inspired by such ruins he had either seen himself or heard about from others, Gotama sought to mobilize people in a joint endeavor to create a civic space in which they could flourish as a society governed by the rule of law (dharma).[11]

The Parable of the City was a way of responding to the conditions of the turbulent world in which Gotama lived. It offered hope to those whose lives were being transformed by epochal social, political, and economic change. Gotama was born at a time when the first cities were emerging in his homeland. The old political order of clan-based oligarchic republics was breaking down and being replaced by monarchies. Men and women were leaving their ancestral villages and migrating to these new urban centers. The advent of money gave rise to a new class of prosperous merchants and bankers. Potters, goldsmiths, and ivory workers came together to form guilds. These were Gotama's people. They were the ones he sought to inspire with his vision of a restored civic space. His teachings provided the builders and inhabitants of these new cities with the ethical, contemplative, and philosophical tools needed to create a culture that would respond to the needs of their uncertain times.

For men and women to participate in the creation of a civic space that can engender a culture of awakening, they need to be able to think for themselves. To become autonomous and find their own voice, they may have to leave behind the certainties passed down uncritically over generations through their clans and religions. Gotama advocated a radical break with traditional worldviews, and challenged the authority of those who upheld such beliefs. Rather than insisting on a totalizing explanation—such as "whatever I experience is caused by what I did in the past"—he encouraged people to engage with the problems they faced and creatively find their own solutions.

Gotama tended not to argue with others about the nature of reality. "Whatever the wise in the world agree upon to be the case," he said, "I too take that to be the case."[12] He understood such knowledge as provisional and ongoing rather than definitive for all time. He recognized how totalizing beliefs can blind us to common sense. Rather than trying to explain how all experience is due to the mysterious operation of past actions, he pointed to the role played by your state of health, the weather conditions, how well you take care of yourself, and the impact of others' behavior. Yes, your past actions could also have been the cause of what you experience. But there is nothing at all mysterious about this; it is something you can see for yourself.[13] Such a perspective empowered ordinary people to take charge of their lives by becoming independent of the authority of others.

The dialogues recorded in the Pali Canon with Pukkhusāti, Vacchā, Kaccāna, and others reveal Gotama as an intelligent, self-assured, and disruptive figure, who does not hesitate to challenge received ideas. In rejecting the metaphysical certainties of his day he does not replace them with metaphysical certainties of his own. Like Socrates he uses his authority as a teacher solely to empower the student.

14
The Truth of Comedy

The archaeological site of the ancient city of Elis in the western Peloponnese attracts few visitors. On the morning I arrive, the car park is empty and the sole caretaker surprised and not overjoyed to see me. Yet at Socrates's time Elis was one of the oldest, largest, and most prosperous cities in Greece, responsible for organizing the pan-Hellenic games at the sanctuary of Zeus and Hera at Olympia. It was also the birthplace of Pyrrho, the founder of the philosophical school of Skepticism. As I make my way down a footpath towards the site itself, I pass a young man seated on a bench, hunched intently over his mobile phone. He is the only other visitor. The featureless landscape consists of fallow fields and occasional patches of brush that fade into the hazy distance.

As the path approaches the remains of the ancient theater, I am suddenly startled by a furious buzzing of bees, which must have been disturbed by my presence. I look around but can see no swarming bees, which only increases my panic. Then I catch a glimpse of something in the sky. A drone. The young man on the bench was more likely the bored son of the caretaker than a tourist and had not been looking at his phone but operating this machine. My cognitive errors and resultant alarm would have perhaps been allayed had I borne in mind Pyrrho's injunction that since "neither our sensations nor our opinions tell us truths or falsehoods, we should not put our slightest trust in them, but be without judgement, without preference, and unwavering."[1] Years of Buddhist practice have encouraged me to do much the same, but the forces of instinct and self-preservation swiftly override such good intentions.

The theater at Elis today is just a semi-circular hollow on a grassy slope, divided into segments by indentations that may once have been passageways between the rows of seats. Only remnants of the stone foundations of the stage remind us where Aristophanes's *Clouds* and other comedies would once have been performed. Looking across the fields overgrown with grass it is hard to imagine the peals of laughter that once would have erupted from this spot, difficult to picture the bustling agora of Elis or the great gymnasium where for centuries athletes trained for the Olympic Games. Here and there the tall grasses have been cleared to allow the occasional brick floor of a building or the base of a stone column to be visible. Otherwise, only silence and emptiness remain.

The comedies of Aristophanes provide an intimate, albeit comically exaggerated glimpse of everyday life in Athens. Unlike the three great tragedians, Aristophanes came of age during the Peloponnesian War. All his comedies were written and premiered against the backdrop of this conflict. For this reason, perhaps, he takes the firmest and most outspoken stand against the war with his scathing parodies of militaristic leaders who repeatedly threatened to prosecute him. The greatest comic poet of Athens was also its foremost poet of nonviolence. One of his plays was titled *Peace*, and another,

Lysistrata, told the story of a young Athenian wife who devised a simple but ingenious scheme to prevent men from going to war: refuse them sex if they persist in fighting.

Aristophanes's comedy *Law and Order Women* (*Thesmophoriazusae*) is set during the autumn festival of Demeter, goddess of the fertility of the soil, which was attended only by women. In the play, the good housewives of Athens are up in arms about the way Euripides depicts them on stage. Addressing the assembled festivalgoers, one of them, Mica, launches an impassioned attack on the playwright.[2] For Mica, Euripides's commitment to truth telling has exposed the fact that women are no different from men in their lusts, indulgences, failings, and deceptions. His tragedies puncture the convenient illusion of the chaste, meek wife, who is delighted to stay at home all day caring for children and carding wool.

Another woman explains how her husband was killed fighting in Cyprus, leaving her destitute. To support her five children, she has been reduced to weaving and selling the myrtle wreaths used in religious rites. Now, she complains, this scumbag tragedian has persuaded people to no longer believe in the gods and as a result her trade in myrtle wreaths has suffered. Euripides is accused of weakening the social and religious bonds that hold Athenian society together. As citizens become more rational and less pious, the lot of this poor widow and others like her becomes even harder to bear. The women at the Law and Order festival unanimously agree on the solution. Euripides has to be assassinated. By any available means. Poison is suggested.

Aristophanes intended his comedies to induce side-splitting laughter, but he knew full well that tragedy lay just below the surface of his jokes. The old man Strepsiades in *Clouds* appears as a ridiculous buffoon, but it takes only a slight shift in perspective to reveal him as a pitiful creature, lost in a world he barely understands and over which he has little control. The genuine tragedy of his situation is that he completely fails to understand Socrates. He knows what the philosopher looks like but has no clue what he does.

Having internalized the popular caricatures of philosophers, Strepsiades uncritically shares the disdainful mockery of the crowd, which ridicules those who pursue a life of the mind. He dismisses Socrates as just another unworldly, puffed-up, slightly mad intellectual. In thrall to his petty fears and desires, it never occurs to him to stop for a moment and wonder about what he is saying and doing. To put himself into question, which is the beginning of philosophy, is alien to him. He blindly lets himself be borne along on waves of prejudice and opinion. Yet as the darker, deeper insights of the comedy sink in, some of the laughing spectators might arrive at the disquieting realization that they are laughing at themselves.

Comic playwrights like Aristophanes are not taken in by the grand displays of heroic deeds and self-sacrifice that are the staple fare of much tragic drama. Comedies reveal instead the tragic innocence of the simpleminded, those ordinary men and women who muddle through life with no thought of personal glory. Like peasants in the paintings of Bruegel, they attend wedding feasts and seasonal processions, reap harvests and trudge through the snow in search of game but seem eternally bemused and distracted. Inspired by Bruegel's painting of the fall of Icarus, W. H. Auden recognized how the old masters were "never wrong" about suffering.[3] For even something as horrific as a boy falling to his death from the sky takes place in the midst of banal, everyday events. As long as the sun keeps shining and the routines of daily life are not interrupted, the farmers tilling fields fail to notice the mythic tragedy that is unfolding in their midst. The tiny arm and head of the drowning Icarus in a corner of the painting are barely discernible.

For an angry group of women at a religious festival to sentence a playwright to death for contributing to a collapse in the market for myrtle wreaths might be amusing for theatergoers. But sitting on a dusty roadside hawking wreaths to scrape together a living is not at all amusing for a destitute mother of five. As more and more men died in battle, indigent, desperate women like her would have been an increasingly common sight in Athens. Yet like Bruegel's fallen Icarus they are marginalized, the tragedy of their humble lives conveniently ignored. By bringing their plight to attention, even as part of a comedy, Aristophanes renders it visible. The audience's belly laughs may have been tinged by uncomfortable pangs of conscience. Nor is it a joke, then or now, to condemn poets, writers, and artists to death simply because something they said is deemed offensive. These comedies are funny but not funny at the same time.

Since very few if any women attended these theatrical performances, it is striking how so many plays featured women—Electra, Antigone, Hecuba, Medea, Clytemnestra, Iphigenia, Cassandra, Helen, Phaedra—in principal roles. The authors of these plays were not feminists in the sense we would understand today. There is no indication that any of them questioned, let alone sought to change, the status and role of women in Athenian society. Yet they empathized with the suffering of women and enabled their voices, albeit through the mouths of male actors, to be heard in public.

The numerous funerary steles from the fifth century BCE on display in Athenian museums today depict bas-reliefs of family life, which movingly show the tenderness and love that existed between husbands, wives, and their children. These images reveal a palpable intimacy and joy that we are likely to overlook if we reduce the treatment of women in Athens to one of oppressive confinement alone. Just because women were subjected to conditions that would be unacceptable in a modern liberal democracy does not mean they led lives of misery and frustration devoid of any happiness.

By suspending social conventions, the Dionysian festivals created a space for the hidden feminine to become visible and audible. In psychological terms, this allowed the predominantly male audience to pay heed to the buried intuitions, feelings, and instincts they shared with their womenfolk but were unable or reluctant to acknowledge. In allowing the Athenian unconscious, its *Anima* in Jungian terms, to be brought into the light of day and made conscious, the playwrights served as civic therapists. The women depicted in the plays were not just stand-ins for the wives, sisters, and daughters of the spectators but also stood for the spectators' own unconscious anxieties and fears.

For Aristotle, the defining purpose of tragic drama was to induce the fear and compassion (*eleos*) needed to trigger catharsis: a liberating and purgative experience in which a sense of wholeness was briefly restored.[4] In the end the aim of comedy seems much the same as that of tragedy. The spectator of *Clouds* may likewise experience the fear of seeing himself in the befuddled innocents on stage, thereby giving rise to compassion for their (and, by implication, his own) tragic plight. In comedy, catharsis is reached through moments of insight into what it is to be such a fickle, selfish, sad, yet comic creature. Perhaps this is what Bertolt Brecht meant in saying that "tragedy deals with the sufferings of mankind in a less serious way than comedy."[5] Rather than the emotional release of pent-up feelings triggered by tragic drama, comedy offers a less sensational but more sobering reflection on the humdrum fact of simply being human.

15
Ataraxia

Once a particular account of a philosophical or religious tradition achieves the status of an orthodoxy, repeated uncritically over generations, it becomes very difficult to dislodge. Those who challenge it are condemned as heretics or fools, while those who perpetuate it become attached to the authority it grants them. No matter how compelling the counter-evidence, any new story will be firmly resisted (or simply ignored) by those who are emotionally invested in maintaining the status quo and accustomed to being obeyed. To risk telling another story may incur wrath or ridicule, but it may also open up new creative possibilities for those who feel shackled and silenced by the dogmatic certainties on which orthodoxies thrive.

Around twelve years after Socrates's death, Plato founded his Academy in Athens on a plot of land he had inherited to the north of the city. The seventeen-year-old Aristotle arrived there in 367 BCE and studied with Plato for twenty-five years until he was invited by Philip II of Macedon to serve as tutor to his twelve-year-old son Alexander. Five years later, Philip's armies defeated Athens and Thebes, making Macedon the dominant power in the Greek world. Philip intended to continue his conquests by invading the Persian Empire, but he was assassinated two years later, in 336 BCE, at which point Alexander, now twenty, became king. The following year, Aristotle returned to Athens and founded his own school at the Lyceum.

Once at the Lyceum, Aristotle focused on providing a fully rounded education (*paideia*)—from arithmetic to music, from philosophy to wrestling—that would prepare aristocratic young men like Alexander for rulership. Yet when Alexander set out to conquer the Persian Empire, he included among his entourage two philosophers who were neither Athenian nor students of Aristotle. These were Anaxarchus, from the city of Abdera in Thrace, and his student Pyrrho, from the city of Elis, who subsequently became the founder of Skepticism. Both of these thinkers traced their lineage back to Democritus, also a native of Abdera, known to posterity as the "laughing philosopher."

As a young man Democritus is said to have traveled widely in search of wisdom, throughout Egypt and Persia and possibly went as far as India.[1] If Democritus did in fact reach India, he would have done so during the lifetime of Gotama but would likely not have traveled far enough into the subcontinent to have met him or his followers. On returning to Greece, he assumed a life of poverty in a small dwelling in his garden where "he used to train himself in a great variety of ways to test his sense impressions, sometimes living in solitude and spending time in tombs," all of which are suggestive of Indian ascetic practices.[2] Democritus is said to have visited Athens but kept a low profile. Although he knew of Socrates, apparently Socrates ignored him.[3]

The practical goal of Democritus's philosophy was the attainment of joy (*euthymia*) and flourishing (*eudaemonia*). He was also one of the first Greek thinkers to develop an atomic theory of the universe. This view led him to cast doubt on the reliability of the senses or reason as means of ascertaining truth, since neither was capable of apprehending the atoms themselves. Democritus is remembered for saying, "In reality, men know nothing; for truth lies in an abyss."[4] Because his philosophy was grounded entirely in the physical world and the senses, Democritus was condemned by the Idealist Plato, who sought to have his work suppressed and burned.[5]

In contrast to how we use the term "skeptical" today, the Greeks understood *skepsis* in its original sense as examination or inquiry. A skeptic was someone who persistently questioned what was presented to his experience rather than immediately adopting an opinion about it. This dimension of Democritus's philosophy was taken up by his disciple Metrodorus of Chios, who once declared that "we know nothing, nor do we even know just this: that we know nothing."[6] Such radical not-knowing would underpin the sense of wonder found in another saying attributed to Metrodorus: "A single ear of wheat in a large field is as strange as a single world in infinite space."[7] Like Socrates, these Democriteans regarded wonder as the origin of philosophy.

When Alexander reached Taxila, the capital of Gandhara, Pyrrho is said to have studied with the local sages and "as a result seems to have adopted a profoundly noble philosophy, having introduced the notion of inability to attain conviction and that of suspension of judgement."[8] This is the only instance of a Greek source ascribing an Indian origin to a Greek philosophical school. Yet since the Democritean tradition, to which Pyrrho belonged, included similarly skeptical ideas, it is difficult to know whether the Indian sages introduced him to an entirely new perspective or simply reinforced and refined notions with which he was already familiar.

Since Pyrrho, like Gotama and Socrates, did not write anything, all we know of his teachings are contained in fragments of text written by his followers. The longest fragment, attributed to Pyrrho's disciple Timon, reads:

> Pyrrho declared that things are equally in-different, un-measurable, and un-decidable. Therefore, neither our sensations nor our opinions tell us truths or falsehoods. We should not put our slightest trust in them, but be without judgment, without preference, and unwavering, saying about each thing that it no more is than is not, or both is and is not, or neither is nor is not. The result for those who adopt this attitude will first be speechlessness (*aphatos*), then untroubledness (*ataraxia*).[9]

This passage has often been cited as a possible case of Buddhist ideas finding their way into Greek thought. Like Gotama, Pyrrho proposes a contemplative practice, which entails relinquishing the binary habit of "is" and "is not," thereby releasing one from dogmatic views into a condition of speechlessness. This wordless unknowing and wonder are likewise the precondition for coming to rest in a still and untroubled state of mind (*ataraxia*), which is strikingly similar to nirvana as a radiant, open-hearted equanimity, unconditioned by the reactive fires of greed, hatred, and opinionatedness.

Just as Gotama declared that it would be a "mere empty boast" to claim that anything existed apart from what appeared to the senses,[10] so Pyrrho is remembered for his use of the Democritean slogan "no more."[11] In each case, one trains one's attention to focus on the immediacy of what is before one's senses while letting go of any idea that there might be "something more," such as God or the Unconditioned, waiting to be uncovered. Not only did Gotama and Pyrrho alike consider it unjustified to posit anything more real concealed behind or beneath or within what appears, in clinging to such beliefs one blinded oneself to what is hidden in plain sight before one's very eyes.

Who were the "naked sages" ("gymnosophists") with

whom Pyrrho, and possibly Democritus, associated while in India? "Gymnosophist" was an all-purpose term used by the Greeks to denote Indian ascetics in general, who were purported to wear little if any clothing, much like the sadhus one encounters in India today. Although Jain monks are famous for going around "sky-clad," that is, naked, they are unlikely to have been present in Taxila at Pyrrho's time. Since the university of Taxila was a renowned center of Vedic learning, Pyrrho would certainly have encountered brahmin priests and ascetics. However, ideas such as "nonjudgment" and the "inability to reach conviction," which so impressed Pyrrho, are alien to what we know of early Brahmanic thought. It seems possible, therefore, that his interlocutors were Buddhists.

The Pali *Dhammapada Commentary* records how Gotama's disciple Kaccāna was staying in or near Taxila when Soreyyā, then still a woman, apologized to him for having lusted after his body and miraculously became a man again. When Pyrrho arrived in Taxila, it is possible that a community based on Kaccāna's teachings still survived there. What gives weight to these admittedly tenuous connections is how closely Pyrrho's teaching resembles that of Kaccāna's in the *Chapter of Eights*.

Compare the fragment above attributed to Pyrrho with these verses from the *Chapter of Eights:*

> Nowhere does a lucid one
> hold contrived views about *is* or *is not*.
> How could he succumb to them,
> having let go of illusions and conceit? He's uninvolved.
>
> He lets go of one position without taking another—
> he's not defined by what he knows.
> Nor does he join a dissenting faction—
> he assumes no view at all.[12]

Both Pyrrho and Kaccāna encourage us to remain without judgment or preference in the face of life's complexity and demands. Both men aspire to rest in a silent, nonreactive awareness, which for Pyrrho is ataraxia and for Kaccāna, nirvana. When no longer trapped in opinions and views, one is freed to respond to situations in creative, spontaneous, and unpredictable ways.

Shortly after Pyrrho's death, the philosopher Arcesilaus became head of Plato's Academy. For the next two centuries, Skepticism became the prominent doctrine taught within its walls. Returning to Socrates's claim that he knew nothing, the Academy moved away from the study of Plato's Idealist doctrines towards the kind of Skepticism taught by Pyrrho. Henceforth, uncertainty and not-knowing came to be valued more highly than attempts to reach philosophical certainty and knowledge.

The Skeptics were not the only philosophical school to make ataraxia a central focus of their practice. This was also the goal of Epicurus and his followers, who likewise regarded such nonreactive, nirvana-like awareness as the source of human well-being and wisdom. Epicurus was born to Athenian parents in 341 BCE on the island of Samos, sixty years after the deaths of Socrates and Gotama. Although he may have studied Platonism as a teenager, he was drawn to the materialistic philosophy of Democritus. Some sources suggest that he admired Archelaus, the natural philosopher who taught and loved the young Socrates,[13] and was influenced by the views of Socrates's disciple Aristippus, who regarded pleasure to be the goal of human life.[14] In his mid-thirties, Epicurus bought a property in Athens, known as the Garden, where he and his followers lived a communal life of simplicity, frugality, and friendship.

For Epicurus, philosophy was for everyone. It was a way of life rather than a specialized activity of professional intellectuals or provocative ascetics. Anyone could do it. Epicurus welcomed both women and slaves into his community in the Garden. From his surviving letters, verses, and other fragments, Epicurus appears as a kind, wise, tolerant, and gentle soul, who would have been entirely at home in the Jeta's Grove at Savatthi among the sangha of Gotama's followers. Like Gotama, he valued friendship as the greatest good and renounced involvement in political life; he encouraged but did not insist on celibacy; and while not denying the existence of the gods, he believed they played no role in human affairs. Both men valued empirical observation, reason, reflection, and thoughtful conversation as means to free oneself from the paralyzing grip of dogmatic beliefs. Both understood the destructive power of uncontrolled emotion and encouraged a disciplined way of life that led to ataraxia.

Epicurus was a materialist, who maintained that ataraxia came about in part as a result of understanding the true nature of the world to be nothing but atoms moving through the void. Building on Democritean atomism, Epicurean physics argued that the extraordinary diversity of living things was made possible because atoms occasionally "swerved" unpredictably to amass in new configurations and forms. For Epicurus, consciousness or mind was merely a subtle vibration of atoms rather than a separate, nonphysical entity that could survive bodily death. As a result, he taught that death was nothing to be feared since when it occurred you were no longer alive to experience it, and as long as you were alive you were necessarily not dead.

Atomic theories were developed by Buddhist schools of thought after Gotama's death, but atoms, let alone the void through which they move, are not mentioned at all in the Pali discourses. Gotama was neither a materialist nor an idealist. He refused to answer questions about the relation between body and mind, the material and the mental. Like the Skeptics, he provisionally and pragmatically accepted views about the nature of the world that were current at his time.

That everything in the universe results from the unintentional interactions between mindless atoms racing around in a void does not diminish the sense of awe that there is anything at all rather than nothing. Two centuries after the death of Epicurus, the Roman Epicurean Lucretius invited his readers to imagine what it would be like to see the everyday features of the natural world as if they were suddenly and without warning shown to them for the first time. "What," he asks, "could be declared more wondrous than these miracles no one before had dared believe could even exist?"[15] Again, the origin and foundations of philosophy are seen to lie in experiences of wonder, astonishment, and awe at the sheer fact that there is something rather than nothing.

Like Gotama and Socrates, Lucretius seeks to awaken people from their sleepwalking in order for them to be fully alive. To achieve this he advocates a life grounded in the peace of ataraxia, which would enable them to witness the struggling, conflicted world of human beings without being overwhelmed or seduced by it. Renouncing worldly riches and success, he praises a life of simplicity and contentment, where one can enjoy sitting quietly by a brook beneath the shade of a tree in awe at the beauty and abundance of the freely given world of nature.[16]

16
A Dialogical Self

Whether or not Socrates had disciples whom he encouraged to carry on his work after his death depends on which sources you read. While Plato's account of his defense speech presents Socrates as having nothing to teach and no students, Xenophon paints a picture of a more conventional teacher with followers, many of whom (like Plato) were devoted to him and at least one of whom (Xenophon himself) may have been deliberately recruited. Socrates, like Gotama, was a magnetic personality who attracted around him a diverse circle of people with widely contrasting backgrounds, motives, and views. Among his followers we find the worldly Aristippus, who regarded pleasure as the highest good, as well as the unworldly Antisthenes, who declared, "I would rather go mad than feel pleasure."[1] Yet both men were drawn to Socrates. And in spite of their differences, they both loathed Plato.

Such diversity among his followers suggests that Socrates had no interest in preaching a doctrine that all his followers would be expected to study, adopt, and then disseminate. Instead, he tested and questioned them in such a way as to get them to start thinking for themselves. He wanted each of them to become independent of him or any other authority figure. Thus Plato developed his theory of Ideas, imagined an ideal state, and founded the Academy; Aristippus charged money for his teachings, enjoyed luxuries and love affairs, and trained his daughter Arete to succeed him as the head of the now forgotten Cyrenaic school; and Antisthenes sought to emulate Socrates's radical commitment to simplicity and virtue, which eventually gave birth to the schools of Cynicism and Stoicism.

Gotama too attracted a wide range of followers from all levels of society, yet Buddhist tradition presents him as a teacher with a consistent set of doctrines and precepts that he delivered to all his students largely irrespective of their individual differences and needs. If we imagine Gotama engaging with his students in a more fluid and impromptu fashion like Socrates, not only would this accord with his description of himself as an "open-handed teacher" who does not think in terms of being in charge of his community,[2] it would also accord with his encouragement for his followers to become independent of others and for no two of them to "follow the same path."[3] Yet instead of allowing for a broad range of different approaches to the dharma to emerge from Gotama's example and teachings, the council of elders convened by Kassapa shortly after his death sought to impose an orthodoxy to which everyone was expected to conform.

The dour Antisthenes appears, along with Socrates, as one of the speakers in Xenophon's *Drinking Party* (*Symposium*), where, as in Plato's eponymous dialogue, the theme is love (*eros*). When Socrates teases Antisthenes that he seems to be the only person in the room who is not in love, Antisthenes objects that he has "a violent love" for Socrates.[4] What Antisthenes loves about Socrates is his unique character, his extraordinary capacity for being in the world but not of the world. Like Socrates, he disdains material goods. Living in poverty with few possessions, he recognizes that he still has enough to eat and drink and a cloak to keep him warm. Liberated from the ongoing struggle to acquire unnecessary things, he understands that the practice of virtue alone is all one requires to achieve dignity, self-sufficiency, and happiness. When asked what advantages philosophy brought, he replied, "To be able to live in company with oneself."[5]

Antisthenes was impressed by Socrates's exemplary way of life. This he sought to emulate through his own austere behavior and instructed his followers to do the same. Like an order of wandering mendicants, they wore the same simple cloak, carried a knapsack with their scant possessions, and walked with a staff. Antisthenes heralded a movement in Greek philosophy towards greater self-scrutiny, dispassion, and disdain for the vanity of the world.

The most celebrated follower of Antisthenes was Diogenes of Sinope, who took his teacher's asceticism to even greater lengths. Exiled from his homeland after a financial scandal, Diogenes came to Athens in search of a teacher who embodied and lived what he taught. Rather than attend lectures at Plato's newly founded Academy, he sought out the elderly Antisthenes, who initially refused to have anything to do with him. After repeated entreaties, Antisthenes—like a Zen master—threatened to hit him with his staff, but instead of withdrawing, Diogenes—like a good Zen student—stepped forward and proffered his head. From then on, it appears, he was accepted as a disciple.[6]

Diogenes adopted a life of uncompromising renunciation, choosing to live on the street in a large, earthenware pot used for making wine; eating and drinking whatever he could beg; urinating, defecating, and masturbating in public; and heaping scorn on others. He dismissed the doctrines of Plato as "a waste of time" and the theatrical performances at the Dionysian festivals as "a spectacle for morons."[7] Scorning pride in one's nationality or regional identity, he declared himself "a citizen of the world" (*cosmopolites*). People compared him to a dog (*kynikos*), transcribed in English as "Cynic."

In both Greece and India you could find men like Diogenes who had opted out of conventional society, dressed in rags or sackcloth, went barefoot, gathered to study and debate around teachers, preached to anyone who would listen, and berated those they regarded as fools. Sunakkhatta, Gotama's former attendant who denounced his elderly teacher to the Vesali assembly as a barren intellectual, is said to have been awed by the saintliness of Korakkhattiya, an ascetic known as the "Dog Man," who went around "on all fours, sprawling on the ground, and chewing and eating his food with his mouth alone."[8] Likewise, on seeing children drinking water from their cupped hands, Diogenes threw away his bowl as yet another unnecessary encumbrance. Gotama scorned this kind of extreme behavior as ascetic showmanship, predicting that it would only lead the Dog Man to fatal indigestion followed by rebirth as a low-ranking titan.

While on a sea journey Diogenes was captured by pirates and sold into slavery. He was bought by a wealthy Corinthian called Xeniades, who put him in charge of educating his children, whom he trained to behave like Buddhist monks, instructing them to "crop their hair close and to wear it unadorned, and to go lightly clad, barefoot, silent, and not looking about them in the streets."[9] The grateful Xeniades remarked that "a kindly deity" had entered his household. Diogenes rejected his friends' offer to purchase his freedom from slavery as imbeciles, saying that lions are not the slaves of those who feed them.[10] He died in Corinth at an old age and was buried near the city gate beneath a column on which was placed a dog carved in marble.

The link between the Cynics and Stoics can be traced

to a student of Diogenes called Crates of Thebes. When Zeno of Citium, the founder of Stoicism, arrived in Athens around 300 BCE—a century after Socrates's death—he found himself sitting in a bookshop listening to its owner read Xenophon's *Conversations of Socrates*. On asking whether such a man could be found in Athens today, the bookseller pointed to Crates, who happened to be walking past, and said, "Follow him."[11] Zeno studied Cynic philosophy with Crates but was reluctant to adopt the dog-like behavior of Diogenes and others. He set himself up as a more conventional teacher in the Painted Stoa on the north side of the Athenian agora, which gave the school its name "Stoicism."

Stoicism made Cynicism more reasonable, respectable, and feasible. While adhering to Antisthenes's and Diogenes's commitment to a life of dispassion and virtue, the Stoics developed a psychological and philosophical framework for this practice that included elaborate theories on physics, ethics, and logic. Just as Socrates evolved from the gadfly who claimed to know nothing into a mouthpiece for Plato's Idealist and political theories, so Diogenes the Dog was replaced first by erudite scholars and, a few centuries later, by some of the most powerful and cultured figures in the Roman world—Seneca, the tutor of Nero, and Marcus Aurelius, the emperor himself.

The Stoics recognized that nearly everything that occurs to people in the course of their lives is out of their control. Whether one likes it or not, things just happen: from the firing of neurons in one's brain and the digestion of food in one's stomach to an earthquake that levels a city and the asteroid that wiped out the dinosaurs. The Stoics understood these things as the irrepressible unfolding of the natural world. They described this as the *Logos* (the "logic" of reality), which they equated with the divine activity of Zeus. Since one can do nothing about this primal outpouring of life, the wise per-

A Dialogical Self

son accepts things as they are and, if they are painful or troubling, patiently endures them. For the Stoics, what happens to us is neither good nor evil. It is simply the way life pours forth. The terms "good" and "evil" apply only to how we react or respond to what's happening. Thus it is here, in the solitude of one's own mind, that one can attain sufficient dispassion (*apatheia*) to make wise rather than unwise judgments. For the Stoics, this is the only place where you are free to exercise control over what is happening to you. You may be powerless over external conditions, but you do have the power to control how you respond to those conditions.

This is not quite as straightforward as it might seem. For external things like earthquakes are not the only things that "just happen" to me. The dread and terror I experience on seeing the walls of my house shake like jelly also "just happen" to me. Stoic practice, therefore, requires focusing and stabilizing one's attention to maintain the inner stillness and dispassion that are constantly threatened by the impact of the world upon one's senses, on one hand, and the emotional turbulence of one's soul, on the other.

The Buddhist-like echoes in these passages are unmistakable. Yet, as far as we know, the Stoics had no contact with Buddhist thought. Particularly striking are the parallels with what tradition regards as Gotama's second discourse: *On Not-Self*. In his first discourse, *Turning the Wheel of Dharma*, Gotama had defined awakening as the recognition, performance, and mastery of four tasks: embracing suffering, letting reactivity be, seeing its cessation, and cultivating a path. Now he analyzes what it means to be the person or self who practices these tasks.

> "The body," Gotama declares, "is not self. If it were, it would not get sick. You could tell your body: 'be like this,' or 'don't be like that.' But because the

body is not self, it does get sick. You cannot tell it: 'be like this,' or 'don't be like that.'"[12]

Or as the Stoics would say: *your body is not under your control.* Sickness is something that just happens to it. No matter what measures you take to stay healthy, cancers, strokes, and viruses will get you nonetheless. And no matter how long you manage to prolong your bodily existence, in the end it will fail you at death.

Ironically, a Stoic reading of *On Not-Self* reveals Gotama's understanding of what it means to be a self. The key characteristic of a self is the ability to issue silent *commands* to oneself: "Be like this!" "Don't be like that!" So if the body really were you, then you (the self) should be able to tell it what to do just as you are able to tell yourself what to do when faced with a choice. But you cannot command your body not to fall sick on feeling the first symptoms of flu, whereas you can command yourself to respond to the flu with acceptance, understanding, and care. The self is essentially *dialogical*. It gives commands as though to someone else, to "another" self with whom you cohabit, who either obeys or fails to obey those commands. As we go through each day we constantly speak to ourselves, argue with ourselves, congratulate ourselves. We are thus "two-in-one" as the political theorist Hannah Arendt names this paradoxical feature of the human condition.

The self is the one who wills. In issuing commands to yourself, you seek to initiate an action that will have consequences both for yourself and for others in the future. In pondering over whether or how to intervene in the world, this dialogical self discloses itself as essentially ethical. Much of our internal dialogue takes the form of a debate with ourselves about what we should think or say or do in response to a particular situation in our shared world. Thus, despite being a single being, we can speak of being "torn apart" as well as "living in company with oneself" (Antisthenes) through the practice of philosophy.

In *On Not-Self,* Gotama observes that just as you do not choose your physical sensations, you do not choose how you feel about them, how they appear to you, or how you find yourself inclined to respond to them. Even these most intimate and subjective experiences *happen* to you. Hence Gotama encourages his students to always bear in mind "This is not mine. I am not this. This is not my self." By training yourself not to identify with either the physical or mental elements of your experience, you gradually "disengage" from them until you achieve "dispassion" (*virāga*). And through such dispassion you then gain freedom (*vimutti*) from the habits, conditioning, and constraints that hold you back from becoming an autonomous ethical agent.

Whether Stoic *apatheia* or Buddhist *virāga,* dispassion is the indispensable condition for establishing and sustaining a space of nonreactive awareness. In contrast to the pathological state of disassociation, which is a withdrawal from the world into alienated isolation, such dispassion becomes the ground for a new way of understanding and engaging with the world. This space allows the freedom for the emergence of an imaginative and creative self, no longer hamstrung by convention and received opinion. Such a self is neither an eternal soul nor a mere illusion.

Each person is a contingent, ever-changing, fluid, and sentient being, formed by a biological and historical past that predates their birth, committed to becoming the kind of person they aspire to be, and dedicated to forming the kind of world they hope will flourish during their lifetime and after their death. Gotama compared the self to a field to be irrigated by a farmer, an arrow to be assembled by a fletcher, and a block of wood to be fashioned by a carpenter. He understood the self as contingent and transient, an ongoing project, a work-in-progress, which chooses to detach itself from the world to find the clarity, compassion, and courage needed to fully engage with the world.[13]

Skepticism, Epicureanism, and Stoicism all bear close family resemblances to early Buddhism, but none of them is significantly closer to Gotama's teaching than any of the others. Each contains elements that have a discernibly Buddhist flavor. Skepticism shares Gotama's emphasis on uncertainty and inquiry; Epicureanism his emphasis on well-being, friendship, and community; and Stoicism his emphasis on ethics and virtue. Are these commonalities the result of cross-cultural borrowing or do they simply reflect similar human responses to the same existential questions being asked under comparable historical conditions? It is difficult to say. Central to each tradition, though, is the need to cultivate a non-reactive space at the heart of one's life to flourish as a person. Skeptics and Epicureans call this state of mind *ataraxia*, Stoics *apatheia*, and Buddhists *virāga*.

On learning that Hellenistic philosophers aspired to a nirvana-like state of nonreactivity, Buddhists may wonder what sort of contemplative practices were used to achieve it. For Pyrrho to instruct his followers to be "without judgement, without preference, and unwavering" is all very well, but anyone who has ever tried to meditate knows how difficult it is to bring the restless mind to such a balanced, collected, and tranquil state. You can't just command yourself to be unwavering. In most cases, to attain this degree of inner calm and clarity requires a sustained contemplative practice over time. Thus Buddhist texts not only emphasize the importance of mindfulness, focus, equanimity, and stillness, but they pro-

A Dialogical Self

vide psychological tools and meditative techniques for cultivating them. Yet nowhere in the surviving writings of the Hellenistic philosophers do we find anything comparable. How, then, did Stoics, Skeptics, and Epicureans actually achieve their stated objectives of *apatheia* and *ataraxia*?

The French scholar Pierre Hadot, a key figure in the recent revival of interest in Hellenistic philosophy as a way of life, maintains that these philosophers practiced formal "spiritual exercises" as means to realize a serene, nonreactive awareness. Yet Hadot is unable to provide any convincing examples of such exercises, let alone point to texts that Buddhists would recognize as meditation manuals. The *Chief Maxims* of Epicurus and the *Enchiridion* (*Handbook*) of Epictetus, for instance, do provide instructions for practice, yet these mainly consist of philosophical and moral precepts to follow in regulating one's attitudes and behavior rather than exercises in how to tame the "mad elephant" of the mind.

Nonetheless, Plato records how Socrates would enter prolonged states of contemplative absorption, and Diogenes Laertius describes how Democritus "tested perceptions" in the solitude of his garden hut, both of which are suggestive of the kinds of meditative practice found in Buddhism. One cannot rule out that Stoic, Skeptic, and Epicurean teachers gave instruction in spiritual exercises only orally and privately to their students, which is also common in Buddhist and other contemplative traditions. What has been lost in the Hellenistic philosophies, which, unlike Buddhism, died out as living schools of thought, is the continuity of generations of practitioners who convey through their personal example and oral instructions the spiritual heartbeat of their tradition.

To think of practice (*bhāvanā*) as the cultivation of a way of life rather than becoming proficient in a spiritual exercise allows us to address this question in another way. For moral precepts and meditation instructions alike consist of commands: "Do this." "Don't do that." That is what unites them as *practices*. Initially, such commands are either read from a text or spoken by a teacher. Over time, though, they become internalized and automatic. One finds oneself giving instructions to oneself in one's own words according the needs of the situation. In this way, practice has more to do with becoming skilled at internalizing, issuing, and heeding commands—whether of a moral, philosophical, or contemplative nature—than with mastering a particular meditative technique.

To practice either Buddhist or Hellenistic philosophy becomes a full-time exercise in remaining sufficiently detached, mindful, and vigilant to respond appropriately to whatever life throws at you. Whether or not you call it "meditation," sustaining such mindful attention is what shapes and transforms one's character, bringing it into closer alignment with the goal of remaining, for example, "without judgment, without preference, and unwavering." Epicurus may not have sat cross-legged in formal meditation like a Buddhist monk, but his ability on the final day of his life to experience joy while afflicted with "the worst possible sufferings,"[14] implies that he had achieved a similar kind of detached, nonreactive awareness.

V
Impossible Questions

17

The Foolish and the Wise

As someone who thinks in pictures, I found an aesthetic delight in the complex simplicity of the Sutrist way of thinking. Once its key elements had fallen into place, I could visualize the entire system in a single glance. It remains as clear to me now as it was forty years ago. This was facilitated by Geshe Rabten's request that I translate and compile what we were studying into a book, which the monastery published in 1978 under the title *The Mind and Its Functions: A Textbook of Buddhist Epistemology and Psychology*. Rather than follow the format and style of Tibetan monastic textbooks, I reorganized the material in a way that reflected Geshe Rabten's oral teachings as well as my own sense of how it all hung together.

For me the primary strengths of Sutrist philosophy were its recognition that ultimate truth lay in ordinary experience and that spiritual development required the integration of rational inquiry and mindful attention. Its primary weakness lay in its being a closed system anchored to the worldview of late Indian Buddhist thought and science, which had little room for any further development. For centuries, Tibetan scholar-monks had debated and further refined its epistemological doctrines, but they did not question its axiomatic assumptions about the nature of the phenomenal world and the structure of the path to awakening. When the Dalai Lama lectures on the Buddhist "science of mind" at conferences worldwide, he bases much of what he says on the Sutrist ontology and epistemology he learned as a young monk in Tibet.

From where I stand now, a more serious difficulty with Sutrism is its unquestioning commitment to binary ways of thinking. Sutrists take it for granted that human experience is split along binary lines. They begin by asserting two fundamental categories: existents (what *is*) and non-existents (what *is not*). When existents are further analyzed, they are again divided into two: ultimate truths and conventional truths, the former being established by valid perceptions, the latter by valid inferences. This leads to an epistemology premised on the binary distinction between nonconceptual and conceptual ways of knowing, which serves as the basis for describing the path from ignorance to enlightenment, from confusion to certainty, from bondage to freedom.

The tidiness of such binary thinking does not fit well with either the complexity and ambiguity of human experience or the ethical skepticism of Gotama. The pouring forth of life itself cannot be contained within binary categories. For the world is not divided in two along the lines of logic and grammar. Despite belonging to a school that claimed to return to the early discourses, the Sutrists ignored Gotama's advice to Kaccāna to avoid "the binary of 'is' and 'is not,'" thereby losing sight of the middle way. Sutrism aspired to a metaphysical perfection that alienated it from the ultimate but contingent and imperfect facts of life it claimed to capture and explain.

Sutrists maintain that concepts are "mixed inseparably" with their objects. When you read these words, for example, you do not consciously distinguish between the marks on the page and the meanings those marks convey to you as a speaker of English. The world we experience only makes sense to human beings because, in an analogous fashion, we have learned how to "read" it. A person born blind, whose sight is then surgically restored, sees only a chaos of colors and shapes when she opens her eyes after the operation. It takes her years to learn how to make sense of what she sees.[1] In human consciousness, conceptuality and non-conceptuality are inextricably bound up with one another. No matter how much you quieten your mind and empty it of thoughts in meditation, the words you see on this page—as well as everything else you see, hear, smell, taste, and touch in the world—continue making sense to you.

Concepts can distort or occlude human experience, but their primary role is to enhance it. Concepts render the world more differentiated, vivid, and bright. They illuminate rather than darken it. Accompany a botanist on a walk through a woodland or an art critic through a gallery of paintings and you will realize how impoverished are your own perceptions of what you see. It is not that you and your companion see the same things but think about them differently. You *experience* them differently. Through having learned to distinguish different wild flowers or artistic styles, the perceptual experience of the botanist and critic is enriched. The images on our retina might be the same, but the consciousness of the expert is quite different to that of the layperson. Concepts are not elements that can simply be added or subtracted like slides in a projector. They are inseparable from and transform your perceptual reality.

I struggled to understand how, in the Sutrist account of the path to enlightenment, the practice of meditation could lead you from a conceptual to a nonconceptual understanding. The crucial shift from inferential knowledge to direct yogic perception, whereby you transition from the path of unification to the path of vision, involved eliminating concepts so you could see things "as they really are." Deep, sustained meditation appeared to function as a kind of solvent in which concepts were dissolved. This would imply that a botanist's consciousness of flowers would be enhanced if only she could delete from her mind the concepts she had formed of them and come to see them as they "really" were. Surely the eradication of concepts would *diminish* rather than enhance her experience. Why would this not also be the case for the meditator? Would eliminating conceptuality through meditation not lead to something closer to catatonia than enlightenment?

Sutrists understand concepts as universals. Concepts are what enable humans to participate in a shared linguistic world of meanings and values that transcends the immediate environment presented through the physical senses. Without concepts and language there would be no culture, no science, no philosophy, no religion. There would be no world, no society, no sense of community. Everything that is distinctive about being human would be lost. Conceptuality and nonconceptuality are two interdependent poles of the cognitive spectrum within which our life unfolds.

Whether it be the absence of reactivity or the absence of a permanent, single, independent self, such absences cannot be directly perceived with the senses, no matter how yogically refined those senses might be. Absences, in the Sutrist system, can only be grasped by conceptual cognition. Nor is this problem solved in the philosophy of Centrism. In their continuing to employ the Sutrist epistemology and soteriology, Centrists face exactly the same difficulty. How can the ultimate truth of emptiness possibly be known by a nonconceptual mind? To directly perceive with your senses something as abstract as the absence of inherent existence is incoherent.

Because both Sutrists and Centrists regard the mind of a buddha as completely free from any distortion, for them such a mind has to be free from the admixture of concepts that unavoidably "distort" what is perceived. For a fully purified and perfected mind, which Gotama supposedly possessed, concepts are no longer necessary. Buddhist scholars thus came to think of Buddha-mind as exceptional, as no longer subject to the rules that govern the working of unenlightened minds, and thereby beyond the reach of ordinary understanding.

For both Sutrists and Centrists, to be fully awakened means to have attained certainty about everything that *is*. They came to consider Gotama as omniscient, one who can understand even the mysterious workings of the laws of karma, which account for why the world is the way it is, why a person experiences what she experiences, and what will be the future consequences of her acts. Gotama's supposedly infallible insight into the laws of karma thereby granted him the God-like authority to prescribe the lay precepts and monastic rules by which his followers were expected to lead their lives.

In this way, epistemological certainty established the foundations for ethical certainty. With faith in Gotama and his teachings you no longer have to be concerned about what is virtuous or just. That has already been revealed to you by an infallible, omniscient authority. The Buddha has effectively become God. The practice of ethics ceases to entail uncertainty and its concomitant risks. It becomes a matter of cultivating virtuous states of mind, abandoning nonvirtuous states, and adhering to precepts and rules according to how Gotama has presented them. If you correctly follow all the steps laid out from the path of formation to the path of cultivation, enlightenment is guaranteed.

The Pali Canon includes a text called *The Great Discussion*. It consists of a dialogue between a monk called Koṭṭhita and Gotama's senior disciple Sāriputta. Gotama compared Sāriputta to the "mother" of his community because of his skill in leading people into the stream of the eightfold path. Koṭṭhita was an intellectual, who seemed more concerned with finding exact definitions for the terms Gotama used rather than with putting the dharma into practice.

> KOṬṬHITA: What makes a person foolish or wise?
> SĀRIPUTTA: People are said to be foolish because they do not understand the four [tasks]. They are said to be wise when they do understand them.[2]

Koṭṭhita then asks Sāriputta how the wisdom he has just spoken of is related to consciousness. In Pali, "wisdom" is *paññā* and "consciousness" *viññāṇa*. Etymologically, the two words are very similar. How are these two ways of knowing, which sound so alike, connected to each other? Sāriputta tells him that paññā and viññāṇa are not two separate things but are "mixed up" in such a way that "you cannot dissect them finely enough to understand the difference between them." Koṭṭhita is puzzled and frustrated by this answer. He persists with the same line of inquiry:

> KOṬṬHITA: Wisdom and consciousness—what is the difference between these two mixed up things?
> SĀRIPUTTA: Wisdom, Koṭṭhita, is to be *cultivated*; consciousness is to be *embraced*.[3]

Sāriputta's strategy is now clear. He wants to rescue Koṭṭhita from getting bogged down in a quest for definitions. In terms of human flourishing, what matters is not what wisdom or consciousness *are* but what is to be *done* with them. Sāriputta is employing the language of the four tasks rather than the four truths. As something to be cultivated, wisdom belongs to the fourth task (cultivating a path); as something to be embraced, consciousness belongs to the first (embracing life).

Like Vacchā before him, Koṭṭhita had no idea what was wrong with the way he asked questions. Bewitched by language, he was oblivious to being under the spell of "is" and "is not." In his eagerness to analyze wisdom, he did not register how foolish he must appear to Sāriputta. When told that a fool is one who does not understand the four [tasks], he failed to take the hint and blundered on with his endless quest for definitions. Sāriputta played along by offering Koṭṭhita joke definitions. "Perception is called perception," he told him, "because it perceives. . . . Feeling is called feeling because it feels." In the end, he brought the dialogue to a halt by shifting to the language of tasks. He bluntly told Koṭṭhita that he ought to *cultivate* wisdom and *embrace* consciousness rather than endlessly speculate about what they *are*.

This ethical turn in the conversation from *is* to *ought* forced Koṭṭhita to recognize that he already understands enough about wisdom and consciousness to practice the tasks associated with them. His ability to participate in this conversation showed that he knew perfectly well how to use the words *paññā* and *viññāṇa* in the language game known as Pali (or one of its demotic cousins). To keep on analyzing these terms might be useful for a philologist or psychologist, but it only served as a delaying tactic for one who supposedly aspired to practice the dharma. Koṭṭhita seemed reluctant, afraid perhaps, to abandon the quest for certainty and set foot on the path itself. He behaved like the man wounded by a poisoned arrow, who refuses to have it removed until he knows whether the feathers of the arrow's fletch belonged to a vulture, a crow, a peacock, or a stork.

Sāriputta cared for Koṭṭhita and tried to stop him prevaricating and going off at tangents. He encouraged him to embrace fully the fact of being a conscious being who suffers, and to cultivate the kind of wisdom that could free him from the entanglements of reactivity that prevent him from responding wisely to life. This is demanding work, which will push against many of the instinctive inclinations and habit patterns that drive him. If Koṭṭhita was to engage wholeheartedly in the ethical practice of the four tasks, he needed to put aside his intellectual obsessions and risk embarking on a new relationship with life itself.

Consciousness is part of the givenness of life, an inevitable consequence of being an embodied creature with feelings, perceptions, and inclinations. Such consciousness is not to be expanded, cultivated, or transformed: it comes with the raw fact of being human. You have no control over it. For Gotama, to embrace the experience of being conscious means to comprehend it in a way that is no longer colored by your habitual wants, dislikes, and opinions. Such comprehension is a generous, loving, lucid, and ironic openness to your being an empathetic and thoughtful person, a fragile harbor of memories anticipating a tentative future. To embrace your life in this way is to radically accept yourself for who and what you are. It is the foundation of care, both for yourself and other sentient beings.

Wisdom, by contrast, needs to be cultivated and refined over a lifetime. At the beginning of their dialogue, Sāriputta explained to Koṭṭhita how wisdom emerges from the practice of four [tasks]. Elsewhere, he describes wisdom as the result of three distinct human activities: listening, thinking, and cultivating. Wisdom is nurtured over time through listening to what wise people have said, by reading and rereading the works enshrined in the canon of your culture, by absorbing the insights of poetry, art, theater, and music. It is refined by continually reflecting on what you hear and read, struggling to resolve inconsistencies and contradictions, discussing and debating ideas with others. As an integral dimension of your humanity, it is matured by training your mind to be more still and attentive, in finding your own voice, and through acquiring the know-how developed in the course of your work.

In the version of the dialogue between Sāriputta and Koṭṭhita found in the Pali Canon, the text does not mention four noble tasks (which is why I have enclosed "task" in square brackets). Instead, Sāriputta describes the wise person as one who understands the Four Noble *Truths*:

> He knows: this is suffering; this is the origin of suffering; this is the cessation of suffering; this is the path that leads to the cessation of suffering.

The doctrine of the Four Noble Truths employs the language of *is* rather than *ought,* of ontology rather than ethics. From the orthodox Buddhist perspective of the Four Noble Truths, the wise are those who have achieved certainty about four propositions of fact, irrespective of whatever else life might have taught them. At some point, I believe, the language of Truths came to overshadow the language of tasks. As a result, the dialogue between Sāriputta and Koṭṭhita lost its dramatic tension and was reduced to a series of questions followed by the "correct" answers of orthodoxy. For the habit of thinking in terms of truths (*what is*) rather than tasks (*what ought to be done*) is precisely what Sāriputta is seeking to expunge from Koṭṭhita's mind.

Reading this dialogue as literature rather than doctrine allows you to recover a narrative that has been buried and forgotten. Such an archaeology of early Buddhist texts may yield only a handful of fragments, but when patiently reassembled these excavated words and phrases begin to reveal the contours of another vision of Gotama's dharma.

The dialogue between Sāriputta and Koṭṭhita is another piece of the puzzle, which confirms my hunch that Gotama taught a task-based ethics that came to be supplanted by a truth-based metaphysics. At the conclusion of his first discourse, Gotama declared that he only considered himself to be awake because he had recognized, performed, and mastered four tasks. We then hear virtually nothing more about these tasks in the hundreds of discourses that have been preserved in the canons of the different schools of Buddhism. It is as though an entire narrative has been erased, and only fragments—like this dialogue between Sāriputta and Koṭṭhita—now survive like a barnacle-encrusted amphora in a sunken ship.

18
Only Tragedy Can Save the City

The tragedies of Euripides and the comedies of Aristophanes reveal how the citizens of Athens struggled to preserve democracy and achieve peace. Democracy was central to Athenian identity yet constantly under threat from powerful oligarchs and potential tyrants. In *Suppliant Women* and *Trojan Women,* Euripides reminds the spectators of their responsibilities to uphold democracy and, as democrats, of their responsibility in unleashing Athenian violence on others. Both poets used their plays to reflect on the sufferings of the Peloponnesian War and deliver impassioned calls for peace. As the fighting intensified, the citizens who attended these performances would have grown increasingly fearful that their world might be coming to an end.

These theater pieces from antiquity continue to shed an unsettling, penetrating light on the times we live in now. For today democracy is also coming under increasing threat from oligarchs and tyrants, populists and tech billionaires, who will use whatever means available to gain power for themselves. We too yearn for peace while military conflicts rage around us, taking thousands of lives, destroying cities, forcing populations to flee. We too witness democratically elected governments supply vast quantities of arms to combatants in wars around the world. Like the Athenian spectators at the plays of Euripides and Aristophanes, we may worry that our civilization too might be heading for a catastrophic collapse. Yet instead of the fate of Athens and its colonies in the Aegean, we fear for the fate of humanity itself.

In the late summer of 406 BCE, eighteen months before the defeat of Athens, Socrates, then in his early sixties, volunteered for the first time in his life to serve on a democratic council in Athens. The task of this council was to pass judgment on a group of six generals accused of failing to retrieve the bloodied remains of those who had fought against Sparta at the recent naval battle of Arginusae, a cluster of rocky islands off the coast of Lesbos.

On the day the generals were to be charged, Socrates was appointed by lot to be presiding officer of the council. As many as six thousand male citizens gathered on the Pnyx to participate in the proceedings. Socrates insisted that under Athenian law it was illegal to prosecute groups of people, that only individual citizens could be held accountable for their deeds. This prompted an uproar from the crowd, including calls for the philosopher to be prosecuted for treason. Socrates stuck to his principles and refused to be swayed. The next day, another presiding officer was chosen and the show trial went ahead. The disgraced generals were promptly found guilty, condemned to death, and ordered to drink hemlock. Socrates's sole foray into the political life of his city coincided with a descent of democracy into mob rule.

Despite a growing sense of hopelessness, public life in Athens continued. In January the following year, the Lenaea festival of Dionysus went ahead as usual. And it was here on a cold winter's day that Aristophanes's comedy *Frogs* was performed for the first time.

Frogs is a comedy about tragedy. It addresses both the increasingly desperate state of Athens and the purpose of tragic drama itself. Its central character is none other than the god of theater: Dionysus. Since both Sophocles and Euripides had died a few months earlier, the god bemoans the fact that Athens no longer has poets capable of writing tragedies suitable to be performed at the Dionysian festivals. "Like the craving for a good bean soup," declares Dionysus, "I'd love a good Euripides."[1] There is only one solution: the god will have to travel to the underworld to retrieve the playwright and bring him back.

Dionysus believes that only a new tragic drama can now save the city. Like a bean soup, Dionysus suggests that Euripides's tragedies were a modest but substantial staple required for survival. By serving as a mirror in which to contemplate the anguish and traumas of one's world, his plays nurtured a keen sense of one's values and responsibilities. In a sanctified theatrical space, the emotional turmoil of day-to-day political life was suspended, allowing a more thoughtful and imaginative response to the city's crises. For Athens to be saved, its citizens were in urgent need of dramas that would provide them the inner strength and vision needed for their democracy to survive.

On arriving in Hades, Dionysus discovers that Euripides, the new arrival, and the venerable elder poet Aeschylus, who has been there for fifty years, have locked horns in a furious row about which of them is the superior tragedian. To settle this dispute, Dionysus agrees to judge which of the two is the better playwright.

Aristophanes comically presents Aeschylus as a noble figure from an earlier age of chivalry and high culture while portraying Euripides as a coarse populist, whose work appeals to the uneducated masses. As the contest between the two dead poets heats up, Euripides ridicules Aeschylus for his aloof and bombastic style, while describing his own approach to tragic drama as "straightforward democracy." He turns to face the audience:

> I taught you people the art of conversation and . . . some of the nicer subtleties of how to make words tell; how to think and observe and decide; how to be quick off the mark and shrewd; how to expect the worst and face reality in the round.[2]

By "putting logic into art," his plays aim at "teaching people to think." Euripides enacts Socratic philosophy on stage, blurring the line between philosophy and art. When Aeschylus haughtily asks him to name the attributes that make a poet renowned, Euripides replies: "The skills and strengths of mind by which we are able to make ordinary people better citizens."

Aristophanes employs the characters in *Frogs* to advance his plea for peace. When Aeschylus boasts of "shoving Ares [War] into everything," Euripides retorts by deploring how as a result he "left poor Aphrodite [Love] out."[3] In line with his antiwar comedies *Peace* and *Lysistrata*, Aristophanes would have shared Euripides's abhorrence of violence and his compassion for its victims. He may have sincerely believed that only a new tragic drama by Euripides would be able to inspire the audience to embrace the suffering of their fellows and finally turn their minds away from war.

Since the purpose of Dionysus's journey to the underworld was to bring Euripides back to Athens, it seems a foregone conclusion that the god would judge him the better poet. But Dionysus has had a change of heart and announces that he has chosen Aeschylus instead. Two guards appear, seize Euripides by both arms, and drag him kicking and screaming offstage to spend the rest of eternity in Hades.

The chorus praises Aeschylus's victory as proof that intelligence, integrity, and nobility will always prevail over clever word play and sensationalist mass appeal. While for Euripides, the ignominy of defeat should persuade him at last to stop "stylishly sitting beside Socrates, blabbering away, discarding artistry and ignoring the most important things about the tragedian's art."[4] Yet given Aristophanes's prominent position in the world of Athenian theater, he would have known that a new play by Euripides—*Ecstatic Women (Bacchae)*—had been found after his death and was due to be premiered at the City Dionysia that March, only three months later. He must have known all along that Euripides, rather than Aeschylus, would soon be "returning from the dead" to stage more plays in Athens.

By articulating on stage the unspoken fears for the future that silently troubled the members of the audience, these poet-playwrights served as weather vanes for Athenian society. As in *Frogs*, the protagonist of Euripides's *Ecstatic Women* is also Dionysus. This play too addresses the impending crisis in Athens but from the perspective of the divine powers believed to control human destiny rather than that of feeble humans attempting to preserve democracy and find peace. *Ecstatic Women* offers no hope of Athens being saved through the mere performance of a theater piece. It recognizes the overwhelming power of nature herself to overturn the dreams and longings of humankind. For us today, it is hard not to read this play, like Gotama's *On Fire*, as a prescient allegory of the climate crisis.

Ecstatic Women opens with Dionysus standing alone on the stage. Fathered by Zeus, Dionysus was conceived by a mortal woman. He is and is not a god. He is and is not a human. He cannot be contained by either concept. He slips between categories. He turns the world upside down. Dionysus is polymorphous, shape-shifting, abundant, intoxicating, sublime, impossible to pin down as "this" or "that." As a personification of the sheer uncontrollability of nature herself, he triggers earthquakes and causes fires to ignite spontaneously. His devotees celebrate him through casting off the shackles of conventional mores and fleeing to the wilderness, where they shake tambourines, wave fennel wands, dance, and sing. These rituals are fueled by the sacrament of wine, probably mixed with other psychoactive substances, which send the women into ecstasies.

The current ruler of Thebes is Pentheus, a level-headed young man, a champion of law and order, a control freak with no interest in altered states of mind. He is quite certain about what is right and wrong, just and unjust. He is scandalized by the presence of this effeminate stranger, who has inspired the women of Thebes to abandon their wifely duties to perform Bacchic rites in the hills. Pentheus vows to hunt Dionysus down, slit his throat, and decapitate him as punishment for his wickedness. The blind Theban sage Tiresias warns Pentheus against carrying out this plan. Pentheus ignores his advice and hastens to the craggy slopes of Mount Cithaeron.

On reaching the mountain Pentheus clambers to the top of a tree to have a better view of the celebrants. The women spot him, gather round the tree, and together manage to uproot it, causing their prey to crash to the ground. The first woman to fall upon Pentheus is his own mother, Agave, who fails to recognize him. She presses a foot against his ribs, grabs his wrist, then rips his shoulder from its socket. The other women join in, tearing him to pieces with their nails and bare hands, scattering clumps of flesh and shards of bone all over the nearby rocks and woodland. Agave gleefully picks up his severed head, secures it to her wand, then runs back in triumph to Thebes to show off her prize.

Pentheus is Athens. And Athens is in pain. Euripides

puns on the name "Pentheus" and the Greek word *penthos*, which means suffering. The translator Emily Wilson renders the pun in English as "Pain-theus." Just as Pentheus's body is ripped apart and eviscerated, so Euripides imagines the imminent destruction of his city, its lifeless fragments scattered over the territories it once ruled (like the body parts strewn over the rocks at Arginusae). Many watching *Ecstatic Women* on that spring day in 405 BCE would have known in their hearts that Athens was doomed.

By casting Dionysus in the role of an avenging deity, Euripides allows his audience to see this impending disaster as the city's ineluctable fate. In the end, the gods, rather than we frail, conceited mortals, are responsible for the unfolding of events on earth. Mere humans are incapable of understanding their seemingly capricious behavior. In *Ecstatic Women*, Euripides's voice shifts to a different register. The poet rises above the immediate context of the Peloponnesian War to ask what it means to be human in a world that can devour you and reduce you to nothing. If you do not respect and honor Dionysus, who embodies the power of nature itself, then he will destroy you as casually as if swatting an annoying fly. There is no wise Theseus here, as in *Suppliant Women*, to offer consoling, rational solutions. For you cannot argue with Dionysus any more than you can argue with melting ice caps and rising sea levels.

Euripides's play shows how human insistence on being in control reaches a tipping point where the earth, no longer able to tolerate the unsustainable demands inflicted upon her, strikes back. By contrast, Socrates's relentless questioning and not-knowing allow for a radically different relationship to the world. Paying close attention to the poignancy and mystery of each moment dissolves the habit of distancing oneself from life and judging it from a stance of alienated self-interest. Instead of arrogance, there is humility; instead of opinionatedness, wonder; instead of certainty, uncertainty.

Six months after the performance of *Ecstatic Women*, Sparta destroyed the Athenian fleet at the battle of Aegospotami. The Spartans then laid siege to Athens, whose terrified inhabitants feared they were about to be slaughtered and sold into slavery just as they had murdered and enslaved the people of Melos ten years earlier. Socrates, who had always advocated a simple life, remained calm and collected. He recalled how during the blockade, "while others were filled with self-pity, I was no worse off than when the city's prosperity was at its peak. For while others acquire their shop-bought luxuries at a high price, I arrange for greater, mental luxuries at no cost at all."[5]

The people of Athens managed to survive the winter. Despite their desperate straits, as a final hurrah they celebrated the City Dionysia as usual over the spring equinox in March. Shortly after the festival ended, Athens surrendered, bringing the war to an end. The victors ordered the great walls of the city to be breached and dismantled, abolished democracy, and imposed an oligarchy made up of sympathetic Athenian aristocrats, headed by Plato's great-uncle and Socrates's onetime student Critias.

Two of the greatest works of Attic theater—*Frogs* and *Ecstatic Women*—were thus forged in the heat of extreme conflict and despair. Yet the performance of a new play by Euripides did not save Athens from defeat. At best it allowed its citizens a perspective from which better to understand their plight and how to respond to it wisely, thereby saving their dignity and self-respect. The end of the Peloponnesian War marked the end of the golden age of Attic theater. The classic works continued to be performed throughout the Hellenistic world for centuries, but no plays of comparable stature were ever written again. War, paradoxically, served as the ideal condition for producing works of art that championed peace.

Drama has lost none of its power to address how to live in a violent and unpredictable world. Instead of watching plays by Aristophanes and Euripides at amphitheaters in religious sanctuaries, we now read novels, stream movies, and binge on TV series in the sanctuaries of our own homes. We too observe and empathize with fictional characters as they struggle to resolve their conflicts. By vicariously participating in their tragic and comic dilemmas, we refine our own ethical intuition and imagination. We suffer with the protagonists, judging their actions to be just or unjust, wise or foolish, courageous or cowardly, thereby honing the human consensus as to what constitutes good and evil. The greatest legacy of the Greek playwrights is to have given birth to an art form that continues to provide an embodied education in ethics for ordinary mortals today.

19

The Great Matter of Birth and Death

In January 1985 I traveled by train from Loyang to Chengdu on my way to the Tibetan capital Lhasa, recently declared an open city that could now be visited by unsupervised backpackers like myself. As the train trundled through the bleak, wintry landscape of rural China, I passed my time reading Keiji Nishitani's newly translated book *Religion and Nothingness*. Nishitani was a central figure of the Kyoto school of Japanese philosophy, a movement that sought to integrate contemporary European thought with Buddhist ideas and values.

One of the passages of Nishitani's book that I underlined in pencil as I sat in the train could have served as an epigraph for what I am writing now. It reads:

> The very condition of basic uncertainty regarding human existence in the world and the existence of self and others, as well as the suffering this gives rise to, are surely matters of the utmost, elemental concern. As the Chinese adage has it, "Birth and death—the great matter."[1]

As a practicing Zen Buddhist as well as an academic philosopher, Nishitani was keenly aware of the tension between a detached analysis of uncertainty in a scholarly article and the practice of uncertainty in daily life. The very notion of *practicing* uncertainty may seem strange if not incoherent to us. Yet this practice has been central to Zen Buddhism since its inception in China around the fifth century CE. As a practice it involves the systematic cultivation and refinement of "great doubt," that is, one's core existential perplexity about what it means to be born and die.

Nishitani quotes the eighteenth-century Japanese Zen master Takusui, who incites the meditator to focus intently on this feeling of doubt until one becomes like "a child within your own breast."[2] No strenuous exertion is required to dwell in this childlike simplicity and innocence. It requires letting go of one's spiritual ambitions, relinquishing the very idea of being or not being enlightened. To doubt in this way is to dwell in the raw mystery of life itself.

In the case of Gotama, his first encounters with and response to the great matter of birth and death were worked into a well-known legend, which has come to serve as the paradigmatic Buddhist account of his renunciation. The story tells of how on leaving the comfort and security of his palaces, the young Prince Siddhartha stumbled across an elderly person, a sick person, and a corpse. These encounters shocked him into realizing that this was the inescapable fate of being mortal. Then a fourth encounter, with a wandering ascetic, showed how there might be a way out of this endless misery, inspiring him to reject the world and devote himself to attaining liberation from birth and death.

In keeping with the norms of Indian renunciant tradition, these encounters produced in the buddha-to-be a sense of revulsion towards existence and a longing not to be born again. Had he been raised in China or Greece, the very same encounters might have given rise to a sense of astonishment and wonder at the fact that he was alive at all. For the first time, he would have glimpsed his life from a perspective other than that of his own egotistic wants and fears, thereby replacing the safe dullness of familiarity with the overwhelming poignancy of awe. Yet rather than prompting uncertainty about the human condition, the four "heavenly messengers," as they are called, granted Prince Siddhartha enough certainty about the human condition to make him resolve to reject it.

Although this legend is found in a discourse in the Pali Canon, it refers not to Gotama but to a mythological buddha of the past called Vipassī.[3] In response to the first three sights of a sick person, an aging person, and a corpse, Vipassī declares: "Damn this thing called birth! Since to him who is born, old-age, sickness and death must follow." In response to the fourth sight, he tells his driver to take the chariot back to the palace without him. He then shaves his head and beard, puts on yellow robes, and goes forth into a life of homelessness.

If birth is the indispensable condition for aging, sickness, and death, then why is it not included among the four encounters? Why does the buddha-to-be not stumble across a bloodied, screaming infant who has just emerged from a woman's womb? Does this omission reflect monastic squeamishness about women's bodies, sex, and childbirth? Or does it reflect a reluctance to have a future buddha peer into the wide open gaze of a newborn only to declare, "Damn this thing called birth!" Birth may be extremely painful for mother and child, but it delivers an unprecedented being into the world, filled with potential for new beginnings. Takusui encourages us to recover a childlike innocence and openness in order to practice Zen. Yet instead of encountering a child still attached to its umbilical cord, the legend of Gotama's renunciation has him encounter a shaven-headed ascetic, a patriarchal figure embodying religious certainty.

In Gotama's first discourse, he does not say that birth, aging, sickness, and death are to be rejected and abandoned. He says they are to be embraced without attachment, aversion, or prejudice. For it is here, in the still heart of non-reactive awareness, that the path of awakening begins. For this is one's existential condition: you are born, you get old, you fall ill, you die. Instead of holding an opinion about this great matter, in Zen practice you just rest in silent, awed perplexity before the primordial fact of simply being here. Rather than seeking certainty about what birth, sickness, aging, and death *are*, you amplify your uncertainty about them until it fills you with speechless wonder.

Keiji Nishitani's *Religion and Nothingness* was published in Japanese under the title *What Is Religion?* For Nishitani, what distinguishes religion from philosophy is that religion leads to the embodiment of doubt whereas philosophy treats it as a detached theoretical reflection.[4] By "religion" Nishitani clearly has his own Rinzai Zen Buddhism in mind, while by "philosophy" he refers to the modern academic discipline alone. But if we think of wisdom as Socrates practiced it, or the dharma as Gotama articulated it, then the conventional distinction between philosophy and religion begins to break down.

Zen emerged in China as a reaction against the institutionalized forms of Indian Buddhism that had been established in the country. An increasing number of Chinese monks found that the rarified doctrines taught in large, prosperous monasteries were leading them to lose touch with the great matter of birth and death. They sought to recover the urgent, elemental question of being human here and now that had prompted Gotama's quest before Buddhism began. They no longer had any patience for the earnest, scholarly debates I had been taught by Geshe Rabten. "Here," declared the ninth-century Zen master Deshan in characteristically rebellious language, "there are no ancestors and no Buddhas. Bodhidharma is a stinking foreigner. Shakyamuni is a dried-up piece of shit. 'Awakening' and 'nirvana' are posts to tether donkeys. The scriptural canon was written by devils; it's just paper for wiping infected skin boils."[5]

Zen confronts its practitioners with impossible demands: "If you speak," Deshan would say, "you get thirty blows. If you don't speak, you get thirty blows."[6] You find yourself trapped in a logical impasse of uncertainty and perplexity, incapable of giving an answer while desperate to do so. In being forced to release the binary grip of "is" and "is not," you have no choice but to endure a state of speechlessness.

The Zen tradition that flourished during the Tang period in China was inspired by indigenous Chinese luminaries, such as Huineng, Linji, and Deshan, but it traced its origins back to a shadowy figure from the west called Bodhidharma. Some Chinese sources describe him as an ethnic Persian from one of the Buddhist countries in Central Asia, others as a prince from south India. Whoever he was, he would have been active in China at some point during the fifth century CE. The stories about him may not be historical, but they illustrate well the provocative and radical approach of the Zen school.

Shortly after arriving in China, Bodhidharma is said to have been invited to the court of a certain Emperor Wu of Liang, a man who regarded himself as a generous patron and enthusiastic student of Buddhism. At their first meeting, the emperor asked Bodhidharma, "What is the meaning of the holy truths?" Bodhidharma replied, "Unholy emptiness." "Then who is standing before me?" rejoined the puzzled emperor. Bodhidharma shrugged, "I don't know."[7] By dismissing the conceptual foundations of Buddhism—the Four "Holy" Truths—and confessing his utter ignorance, Bodhidharma is the ideal precursor of Zen. The exchange punctures the emperor's conceit of being a good Buddhist, leaving him equally bewildered about both the dharma and himself.

Bodhidharma is credited with the well-known definition of Zen as "a special transmission outside the scriptures, not founded on words or letters." He shares with Socrates a suspicion of the written word and a love of confrontational dialogue. Like Socrates, a Zen teacher ruthlessly tests her students' understanding until they reach an aporetic, nonreactive silence where the chattering mind comes to a stop. Gotama too is reported as testing his student Sariputta's state of mind as rigorously as a goldsmith would test a nugget of metal to ascertain whether or not it is gold.[8]

The Chinese Zen master Yunmen forbade his students from writing anything down for fear that they would cling to his words rather than arrive at fresh insights for themselves. This approach dispenses with the authority of sacred scriptures and empowers each practitioner to find his or her own voice. Zen rejects Buddhism in order to recover the sublime banality of the everyday. When Yunmen asked his students to describe the radiant light of their innermost nature, they remained silent. Yunmen answered on their behalf, "The monks' hall, the Buddha hall, the kitchen pantry, the main gate."[9] In other words: stop yearning for transcendent states of enlightenment and start paying attention to the stuff of the world all around you.

Not only do Bodhidharma and Socrates have the same provocative teaching style, they look the same. Both are depicted with bulging eyes, thick lips, big nose, scruffy beard, hairy chest, and a bald pate, features that are the exact opposites of the prevailing cultural ideals of human beauty in both China and Greece. Stone busts of Socrates and brush paintings of Bodhidharma alike depict a person who simultaneously evokes both revulsion and reverence. Just as Socrates's ugly outer appearance conceals a divine inner beauty, so Bodhidharma's scowling countenance disguises the sublime enlightenment of a sage. These portraits transcend the binary opposites of ugliness and beauty to disclose an all too human embodiment of the highest ethical and spiritual values of the culture.

The cover of Alan Watts's *The Way of Zen,* one of the first two books on Buddhism I bought in London as a teenager, was illustrated with a brush painting of Bodhidharma by the eighteenth-century Japanese Zen Master Hakuin. With no formal training, Hakuin's many brush paintings of Bodhidharma were executed in a naive, forceful style. Rather than scowl, Hakuin's Bodhidharma looks at you askance with a piercing, doleful gaze. You encounter the same uncertainty and childlike wonder that peer from Hakuin's own eyes in his extraordinary self-portraits.

The aim of Zen practice is not to leave you suspended in doubt, uncertainty, and speechlessness; it is to empower you to respond compassionately to the suffering of life from the perspective of wonder. Zen teachers want you to think outside the box, to respond in a spontaneous and creative way to the uniqueness of the situation at hand rather than follow the well-oiled prompts of habit, custom, and conditioning. Hence we often find in Zen writings accounts of monks who respond to a perplexing question by raising their fist in the air or by putting their straw sandals on their head and silently leaving the room. "In my forty-first year," recalled Hakuin, "I at long last penetrated into the heart of the great matter. Suddenly, I saw it—as clearly as if it lay in the palm of my hand. What is the mind of awakening? It is, I realised, a matter of doing good, of benefitting others."[10]

20
What Is This Thing?

In 1980, I abandoned my Tibetan Buddhist studies in logic, epistemology, and soteriology and traveled to Songgwang Sa Monastery in South Korea to train in Zen. I remained in this remote, twelfth-century mountain retreat for nearly four years under the guidance of Kusan Sunim, the Zen master of the temple. The routine never varied. For three months each summer and three months each winter, a small group of us would alternately sit for fifty minutes and then walk for ten minutes on a heated stone floor in a plain white room with latticed doors and windows covered with rice paper. Seated cross-legged on a cushioned mat from three in the morning to nine at night, I would face the wall and ask myself, "What is this?"

Songgwang Sa was a Buddhist monastery, but I had not come here to study Buddhism. I had no interest in the idealist "Mind-Only" (Cittamatra) school of Buddhist thought that informed Kusan Sunim's teachings of Zen. I found Śāntideva's and Tsongkhapa's Centrist critiques of Buddhist Idealism persuasive. For Kusan, however, the "this" of "What is this?" referred to an absolute, transcendent, ineffable *Shin—citta,* soul, or mind—which one sought to penetrate and realize through relentless questioning in meditation. To inquire into the nature of *Shin* in the way Kusan instructed made as little sense to me as if he had told us to stare at the wall and ask, "What is God?"

I did not come to Korea in search of an erudite scholar with whom to study and debate Buddhist doctrine. I was fleeing scholarship and erudition. Kusan was a down-to-earth, simple man, who grew up on a farm and worked as a barber before becoming a Zen monk at the age of twenty-nine. He was always kind and considerate towards me but had no interest in discussing the finer points of the canonical discourses. All that mattered for him was whether or not one had the courage to put everything into question by sitting for hours on end staring at a wall.

The question I had brought to Korea was this: "Why is there anything at all rather than nothing?" When I had first read these words a year or so earlier in Martin Heidegger's *An Introduction to Metaphysics,* they sent shivers up my spine and brought my mind to a halt. I had at last found a language in which to express the inchoate, urgent, and unresolved feelings that had been steadily growing within me during my time as a Buddhist monk. This question seemed to be the very wonder Socrates regarded as the beginning of all philosophy. Zen training under Kusan's guidance gave me a disciplined way of enduring and enhancing this wonder.

I was drawn to Zen because it returned to the visceral questions prompted by the great matter of birth and death and put aside the elaborate answers Buddhist monk-scholars had formulated over the centuries—including the Transcendental Idealism that Kusan Sunim and other Zen teachers appeared to endorse. When I consulted the Chinese text in which the question *What is this?* first appeared, I was reassured to discover that it said nothing about Mind. It just said,

"What is this *thing*?" Such blunt, direct, everyday speech, which likewise distinguished Socrates from the Sophists, also attracted me to Zen. In reflecting a Chinese rather than an Indian context, Zen drew me closer to the indigenous East Asian thought of Daoism, exemplified by the sages Laozi and Zhuangzi, who had rebelled against the moral strictures of Confucius just as the first Zen masters had rejected the dry scholarship of doctrinal Buddhism.

Laozi was a semi-legendary Chinese sage active around the same time as Gotama and Socrates. In the *Tao Te Ching* he compared the way or path to water, something so common and ubiquitous that, apart from times of flood, typhoons, and drought, we pay it little attention. Yet for Laozi, "The highest good is like that of water." By carefully observing this humble substance, Laozi came to understand how humans might live ethically on earth. "The goodness of water," he said, "is that it benefits the ten thousand creatures; yet itself does not scramble, but is content with the places that all men disdain. It is this that makes water so close to the Way."[1] Just as water, the essential condition for life itself, naturally and effortlessly settles in the lowest place, so the sage "puts himself in the background, but is always to the fore."[2] The Way (*Tao/Dao*) of which Laozi speaks is not just a way of life that one chooses to pursue but the way life itself uncannily pours forth.

Gotama too compared the path to water. Those who set foot on the eightfold path were said to enter a stream. No longer blocked by reactivity, they found themselves in a creative, dynamic flow of experience. Laozi might have thought of this as more akin to *becoming* a stream. Your pulse, your breath, the synapses firing in your brain became the currents, eddies, and ripples of a life in unimpeded flow. Rather than contemplate the great matter from a safe existential distance, you released yourself into its embrace. In asking "What is this?" you were simply vocalizing the mystery that is within you and around you all the time. You might just as well have asked "What is this that asks 'What is this?'?"

Such radical curiosity brings you up against the limits of language. The more you struggle to respond to such questions, the more you realize how inadequate words are. Zen practitioners in China, Korea, and Japan often chose to communicate the great matter nonverbally. Take Sengai's brush painting of a rabbit crouching on the ground beneath a full moon. The rabbit seems altogether surprised at being a rabbit. With a few rapid brush strokes, this Japanese artist captures the puzzling poignancy of being a living, breathing creature. The same is true for Suiō's *Axe,* Meigetsu's *Bowl,* and Insan's *"Thirty-blows" Stick.* Each is a swiftly executed image of an everyday object weighted with the sweat of human labor and longing. The artist renders the axe, the bowl, or the stick almost unbearably vivid and tragic with the barest minimum of means.[3]

Like Socrates and Gotama, their Chinese near contemporaries were likewise intrigued by the practical, wordless wisdom of artisans. Zhuangzi, an obscure figure who probably lived in the fourth century BCE, described the skills of a cook called Ting:

> At every touch of his hand, every heave of his shoulder, every move of his feet, every thrust of his knee—zip! zoop! He slithered the knife along with a zing, and all was in perfect rhythm.[4]

In response to the admiring comments of Lord Wenhui, Ting laid down his knife and said: "What I care about is the Way, which goes beyond skill." Despite having cut up thousands of oxen over the past nineteen years, Ting claims that he has never once had to sharpen his knife. He recognizes that what he achieves requires far more than just technical proficiency. It took years of practice to align his entire being with the task at hand, so that now his actions are natural and unforced, neither premeditated nor self-conscious. Like the Zen brush painter, Ting has acquired perfect mastery of his art, which he performs with seemingly effortless effort.

Zhuangzi's cook provides an example of how we might live in the world through embodying and becoming the Way rather than treading it. Can we negotiate our world from moment to moment with the same ease and precision as Ting applies his knife to the carcass of an ox? Can we respond effectively to difficult situations without wearing ourselves out or leaving a messy trail of hurt feelings and resentment in our wake? The story of Cook Ting has little to do with cooking and everything to do with human flourishing. "Excellent," declared Lord Wenhui on hearing Ting's words, "I have learned how to care for life!"

The first translators of Buddhist texts into Chinese frequently adopted Daoist terminology to represent Indian ideas. The word they chose for "nirvana" was *wu-wei*—"nonaction," which Laozi and Zhuangzi regarded as the stillness and emptiness of mind needed to act naturally and spontaneously. When Buddhism was introduced into China it seems that nirvana was still understood as the nonreactive space in and from which to respond to the world here and now. "The Way," echoed Zhuangzi, "gathers in emptiness alone." For it is in the absence of compulsive reactivity that we are able to imagine and enact another way of being in the world. "Look into that closed room," counseled Zhuangzi, "the empty chamber where brightness is born."[5] Or, as Gotama might have put it, "Behold the stopping of reactivity, the empty space where the eightfold path is born."

Gotama also admired the skill of butchers. In describing how to be mindful of the body, he said:

> Just as though a skilled butcher or his apprentice had killed a cow and was seated at the crossroads with it cut up into pieces; so too a practitioner reviews this same body, however it is placed, however disposed, as consisting of elements thus: 'In this body there are the earth element, the water element, the fire element, and the air element.'[6]

Here, the skill of the butcher lies in his ability to cleanly separate the cow's carcass into its constituent elements before laying them out before him so that each piece can be clearly identified: the haunch, the liver, the tongue, the intestine, and so on. Likewise, by paying close attention to the solidity, fluidity, warmth, and motility of your embodied experience, you realize how your body is not a single clump of matter but is composed of different elements each with their own function as part of a whole. In refining this contemplative awareness you come to appreciate the complexity, dynamism, and interdependence of your physical experience. You arrive at a more visceral, intuitive sense of the changing, contingent, and impersonal nature of your body.

Pursuing this contemplation further, you realize that all the pieces of the butchered cow are laid out clearly before you but the cow has disappeared. And if you analyze any one of the parts, such as the liver, that too will further break down into cells, proteins, molecules, and atoms. Both Cook Ting and the Indian Buddhist contemplative find themselves moving through an unimpeded emptiness: the space where Ting's knife no longer "touches the smallest ligament or tendon," and the abyss of unfindability in which the contemplative dwells.

Zhuangzi's perspective is that of an artisan who engages with the world in order to modify and transform it, whereas Gotama's is that of a monastic who contemplates the world in order better to understand it. In the language of the Western tradition that goes back to Aristotle, Zhuangzi seems more inclined to the active life—how to effect changes in the world we share with others—and Gotama to the contemplative life—how to see the world more clearly. While both action and contemplation are necessary to lead an integrated human life, individual people and entire cultures tend to privilege one over the other. The challenge is to cultivate a middle way. Zhuangzi describes what lies in between these poles as "a state in which 'this' and 'that' no longer find their opposites." In letting go of a binary perspective, one comes to dwell in and live from this still point that Zhuangzi calls the "hinge of the Way"[7] and Gotama calls nirvana.

The French essayist Michel de Montaigne knew nothing at all about Zhuangzi or Laozi, but his idea of Socrates—"the wisest man that ever lived"—was very close to that of a Daoist sage. Montaigne despaired of the artifice, superficiality, and ostentation of the educated people of his day. Raised by a peasant family until the age of six, for the rest of his life he considered the wisdom of peasants to be superior to that of philosophers. Socrates, he argued, would have passed unnoticed had he appeared in sixteenth-century France. The natural beauty and simplicity of his wisdom would either have escaped the coarse minds of Montaigne's contemporaries or been dismissed as foolishness. "Socrates," he said, "makes his soul move with a natural and ordinary motion. . . . His inductions and comparisons are drawn from the commonest and most familiar actions of men; everyone understands him." Instead of producing vain, speculative theories, Socrates's aim was to "provide us with matters and precepts that are of real and direct service to life."[8]

In the solitude of his tower, the former mayor of Bordeaux and devout Catholic tried to model himself on Socrates. Instead of raising his mind to ever greater heights, Montaigne strove "to humble it and lie it down to rest." Socrates too, he observed, "raised nothing," but brought everything down to his own "proper and natural level." For like peasants and indigenous people untouched by modern civilization, Socrates "moved close to the ground, and dealt with the most useful topics at a gentle and ordinary pace." Here is a portrait of the philosopher, who, like Laozi's sage, moved unnoticed through the world like water finding its own level. Montaigne likewise yearned for anonymity, simplicity, and ordinariness. "I want death to find me planting my cabbages," he remarked, "worrying neither about it nor my imperfect garden."[9]

More than forty years have passed since I first set foot in Songgwang Sa Monastery, faced a wall, and started asking myself "What is this?" I continue to ask the same question every day. I have long given up trying to find an answer. This impossible question has become far more fascinating and revealing than any answer ever could be. For posing such a question leaves one suspended in uncertainty between "is" and "isn't," "yes" and "no," which, I would maintain, is the nonbinary perspective on life that underpins and animates Gotama's middle way. After eight years of pondering the question "What is this?" the eighth-century Chinese monk Huairang informed his teacher Huineng that he had finally understood something. "So what is it?" retorted Huineng. "To say it is like something," answered Huairang, "misses the point."[10]

VI
Starting All Over Again

21
A Cartography of Care

As much as I admired my teachers Geshe Rabten and Kusan Sunim for the choices they had made, the risks they had taken, the hardships they had endured, and the integrity with which they embodied what they taught, I could not embrace their deep doctrinal conservatism. From the outset of my engagement with Buddhism, I was unable to silence the internalized voices of the skeptical, secular humanism in which I had been raised. While both my teachers were committed to the preservation of traditions they justifiably felt to be threatened by modernity, I sensed in my gut that neither Tibetan Buddhism nor Korean Zen could provide an adequate response to the complex challenges of living in an increasingly globalized world.

After disrobing as a monk and returning to Europe as a married man in 1985, I began to read more closely the discourses attributed to Gotama himself. I wanted to get as close as possible to the historical origins of Buddhism. Here I came across Gotama's declaration that he had no intention of appointing a successor, that after his death the dharma and training (*vinaya*) alone would serve as one's teacher.[1] These words liberated and empowered me to imagine what it would be like to return to the sources of the tradition and start all over again. Since the demise of Buddhism in India nearly a thousand years ago, another *systemic* way of practicing the dharma had yet to emerge. Rather than reforming any of the traditional schools of Buddhism, this, I believed, was the challenge of our age.

While lying on his deathbed, Gotama told a wandering ascetic called Subhadda that what differentiated his dharma from that of the other teachers of his day was the practice of the eightfold path. Rather than boasting of enlightened masters who claimed to have realized the Truth, what made his dharma unique was the presence of men and women who had made the eightfold path their own and cultivated it throughout the course of their lives.[2]

Having defined the fourth task as the cultivation of this eightfold path, Gotama implied that all its eight limbs needed to be cultivated as though, metaphorically, you were cultivating a garden. The eightfold path is not something that you mechanically follow step by step. It is inseparable from who you are as a living, breathing person. It is a project that needs to be constantly created, developed, and maintained over time. Ranging from your contemplative practice of mindfulness to your active life of work and social engagement, it is an ethical practice that integrates the cultivation of your inner life with that of your participation in the world you share with others.

The word I am translating as "cultivation" is *bhāvanā* in Pali and Sanskrit, which literally means to "bring into being." As part of Buddhism's turn from ethics to epistemology, the holistic sense of *bhāvanā* as the cultivation of the entire eightfold path came to be replaced by the narrower sense of *bhāvanā* as the practice of meditation alone. This is how the term *bhāvanā* is generally used by Buddhists today. *Bhāvanā*—*sgom* in Tibetan—is what you do when you sit cross-legged on a cushion to practice a formal spiritual exercise. *Bhāvanā* thus mutated into the private, introspective activity of a meditator. In the Indo-Tibetan tradition the Path of Cultivation consisted solely in purifying the mind of increasingly subtle layers of epistemic confusion. The transmutation of *bhāvanā* from the cultivation of the entire eightfold path to the practice of meditation alone encapsulated the fatal turn in Buddhism from ethics to epistemology, from care to transcendence, from four tasks and four paths to Four Noble Truths.

This broader, ethical understanding of cultivation is, however, preserved in a discourse of the Pali Canon aptly entitled *On Cultivation* (*Bhāvanā Sutta*).[3] The text opens with Gotama imagining a person who is tormented by her compulsive patterns of reactivity despite a sincere longing to be freed from them. He then lists the thirty-two virtues that need to be cultivated for her to achieve such freedom. These are divided into six clusters:

The four foundations of mindfulness
The four resolves
The four steps of creativity
The five strengths
The seven facets of awakening
The noble eightfold path

By cultivating these thirty-two virtues a person brings into being the kind of ethical ecosystem needed to achieve the fulfilment she seeks. Even should someone have no interest at all in awakening, adds Gotama, by developing these qualities in her life, she will nonetheless attain it. The process of awakening is rational, natural, and organic. Whether or not you are a

Buddhist is irrelevant. Once the conditions for awakening are in place, the consequences will follow.

Bhāvanā, therefore, encompasses more than just cultivating the eightfold path. It involves cultivating the entire ecosystem in which the path is embedded and nurtured. Since these thirty-two virtues extend across all four paths and tasks, the very process of awakening itself is revealed as fundamentally ethical.

In *On Cultivation* Gotama employs an analogy to describe this process:

> Imagine a hen with eight, ten or twelve eggs, who had not properly sat on them to keep them warm and incubated. Despite her wish that her chicks break out of their shells with their claws and beak and hatch safely, they will fail to do so. But if she has sat on them properly, then even if she *doesn't* want her chicks to hatch safely, they will.[4]

Just as the mother hen turns and rearranges her eggs with her feet to ensure that all will be kept equally warm, so does the practitioner constantly adjust and rebalance the elements of her practice to ensure that no one virtue predominates while others are ignored. Yet over time Buddhist traditions have tended to emphasize contemplative skills such as mindfulness and collectedness over the practical skills of creativity, work, and survival, leaving them, as it were, out in the cold.

A clutch of eggs in a nest has no intrinsic order. The sequence in which the limbs of the eightfold path is traditionally presented is just one of many possible iterations. Imagining the limbs of the path as a clutch of eggs liberates you to arrange them in ways that are adapted to the needs of current circumstances. By reordering them to culminate with survival, work, and voice rather than deep states of meditation, a secular iteration would reconfigure the path to give greater emphasis to those virtues that enable us to flourish in the world. While each egg is a womb that brings a new life into being, the brood of hatchlings (the thirty-two virtues together) could be seen as a metaphor for bringing another kind of society into being.

The ethical ecosystem of the thirty-two virtues is divided among the four paths (formation, unification, vision, and cultivation), each of which, in turn, undergirds one of the four tasks (embracing life, letting reactivity be, seeing it stop, and cultivating a path). This allows us to appreciate the makeup of each task with greater granularity and complexity. Each limb of the eightfold path, therefore, is rooted in, emerges from, and is sustained by this ecosystem that envelops it.

By correlating the paths, tasks, and virtues in this way, we can begin to make out a map that once may have served as an aide memoire for Gotama's community (Table 1). To help remember the thirty-two virtues, they might once have been visualized as the thirty-two parts of one's own body or the thirty-two marks of a buddha's body. Since, for Gotama, care was the virtue that included all other virtues, we could think of this map as a Cartography of Care, which allows us to see at a glance the relationships between the diverse elements that help us find our bearings and make our way within the territory of awakening.

The cartography that emerges from this archaeological excavation of scattered texts also provides a dynamic template for Gotama's vision of a restored civic space. If the fragment of dialogue between Sāriputta and Koṭṭhita in *The Great Discussion* is like a barnacle-encrusted amphora from a shipwreck,

Table 1. Facts, Tasks, Paths, Virtues

	One	Two	Three	Four
Fact	Suffering	Arising	Ceasing	Pathing
Task	Embrace suffering	Let reactivity be	See reactivity stop	Cultivate a path
Path	Formation	Unification	Vision	Cultivation
Thirty-two virtues	**Four foundations of mindfulness**	**Five strengths**	**Seven facets of being awake**	**Eightfold path**
	Body, Feelings, Mind, Ideas	Mindfulness	Mindfulness	Mindfulness
		Confidence	Wonder	Collectedness
	Four resolves	Courage	Courage	Perspective
	Creating conditions . . .	Collectedness	Joy	Imagination
	—for reactivity not to arise	Discernment	Stillness	Application
	—for letting reactivity be		Collectedness	Survival
	—for virtue to arise		Equanimity	Work
	—for sustaining and increasing virtue			Voice
	Four steps of creativity			
	Aspiration, Perseverance, Intuition, Experimentation			

this matrix of interlocking paths, tasks, and virtues is like the skeletal structure of the sunken ship itself. Here lie the outlines of Gotama's task-based ethics of uncertainty, long submerged beneath Buddhism's truth-based metaphysics of certainty. And this, I believe, is where we can start to reimagine and rebuild a dharma for our own uncertain times.

22
Silencing Socrates

Socrates saw himself as a gadfly and Athens as a heavy, sluggish horse. He knew it sounded ridiculous, but he believed the gods had dispatched him to the city to irritate its citizens and wake them up. He made no distinction between cultured aristocrats and the uneducated artisans with whom he argued daily in the agora. In refusing any payment for his teaching, he was accountable to no one. He annoyed whomever he chose. Vexed democrats may have sought to discredit him because of his association with the oligarchic elite, but since he spent much of his time disputing with ordinary people on the street their complaints would have rung hollow. The nobility may have invited him to their fancy soirées, but they looked down on him for his common manners. Socrates belonged to no camp or party. Now, on a spring day in May 399, with Athens still smarting from defeat and struggling to restore its lost dignity, the seventy-year-old philosopher is served with a writ commanding him to appear at the court of the magistrate responsible for religious affairs.

On reaching the courthouse, Socrates runs into a young priest called Euthyphro. "Hey, Socrates," says the priest. "What brings you here?"[1] Socrates tells him that he has been indicted on charges of corrupting the young. Euthyphro finds it incredulous that someone who embodies the very soul of Athens could be treated in such a callous way. The philosopher explains that he has been accused of inventing new gods and rejecting the old. Euthyphro commiserates with him. He knows from experience how spiritually elevated souls like Socrates and himself are easily misunderstood by the unenlightened rabble. "I understand," he sighs. "This is because you say that a divine voice keeps coming to you."[2]

It was common knowledge in Athens that since he was a child Socrates listened to an inner *daimonion*—"a divine something"—to guide his actions. At his trial he explains how this voice only warns him against doing something; it never tells him what to do. It was through heeding this voice that he had stayed away from politics, which had granted him the freedom and leisure to become a philosopher. Socrates was thereby not accountable to anyone; he was only accountable to this "divine" voice within him. He also acknowledged how rare it was to hear such a voice.

Since antiquity, scholars have sought to make sense of Socrates's *daimonion*. While Plutarch speculated whether it had something to do with divination or telepathy, the Oxford professor Armand D'Angour, in a recent book, *Socrates in Love,* pathologizes it as an auditory hallucination. Both accounts reveal the underlying worldviews of their respective authors but neither considers the key role of the *daimonion* in making ethical choices, which is how Socrates understood it.

Could the *daimonion* be no more than what we now call "conscience"? Was Socrates's uniqueness due to his possessing an unusually acute sense of the "gut feeling" that something was ethically wrong? Did his observation about the rarity of such an inner voice reflect a society in which moral authority still lay primarily with oracles, priests, and the law but had not yet become internalized and individuated? In relentlessly questioning and testing people, did Socrates, like Gotama, seek to rouse them from the slumber of conformity to social and religious norms as a means to gain greater moral autonomy through the refining of their conscience?

In encouraging people to think for themselves, Socrates appealed to the authority of an inner moral law, which stood above that of the time-honored and divinely sanctioned laws of Athens. Were citizens to follow his example, it was feared, then society would descend into anarchy, with each person accountable solely to their own conscience. Not only was this prospect unsettling enough, but Athenians could point to the aristocrats Alcibiades and Critias, both of whom had been part of Socrates's circle only later to become traitors and tyrants. Why then should Socrates be permitted to keep spreading his toxic ideas among the young and impressionable?

Euthyphro likewise failed to grasp the ethical dimension of Socrates's *daimonion*. For this vain young priest, the *daimonion* was no different from the ability of soothsayers and prophets to predict the future. Euthyphro has come to the law court to indict his father for the manslaughter of a retainer, who had killed one of the family's slaves in a fit of drunken anger. The family is furious with Euthyphro. They regard the prosecution of one's own father for the inadvertent death of a murderer as deeply irreverent. Yet Euthyphro is convinced that his privileged insight into divine matters grants him the authority to bring his father to trial in order that justice be served.

Socrates appears overjoyed to have met Euthyphro and asks to become his student. By learning from him the true nature of reverence he will then be able to refute the charges of irreverence on which he has been indicted. Tone deaf to Socratic irony, Euthyphro accepts Socrates as his pupil. The stage is now set for Socrates to subject Euthyphro to a ruthless examination whereby every definition of reverence that Euthyphro offers is shown to be riddled with contradictions. Socrates runs circles around Euthyphro and soon has him entangled in conceptual knots. The priest conveniently remembers his pressing business at hand, brings the discussion to a halt, and hurries off.

Euthyphro's innocent question—"Hey, Socrates. What brings you here?"—is the first sentence of Plato's entire oeuvre. For the past two thousand years, anyone who opened the standard edition of Plato in search of philosophical enlightenment would have found themselves puzzling over this zany encounter between Socrates and Euthyphro. Plato had originally aspired to be a tragic poet and playwright. In writing his dialogues, he invented a genre that used the dramatic conventions of theater to frame philosophical inquiry and debate. When Aristotle came to classify forms of literature some decades later, he regarded Plato's dialogues as "dramatic mime," a kind of silent theater that springs to life in the reader's imagination.[3]

Plato may have been inspired by the tragic poets, but Euthyphro could have walked straight out of a comedy by Aristophanes. This pompous buffoon plays the role of a comic book priest just as Socrates had played the role of a comic book philosopher in *Clouds*. Yet the entertaining repartee between the brilliant dialectician and dimwitted cleric as they stand outside the law court has tragic undertones. Each reader of the dialogue will recognize the hollowness of Euthyphro's blithe assurances to Socrates not to worry, that his court case "will likely come to nothing." Whether poring over a handwritten scroll of the *Euthyphro* in the ancient library at Alexandria or a digital copy of the dialogue on a Kindle, we all know what happens next.

With the *Defense* (usually called the *Apology* even though Socrates apologizes for nothing), Plato invents the courtroom drama. Unique among his Socratic texts, the *Defense* is a monologue rather than a dialogue. The case for the prosecution is not recorded. All we have is Socrates's heartfelt, ad hoc speech in his defense to the 501 Athenian men whose votes will decide his fate.

Of greater concern to Socrates than the specific charges for which he was being tried in court that spring day was the body of misinformation about him that had been circulating in Athens for years. Oft repeated rumor and gossip were particularly insidious, he says to the jury, because they are often implanted in the mind at an impressionable age. Once such opinions have taken hold of the public imagination, it is very difficult to do anything about it. You cannot take the public to court and charge it with slander. To combat such generalized prejudice, remarks Socrates, is like shadowboxing: cross-examining an invisible opponent who never answers.

In particular, he singles out the impact of Aristophanes's comedy *Clouds*. The play was first performed a quarter of a century before, but its continuing popularity has reinforced the false impression of him. Aristophanes would have known that the absurd proto-scientist, Sophist, and atheist of *Clouds* was the antithesis of Socrates. In the courtroom, Socrates reminds the members of the jury that at one time or another most of them had stood around listening to him conversing in the agora. But, he asks, did any of them even once hear him mention the kind of things discussed by the comic philosopher of the play? Of course they hadn't. Even the counter-evidence of their own eyes and ears, he implies, would be insufficient to dislodge the fixed opinions that had colonized their minds. With this line of attack Socrates raised the stakes of the trial. He now claimed that he stood accused not just by the three citizens who had formally indicted him but by the members of the jury itself, the very citizens who would judge him. This was a witch hunt, he implied, a sham trial whose outcome was a foregone conclusion.

Socrates acknowledged that young men from rich and leisured families followed him around Athens so they could listen to him interrogate and test people. These youths would then imitate him by subjecting others to a similar examination, which often made those people furious. Yet rather than chastising the young men for their behavior, they blamed Socrates for having recruited the youths as students and then corrupted them. Ignorant of Socratic philosophy, these angry, offended citizens hurled the standard anti-philosophical prejudices at him. But Socrates is adamant that he neither has nor has ever sought a single student. "I have never been anyone's teacher," he declares to the jury. "I cannot be justly held responsible for their good or bad conduct, as I never promised to teach them anything and have not done so."[4]

Like a midwife, Socrates sought to help these young men and the others he encountered to become the kind of people they *could* be. He goaded the citizens of Athens to exercise their own moral judgment. Giving others his complete attention from dawn to dusk showed how much he loved them. His insistent questioning was a pure act of generosity for which he expected nothing in return. His all-too-visible poverty was the greatest testament to his integrity. Socrates did not pursue his inquiries to persuade others of his views or gain admirers. These young men choose to spend time in his company, he argues, not because they are his devotees but because they delight in the way he questions and probes people's minds.

Even if Socrates had succeeded in convincing the jurors of the purity of his motives, that in itself may not have assuaged their concerns about where his actions might lead.

By startling people into greater self-awareness and encouraging them to examine themselves more critically, Socrates was forming a different kind of person and, implicitly, envisioning another kind of society.

In Euripides's *Suppliant Women,* first performed twenty-four years earlier at the same City Dionysia as *Clouds,* the mythical Athenian king Theseus identifies three groups of people in the city: the useless rich, the desperate poor, and between them, a middle group, those who were responsible for keeping the city safe from harm. Who made up this middle group? Euripides may have been alluding to those in the audience who were growing more critically self-aware through a Socratic examination of their souls. Were Socrates allowed to continue subjecting all and sundry to his philosophical and moral examinations, this group could become a third force in Athenian democracy, threatening the vested interests of the factions who sought to silence him.

As the trial drew to a close, Socrates reflected on its possible outcomes. Death held no fear for him, and he realized that might be precisely what made him different from and wiser than other men. He admits that he has no idea what will happen after death, nor does he pretend to have any knowledge of the underworld. All he knows for sure is that "it is wicked and shameful to do wrong."[5] In the end, what matters is how you live your life rather than what you believe about it.

Nor would Socrates accept an acquittal from the court on condition that he hold his tongue and cease to practice philosophy. Under no circumstances, he told the jury, would he be willing to ignore the divine command to exhort people to care for wisdom and the state of their souls. He was convinced that his work was a blessing not a curse for the city. Those who vote to condemn him, he asserted, will cause greater harm to themselves than to him since they will be unjustly executing an innocent man whereas he will simply stop breathing.

The only thing that surprised Socrates about the guilty verdict was that so many jurors voted against it. If thirty votes had gone the other way, he would have been acquitted. While the officers of the court were concluding their business, and those who voted to execute him were leaving the courtroom, Socrates turned to the jurymen who had voted against the conviction. He related how throughout the day his *daimonion*—his conscience—had never once opposed him. He concluded from this that everything he had said and done that day was right, and therefore the death sentence was probably a good thing. He was angry neither with his original accusers nor with any of those who convicted him. "Now the time to part has come," he said. "I go to die, you go to live. Which of us goes to the better lot is known to no one, except the god."[6]

23
A Revaluation of All Values

With his pronouncement "God is dead," Friedrich Nietzsche declared that the ontological and moral foundations of Western civilization had collapsed, leaving in their wake nothing but a dizzying abyss of nihilism. He saw his mission in life as the overcoming of this nihilism through a radical "revaluation of all values," which would enable a superior kind of human being—an *Übermensch*—to emerge. At the heart of this project lay the challenge of abandoning any idea that the ultimate meaning and value of this life lay in a transcendent realm to which one only had access after death. Whether one considered this realm to be that of Platonic Ideas, the Christian heaven, or the eternal peace of Nirvana made no difference. Nietzsche sought an unconditional affirmation of *this* life, an *amor fati:* a love of one's fate so total that one would joyously endure each moment again even were it to be repeated forever.

In 1872, three years after his appointment to the chair of classical philology at the University of Basel at the age of twenty-four, Nietzsche published his first book, *The Birth of Tragedy*. Originally entitled *Socrates and Greek Tragedy*, this short text sought to explain how ancient Greek tragic drama had emerged from "the spirit of music" only to fatally decline under the influence of Socrates. *The Birth of Tragedy* was written at the height of Nietzsche's lionization of Richard Wagner, who was then in the midst of composing his Ring Cycle, in which he abandoned the traditional operatic form in favor of a set of four musical dramas, explicitly modeled on the tetralogies of the Greek tragedians while featuring figures from German and Norse mythology.

Six years later, Nietzsche's friendship with Wagner came to an end. But in 1886, three years before he succumbed to madness, Nietzsche reissued *The Birth of Tragedy* with a long foreword titled "Attempt at Self-Criticism." Despite his ambivalence about this early work, Nietzsche recognized how it had introduced many of the core ideas that he would develop in his later writing. "With this questionable book," he concluded,

> my instinct, an affirmative instinct for life, turned *against* morality and invented a fundamentally opposite doctrine and valuation of life, purely artistic and *anti-Christian*. What should I call it? As a philologist and man of letters, . . . I called it the *Dionysiac*.[1]

The Birth of Tragedy opens with Nietzsche's well-known distinction between the Apolline and the Dionysiac, for him the underlying forces that drive the development of the arts. While the Apolline, for Nietzsche, is epitomized by the pure forms of sculpture and associated with reason, the Dionysiac is epitomized by the nonvisual art of music and associated with sensuality and intoxication. These two tendencies both accompany and oppose each other, and for the most part they are locked in a struggle for dominance. It was only through a "miracle" of the Greek will that they momentarily achieved the union that resulted in Attic tragedy, an art form that was as Dionysiac as it was Apolline.

For Nietzsche, this triumph of Greek tragedy was short-lived. And its death was inflicted by one of its own practitioners: Euripides. For Euripides abandoned not only Dionysus but also myth and the genius of music as well. As a consequence, Apollo abandoned Euripides, leaving the playwright to produce hollow tragedies peopled by masked, counterfeit heroes with fake passions and superficial speeches. For via Euripides, claimed Nietzsche, "everyday man pushed his way through the auditorium onto the stage."[2] Instead of archetypal heroes who held the Dionysiac and Apolline forces in balance, Euripides now showed ordinary men and women preoccupied with the trivial affairs of the world.

Euripides was, for Nietzsche, little more than a mask through which Socrates spoke. One detects here an aristocratic, elitist rejection of the popularization of theater. In *Twilight of the Idols,* Nietzsche denounced Socrates as belonging "by extraction to the lowest of the people."

> Socrates was rabble. We can see for ourselves how ugly he was. Ugliness may be objectionable, but for the Greeks it almost amounted to cancellation. Was Socrates a Greek at all?[3]

In Plato's *Drinking Party* Alcibiades compared Socrates's "ugly" appearance to that of Silenus, the supposed tutor of Dionysus in Asia Minor and thus a non-Greek barbarian. As with the brush paintings of Bodhidharma, the surviving busts of Socrates may not have been attempts at lifelike portraiture, but unconscious, coded ways of marking his otherness as an outsider.

In accusing Euripides of abandoning Dionysus, Nietzsche encountered a problem. For Euripides's *Ecstatic Women* is arguably the most Dionysiac play ever written. Not only is it the sole surviving Attic tragedy where Dionysus himself is the protagonist, the drama shows the utter futility of challenging him. The message is clear: reject Dionysus and you risk being torn to pieces by your crazed mother and aunts. To explain the inconsistency, Nietzsche claimed that towards the end of his life Euripides must have understood the error of his ways and wrote *Ecstatic Women* as a recantation. But no amount of mea culpas, insisted Nietzsche, could atone for, let alone change, the destructive course Euripides had set in motion for tragic drama.[4]

By bringing Dionysus onto the stage in *Ecstatic Women*, Euripides dethrones the god of theater and places him on the same level as the human protagonists. Euripides doesn't abandon Dionysus so much as humanize him, exposing the ambivalence of his birth: fathered by Zeus but conceived by a human woman. Euripides is not recanting his past mistakes but once more experimenting with and pushing the boundaries of tragic drama itself.

I admire in Euripides and Socrates precisely what Nietzsche deplores. By pushing the ordinary man and then Dionysus himself onto the stage, tragedy is not undermined but enriched. The tragic is no longer just concerned with the mythic conflicts of heroic figures offered for our contemplation and edification. It is present in the suffering of each person's life and in the collective struggle to cope with the crises of a shared world. "Socripidean" drama allows us to embrace *our* suffering. In encountering ourselves on stage, the private dialogic self is rendered visible and audible in a public space shared with others. Theater thus functions as a form of personal and civic therapy, addressing both "me" and "us." In taking these innovative steps, Euripides moved towards the kind of drama with which we are familiar today, from the plays of Shakespeare to TV series.

Despite his negative view of Socrates in *The Birth of Tragedy,* eight years later, in *The Wanderer and His Shadow,* Nietzsche prophesied how one day people will look to the accounts of Socrates in Plato and Xenophon rather than the Bible for moral and intellectual guidance. He praised Socrates as being not only more intelligent than Jesus but "able to be serious cheerfully and in possessing that wisdom full of roguishness that constitutes the finest state of the human soul."[5]

Nietzsche was deeply ambivalent about Socrates. He kept oscillating between condemnation and admiration of the philosopher. In his book *The Art of Living,* the scholar Alexander Nehamas argues that this was because Nietzsche regarded Socrates as his principal competitor. For Nietzsche too was a gadfly who sought to awaken his readers from their slumber. Nietzsche too rejected the philosophers who had preceded him and sought to introduce an entirely new way of thinking and being. And Nietzsche too, just like Socrates, strove to be utterly authentic in all he said and did.

Nietzsche never suggested that he might be the Socrates of his time, but this was unlikely due to modesty. For elsewhere he claimed: "I could be the Buddha of Europe."[6] The same ambivalence Nietzsche displayed to Socrates is now directed towards Gotama. In *Thus Spoke Zarathustra,* he includes Gotama among the Preachers of Death, those "consumptives of the soul" who urge us to depart from this life as swiftly as possible.[7] In order to overcome the catastrophic nihilism that followed the death of God, Nietzsche acknowledged the need for some kind of European Buddhism, which might be the perfect philosophical "hammer" needed to deliver the killer blow to Christianity.[8] When it suited him, Nietzsche was only too willing to use Socrates and Gotama as allies in his campaign to discredit the Christian faith. But he could just as easily turn against them.

Nietzsche understood well how his own philosophical project paralleled that of Gotama. Both men sought to overcome metaphysics, abandon concepts of God and immortality, and usher in an entirely new vision of human life on earth. Unlike Schopenhauer, Nietzsche had access to reliable scholarly writings on Buddhism. In 1875, he wrote to a friend praising the early Pali text the *Sutta Nipāta,* singling out the refrain "Thus I wander, lonely as the rhinoceros" as particularly pertinent to himself.[9] Yet as much as he was sometimes drawn to early Buddhist texts, he also recognized that Buddhism shared with Schopenhauer the nihilistic belief that it is better not to exist than to exist. Despite its occasional rays of consolatory wisdom, Buddhism turned out to be yet another world-negating creed.

Nietzsche criticized Buddhism as a religion for the "end and weariness of a civilisation." He noted that its teachings tend to appeal to the scholarly, pacifist, and leisured classes. This was no doctrine for a young, vibrant, and energetic society, but for oversensitive people who have become excessively world-weary and spiritual. But such periods of peaceful decline are also characterized by apathy and a lack of resolve, a retreat from the conflicts of the world into self-indulgent inwardness, which he saw as symptomatic of the decadence all around him.

Buddhism was attractive to artists, philosophers, and Theosophists alike at the close of the nineteenth century because it seemed to provide an alternative metaphysics to fill the gaping void left by the death of God. But since Gotama famously refused to make any pronouncements on metaphysical questions, to recover his radical vision anew requires abandoning the metaphysics of the Four Noble Truths and beliefs in karma and rebirth as totally as Nietzsche abandoned God and morality. For only by clearing away the accumulated debris of Buddhist dogma that clutters the path will we be able to embrace and love this contingent, chaotic life with the same exuberant passion as Nietzsche.

This move turns traditional Buddhism on its head. Instead of treating suffering as a curse that needs to be eliminated forever, Nietzsche saw suffering as a "blessing" that was the source of all human nobility and creativity. For it is suffering rather than happiness that serves as the spur for human flourishing. "As for my long sickliness," observed Nietzsche,

> don't I owe it unspeakably more than my health? . . . *I also owe my philosophy to it.* . . . It is great pain alone, the long, slow pain which takes time . . . that compels us philosophers to descend to our ultimate depths. . . . I doubt whether such pain "improves" us, but I know that it *deepens* us.[10]

Nietzsche was a man who fully embraced the suffering of life, the first of Gotama's four great tasks. He may not have been the Buddha of Europe, but his radical teaching may help pave the way for a fully secular iteration of the dharma.

In 1889, nine months after Nietzsche suffered an irrevocable mental breakdown in Turin, Martin Heidegger was born on the other side of the Alps in southern Germany. In 1927, at the age of thirty-eight, he published *Being and Time*, his most important albeit unfinished work in which he sought to realize Nietzsche's goal of overturning the foundations of Western metaphysics in order to start thinking anew.

When I returned to Europe from India as a young monk I embarked on a quest to discover how Western philosophers had addressed the central ideas addressed by Buddhist thought. I was magnetically drawn to the work of Heidegger and plowed through the dense, idiosyncratic prose of *Being and Time*. With no training in Western philosophy, it was hard work. But it reconfigured the way I saw myself and the world. In order to overturn metaphysics, Heidegger felt obliged to invent another language, which abandoned the classical distinctions—reality and appearance, substance and accident, cause and effect, subject and object—that had characterized the tradition since Plato and Aristotle. Once I became used to the terminology, I realized how well Heidegger's probing analysis of everyday experience both confirmed and was confirmed by my practice of the dharma. For there too, conventional, linguistic distinctions break down to reveal a being-in-the-world where everything is interwoven with and interpenetrates everything else.

Heidegger's work drew me in because he explored topics that were not given much attention in traditional Western philosophy: death, care, authenticity, curiosity, nothingness, anxiety, impermanence. Yet these themes were familiar to me from Buddhism. *Being and Time* came to serve as a crucial bridge between my Buddhist training and my European roots. From there I was led to the work of Christian theologians, who had adopted Heidegger's phenomenological approach as a means to reinterpret Christianity afresh. Something similar, I felt, could be done with Buddhism. This inspired me to write my first book, *Alone with Others: An Existential Approach to Buddhism* (1983), which drew on the ideas of these non-Buddhist philosophers and theologians to help initiate my own attempt to rethink Buddhism.

In 1939 *Being and Time* was translated into Japanese. It was the first attempt to translate a book that is sometimes said to be untranslatable—even into German. Yet such was the esteem in which Heidegger's work was held in Japan that over the next three decades it was retranslated five more times. What was it about Heidegger's work, I wondered, that exerted such a powerful appeal to Japanese readers, most of whom would have been Buddhists?

In the years prior to writing *Being and Time*, several Japanese scholars studied with Heidegger in Germany, the most prominent among whom were Tanabe Hajime and Count Kuki Shūzō. These men were mature thinkers and authors in their own right. Not only did they attend Heidegger's seminars, he invited them to his home to discuss Chinese philosophy, Japanese poetry and art, and contemporary currents in East Asian thought. In 1924—three years before the appearance of *Being and Time*—Heidegger received a generous offer to take up a three-year position at an institute in Tokyo, which, for unknown reasons, he declined. Had he accepted, *Being and Time* would likely have been written in Buddhist Japan.

Other German philosophers before him—Leibniz, Schelling, Hegel, Schopenhauer—had referred to Oriental ideas in their work, but Heidegger was the first major Western thinker to spend extended periods of time in conversation with scholars from a non-European tradition, who did not speak an Indo-Aryan language as their mother tongue and were not raised in a Christian milieu. Just as I had silently absorbed a Buddhist sensibility simply from living with and translating for Geshe Rabten, Heidegger's experience of being questioned by and, in turn, questioning living Asian thinkers would have given him firsthand insight into how the Japanese conceived of and intuited the world. Without citing a single Buddhist or Daoist text in *Being and Time*, these intercultural exchanges may have played a significant role in informing the ambiance, tone, and perspective of his seminal work.

In 1937 Keiji Nishitani—the future author of *Religion*

and Nothingness—arrived in Freiburg to study with Heidegger for two years. When he presented Heidegger with a copy of the first volume of D. T. Suzuki's *Essays in Zen Buddhism*, Heidegger told him that he had already read it. He then gave Nishitani a standing invitation to visit his home every Saturday afternoon to discuss Zen, which Nishitani gladly accepted. After the war, while he was still banned from teaching because of his calamitous association with the Nazis, Heidegger invited the Chinese Christian scholar Paul Shih-yi Hsiao to collaborate with him on translating Laozi's *Tao Te Ching* into German. Reflecting on this experience years later, Hsiao recalls how like many other Asians he was initially puzzled as to why Westerners found Heidegger's work so impenetrable, since what Heidegger articulated had "frequently been said similarly in the thinking of the Far East."[11]

In aspiring to a "revaluation of all values" Nietzsche and Heidegger had to locate themselves outside the mainstream Western tradition. While Nietzsche ventriloquized a pseudo-Zarathustra from distant Persia, Heidegger went back to the pre-Socratic philosophers of Greece. Since the metaphysics Heidegger sought to overthrow originated with Plato and Aristotle, he believed a new beginning could only be found by returning to the philosophical fragments of their Greek predecessors and, without admitting it, to the Chinese classics of Laozi and Zhuangzi. Where does this leave Socrates? While Nietzsche veered between loving and loathing the philosopher, Heidegger solved the Socrates problem by ignoring him.

In the hundreds of pages of his published writings, Heidegger speaks of Socrates only once. "Throughout his life and up to his very death," he wrote in *What Is Called Thinking?*, "Socrates did nothing other than place himself in the draft, the current [of thinking], and maintain himself in it."

> This is why he is the purest thinker of the West. This is why he wrote nothing. For anyone who begins, out of thinking, to write must inevitably be like those people who run for shelter from a wind too strong for them. It remains the secret of a still hidden story that all Western thinkers after Socrates, their greatness notwithstanding, were such refugees. Thinking became literature.[12]

This passage is as baffling as it is revealing. It evokes the image of Socrates absorbed in thought for hours on end as described by Plato. At the same time, Heidegger appears to include himself among those weak-willed philosophers who are incapable of enduring the primal surge of thinking and reach instead for the solace of their pens and typewriters. Rather than letting the storm of thinking "unfreeze what language has frozen into thought," as Hannah Arendt interprets this passage, the refugee holds fast to established concepts and beliefs. Arendt then imagines Socrates as saying, "If the wind of thinking, which I shall now stir in you, has shaken you from your sleep and made you fully awake and alive, then you will see that you have nothing in your grasp but perplexities."[13]

Ten years before Heidegger died in 1976, he granted an interview to the German magazine *Der Spiegel*. The piece concludes with a long exchange about his views on the threat of planetary technology. Heidegger recognizes that an entirely new way of thinking is required to address the unprecedented challenges presented by modern technology but insists that it cannot come about by "the adoption of Zen Buddhism or other Eastern experiences of the world." It could only emerge "from the same place in the world where the modern technological world originated," that is, by returning to the textual fragments of the pre-Socratic Greek thinkers.[14]

The *Der Spiegel* interview appears to offer Heidegger's final word on his relation with East Asian thought. Yet two years *after* he gave this interview, he wrote a foreword to the Japanese edition of one of his books where he acknowledged to his Japanese readers how a radically rethought Western philosophy *could* fruitfully engage with Asian thought. Through finding common ground in what he calls the "clearing" in the forest of Being—a term rich in associations with the non-reactive space of emptiness, nirvana, ataraxia, and *wu-wei*—he believed that such a meeting of minds could "help with the task of saving the essential nature of human being from the threat of an extreme technological reduction and manipulation of human existence."[15]

24
For Love of the World

What immediately struck me on reading Heidegger was the absence of any mention of love, compassion, or ethics in his work. While Nietzsche railed against the slave morality of Christianity and the anemic spiritual love of Buddhism, Heidegger simply ignored these topics. Love is mentioned only once in *Being and Time*. Both men were driven by an intense cerebral passion that paid little if any attention to the suffering of their fellow creatures, let alone how a thinking person ought to respond to it. For many, Heidegger's association with the Nazis fatally compromised his philosophy. Yet two of his Jewish students, Emmanuel Lévinas and Hannah Arendt, continued to admire his work. Lévinas detested Heidegger for being a Nazi but still considered him one of the greatest thinkers in the Western tradition.[1] In different ways, Lévinas and Arendt spent the rest of their lives fleshing out the ethical, social, and political dimensions implicit in some of Heidegger's radical ideas.

The original title of Hannah Arendt's *The Human Condition* (1958) was *Amor Mundi* (love of the world) as opposed to Nietzsche's *amor fati* (love of one's fate). The prologue of the book opens with a reflection on the launch of the Russian Sputnik into orbit the previous year, the first time a manmade object had escaped the bonds of gravity. She bemoaned how many reacted to this event with relief, that it could be the first "step toward escape from men's imprisonment on earth." She worried about how the process of secularization that began with Nietzsche's death of God the Father might one day culminate in the repudiation of "Earth . . . the Mother of all living beings." She shared Heidegger's concerns about the relentless power of scientific technology to shape our futures, envisioning the advent of "artificial machines to do our thinking and speaking," thereby severing our ties with the natural world and turning us into the slaves of our technological know-how. She saw this willful rebellion against human existence as a fundamental betrayal of who and what we are. For "the earth," she observed, "is the very quintessence of the human condition."[2]

Hannah Arendt was born to secular Jewish parents in October 1906 and grew up in Königsberg, the city of Immanuel Kant. After taking courses in classics and theology in Berlin, in 1924 she entered Marburg University to study with Heidegger. She was drawn by his growing reputation as a brilliant, dynamic philosopher who had abandoned dry scholarship and returned to the pure, vital act of thinking itself. Through his example she hoped to reach that passionate state "in which thinking and aliveness become one."[3] They soon fell in love and embarked on a clandestine affair. She had just turned eighteen; Heidegger was thirty-five, married with two children, and immersed in the writing of *Being and Time*. Twenty years later, he confessed to her that she had served as the muse for his magnum opus.

While Nietzsche sought inspiration for a new beginning in Zarathustra, and Heidegger in pre-Socratic and East Asian thought, Hannah Arendt returned to Socrates. In 1954, she wrote an essay on Socrates, which was not published until after her death as part of a collection entitled *The Promise of Politics*. As her primary source of Socratic inspiration, she cites a passage from Plato's *Gorgias*. "It is better," declares Socrates to his interlocutor Callicles, "to be in disagreement with the whole world than, being one, to be in disagreement with myself."[4] Arendt regards this as the "key sentence for the Socratic conviction that virtue can be taught and learned."[5] In other words, to be in harmony with oneself as a rational and ethical agent is the foundation for the *practice* of becoming fully human.

Gotama's second discourse *On Not-Self* plays a similar role to the *Gorgias* passage in revealing what kind of being is capable of pursuing the practice of reason and ethics. As we have seen, this text tacitly reveals the self to be that which issues and receives commands. By clarifying what I am not, the discourse indirectly illuminates what I am: a being in constant, insistent dialogue with itself. In Buddhist logic, the kind of indirect argument used in *On Not-Self* is called "consequential reasoning" (*prasaṅga*), which requires you to draw out the consequences of the argument yourself rather than have them explicitly stated.

Nāgārjuna also employs consequential reasoning in the opening verse of his own analysis of self in *Verses from the Center*:

> If body and mind were me,
> I would come and go like them;
> If I were something else,
> They would say nothing about me.[6]

The first consequence to be drawn from this verse is that you *do not come and go* like the transient sensations, feelings, and thoughts of your body and mind. You remain stubbornly, boringly, and annoyingly the same. The very function of a self is to provide an unchanging point of reference for everything that has happened and is happening to you, from your earliest experiences as a child to your reading these words now. If you did not remain the same through time, you would be either incoherent or psychotic. Yet although you cannot be reduced to the fugitive elements of your mind and body, it is only in reference to your thoughts and words, physical features, and acts that anything meaningful can be said or known about you at all. Instead of denying the existence of self, Nāgārjuna understands how the self is profoundly paradoxical and resistant to definition.

In both these foundational Buddhist texts, Gotama and Nāgārjuna do not even suggest that the self is an illusion that needs to be dispelled. Through consequential reasoning each highlights different dimensions of the complexity, weirdness, and uncertainty of being a self. Gotama reveals the self's dialogical role as the giver and receiver of commands, while Nāgārjuna reveals how the self eludes any attempt to be contained by the basic categories of language. Both are interested in what dynamic and fluid selves *do*, not what they *are*. Their consequential logic is in the service of ethics rather than ontology or metaphysics.

By bringing these insights of Socrates, Gotama, and Nāgārjuna into alignment, we arrive at perhaps the most fertile common ground between early Buddhist and classical Greek thought. Hannah Arendt maintains that Socrates's "fundamental discovery" of our dialogical nature serves as the foundation for *both* logic and ethics, an insight into Socrates that appears unique to her.[7] To lead an examined life entails that we aspire to live without contradicting ourselves *both* in the solitude of our thoughts (logic) *and* in our interactions with others (ethics). This is possible because we are never alone. Even when absorbed in our most silent, intimate thoughts, there is a questioner and an answerer, an advisor and an advised, engaged in an ongoing struggle to reach agreement and overcome discord. Whether we are trying to solve a philosophical conundrum or resolve a dispute with a friend the same dialogic dynamic is at play. In the realm of logic we are called to heed the axiom of contradiction, while in the realm of ethics we are called to heed our conscience. In both cases, the aim is to think, speak, and act consistently and without contradicting either our reason or values. Gotama captures this in his definition of a "true person" (*tathāgata*) as one "who does as he speaks and speaks as he does."[8]

Socrates was a living example of such a true person. He relentlessly tested his interlocutors to expose whatever inconsistencies lay buried beneath the surface of their complacent certainties. Yet he did not do this to impress them with his brilliance and expose their stupidity but to spur them towards leading an ethical life in which their values, words, and deeds would no longer be at odds with each other.

To reach a condition, even momentarily, when one ceases to be in conflict with oneself is equivalent to being in harmony with oneself. The *Gorgias* passage cited above starts with Socrates saying, "I think it better to have my lyre or a chorus that I might lead out of tune and dissonant, ... than to be out of harmony with myself."[9] Gotama uses a similar analogy with the monk Sona, a former lutist. Gotama reminds Sona that when the strings of his lute were either too tight or too loose, the instrument would be out of tune and hard to play. Likewise, if his enthusiasm is too strong it leads to restlessness and if too weak to laziness. In order to proceed along the path, Sona needs to find a harmony within himself comparable to that of a well-tuned lute. In particular, Gotama explains, the five strengths of confidence, mindfulness, courage, collectedness, and discernment need to be attuned with each other in order for inner discord to be overcome and inner balance and unification to be achieved.[10]

When no longer feeling torn apart and destabilized by conflicting emotions, one settles in a space of stillness, focus, and clarity. Such is the quiet, still space where wonder is born and, for Socrates, "philosophy begins." In her interpretation of this passage, Hannah Arendt regards such wonder as an experience or feeling (*pathos*) that philosophers have to *endure*.[11] For the feelings of awe, wonder, and mystery that life provokes can be hard to bear. It is difficult to maintain an open heart and mind when confronted with the overwhelming fact of being here at all, aware that at any moment everything could abruptly stop. Arendt maintains that Plato first encountered this dimension of wonder when Socrates would sometimes remain immobile completely absorbed in contemplation.[12] This sounds very much like sitting in Zen meditation without moving for hours on end while contemplating the puzzle of one's existence.

Speechless wonder is the source both of ultimate questions—*What is this thing? What does life mean? What happens after death?*—and of the firsthand Socratic realization, "*Now* I know that I do not know." It is through the ability to endure such wonder and ignorance that a person becomes "a question-asking being"—a philosopher in the truest sense of the word. It is not that those without any interest in philosophy do not experience wonder. They do. But unlike philosophers or contemplatives they may not be able to tolerate it for long. Instead, they tend to replace wonder (*thaumadzein*) with opinions (*doxadzein*). To overcome the uncertainty, insecurity, and disorientation of wonder, we form views about our existential condition to render it conceptually intelligible and thereby manageable. In this way, opinion serves as an anesthetic that numbs you to the great matter of birth and death.[13]

In claiming that wonder is to be endured, Arendt unwittingly provides a link between the Buddhist contemplation of suffering and the Zen practice of questioning and not-knowing. Instead of insisting that life *is* suffering, one is encouraged to *suffer* life by embracing it unconditionally. Gotama and Zen teachers alike maintain that this requires committed contemplative practice. For Keiji Nishitani, Zen practice became a lifelong commitment to "thinking and then sitting, sitting and then thinking."[14] Zen has no illusions about how hard it is to release the grip of those opinions that inhibit wonder. For such opinions are not just ideas you can adopt or discard at will, they are often deeply entrenched biological, emotional, and cultural habits. In the visceral language of Zen, you have to question with the "marrow of your bones and the pores of your skin" to overcome them.

In *The Life of the Mind* (1971/78), Hannah Arendt poses the rhetorical question "What makes us think?" She then looks for an historical figure who was equally at home in the spheres of thinking (logic) and acting (ethics) and able to move skillfully and fluidly between them.[15] A person best suited for such a role would need to be one who "counted himself neither among the many nor among the few,"

> Who had no aspiration to be a ruler of men, no claim even to be particularly well fitted by his superior wisdom to act in an advisory capacity to those in power, but not a man who submitted meekly to being ruled either; in brief, a thinker who always remained a man among men, who did not shun the marketplace, who was a citizen among citizens, doing nothing, claiming nothing except what

in his opinion every citizen should be and have a right to.[16]

She assumes her readers "will have guessed that I am thinking of Socrates," but this assumes that her readers were cultured Europeans or Americans like herself. Had she posed the same question to an audience in Asia, they would likely have assumed that she was thinking of Zhuangzi, Laozi, or Gotama.

Arendt appears to have had no interest in Buddhism at all. Unlike Nietzsche and Heidegger, she neither mentions nor alludes to it in her writings. There is no record of her having befriended Heidegger's Japanese students whom she would have met in Marburg and Freiburg. Nor is she known to have attended any of D. T. Suzuki's lectures on Zen Buddhism at Columbia University from 1952 to 1957, which attracted many figures from the New York intelligentsia. The only non-European thinker she ever cites is Zhuangzi.[17] She remained deeply wedded to the European traditions of religious, philosophical, and political thought, despite being sufficiently critical of them to long for the onset of another way of thinking, which could give birth to a *novus ordo saeclorum*—a new order of the ages.[18]

Arendt's disinterest in Buddhism may be precisely what makes her work so well suited to providing a language and terminology in which to articulate Buddhist thought and practice anew. Unlike Nietzsche and Heidegger, her writings are not inflected by any overt or covert enthusiasm for non-European ideas. She is not even ambivalent about Buddhism. Her work contains no hint of either Orientalist admiration or Western disdain for Asian thought. As someone who sought to radically reimagine her own tradition through restoring the balance between a contemplative and active life, which she discovered in Socrates, she is perhaps the ideal conversation partner for a secular Buddhist who seeks to do likewise.

VII
A Worldly Eightfold Path

25
The Parable of the Snake

Had I not been exposed to the Indo-Tibetan soteriology of the four paths and trained in logic, I may never have noticed the centrality of the four tasks in the practice of the dharma, which was hidden in plain sight in Gotama's first discourse. For buried beneath the epistemological surface of what Geshe Rabten taught me lay the deep logic of awakening. While the Pali tradition of Theravada Buddhism lost sight of the four paths and their correlation with the thirty-two virtues, this doctrine survived in the Mahayana traditions that made their way to Tibet. What may have been just a historical accident enables us to understand how Gotama's dharma is concerned with cultivating an eightfold path that engages the whole of our humanity rather than the complete end of suffering and thereby of life itself.

The ethical path Gotama advocates is a lifelong project. Its transformative effects on one's character only become apparent over time. And since you are the person undergoing this gradual change, the effects may be more obvious to others than yourself. In letting reactivity be, you need faith in a process that may not deliver either immediate or permanent results.[1] Since reactivity is built into the limbic system of the brain, it is liable to keep flaring up no matter how many years you have devoted to mindfulness, discernment, and collectedness. To be in harmony with oneself is a fragile achievement, constantly threatened by renewed eruptions of reactivity and, as you age, with the breakdown of your physical and mental faculties. This is a faith that requires patience, humility as well as a sense of humor.

In examining the connections between the paths, tasks, and virtues presented in the Cartography of Care, it becomes clear that mindfulness serves as the guiding thread of the entire process of awakening. For among the thirty-two virtues, mindfulness alone is found on each of the four paths and involved in each of the four tasks, working in concert with the other virtues it accompanies. By grounding each task in immediate experience, mindfulness ensures that one's practice is informed by emotional intelligence and embodied knowhow as well as cognitive reasoning. And by holding in mind what each of the four tasks is for, mindfulness serves as the compass that keeps each group of interconnected virtues directed towards one's ethical goals.

As an ethical system founded on a nonbinary perspective, Gotama's dharma is constructed from basic fourfold units—similar to the way four nucleotides make up the structure of DNA, the genetic code for all forms of organic life. This fourfoldness is everywhere: four paths, four tasks, four mindfulnesses, four immeasurables, and so on. When Koṭṭhita asked Sāriputta to explain what perception perceived, Sāriputta answered, "It perceives yellow, it perceives red, it perceives white, it perceives blue."[2] These are the four primary colors in Buddhism, which can be correlated to the four elements: earth (yellow), fire (red), air (white), and water (blue). Rather than providing factual examples of visual percepts, Sāriputta could have been reminding Koṭṭhita to embrace life (yellow/earth), let go of reactivity (red/fire), see its stopping (white/air), and enter the stream of the path (blue/water).

In the Parable of the Snake, Gotama compares practicing the dharma to the handling of a poisonous snake.[3] Such a snake is swift, silent, and lethal. I imagine this creature as having thirty-two vertebrae, which grant it both strength and flexibility. If the dharma is to enable human flourishing, it needs to be treated with the kind of sensitivity, dexterity, and care with which a doctor would handle such a snake to extract its venom. While being neither repelled nor frightened by the snake she holds in her hands, the doctor has no intention to cause it harm. She treats the creature with respect, fully aware that should the snake feel threatened by anything she does, it could bite and kill her.

The manner in which you approach, take hold of, and configure the dharma is likewise crucial. If you organize its elemental ideas and values to "criticize others and win in debates," as Gotama warns, then you risk turning the dharma into an ideology. You are liable to succumb to the conceit of being certain about what is true and what is false, what is right and what is wrong. Given our insecurity, finitude, and ignorance, the craving for certainty can be hard to resist. More insidiously, we may not even notice how deeply we are in thrall to the longing to be right.

As someone who criticizes Buddhist orthodoxy, rejects time-honored doctrines such as the Four Noble Truths, and regards his interpretations of the dharma as closer to the original intent of Gotama than many eminent Buddhist thinkers past and present, I lay myself open to exactly the same charges as those I level against others. For how, despite all my disavowals of dogma, is this "secular dharma" I advocate not laying the groundwork for yet another dogmatic system? Am I any less convinced than other interpreters that my reading of the canonical texts is the right one? In rejecting the very idea of "truth claims," am I not implicitly making yet another truth claim? Is it even conceivable that an author can relinquish the authority that is intrinsic to the very concept of authorship? If I dig beneath the surface of this "ethics of uncertainty," might I not find buried there unacknowledged certainties of which I am barely conscious?

The question that lies at the heart of this book is this: how can a life of rigorous ethical commitment be compatible with the nonbinary perspective of radical skepticism? Here too I appear to contradict myself by framing my argument in terms of yet another binary split: that between certainty and uncertainty. Do I not thereby suggest that certainty is suspect and to be avoided, while uncertainty is desirable and to be adopted? That the former is somehow "bad" and the latter somehow "good"? As long as I persist in using a human language, will I not always be susceptible to its bewitchments, no matter how sincerely I strive to be free from their spell?

Perhaps the only safeguard against such objections is never to lose sight of them. No matter how fervently I believe in what I am saying, I need to keep reminding myself of the contingent and provisional nature of every statement I make. Whenever I use binary terms, I have to recognize them as a structural feature of language rather than a mirror of nature. Binaries are just a convenient shorthand for a spectrum with numerous fine gradations that blur into each other like the colors of a rainbow. In most ethical contexts the polar conditions of "certainty" and "uncertainty" are entangled with each other. Whatever choice I make will contain elements of both. I may have mustered sufficient conviction to embark on a course of action, but lingering doubts still haunt me. I may be viscerally anxious about a decision, but am convinced it is the right thing to do. Such is the consequence of inhabiting an unstable world like ours. I cannot possibly take into account every single variable and unknown that confronts me before making an ethical choice. And whatever I decide to do, with the very best of intentions, I can never be sure in advance that I will not make matters worse.

In comparing the dharma to a snake, Gotama imagines it as a living, breathing creature, rich in vitality and possibility. By treating it as an ideology, you confine it inside a cage. Using the dharma as a Nietzschean hammer "to criticize others and win in debates" reduces it to a set of immutable truth claims, valid for all time, which need to be constantly defended against those who hold conflicting views. The dharma ceases to be a living, evolving current of ideas and practices that adapts to changing circumstances. It freezes into a body of inflexible opinions whose certainties need to be preserved. Handling the dharma in this way paralyzes and incapacitates you. It becomes the very sickness it was meant to cure.

Embracing, letting be, seeing, and cultivating are activities that respond to the contingencies of this fugitive, tragic world. Like a snake they weave their way through the vicissitudes of life, keenly alert to opportunities and threats. Sensitive, creative, and alive, they behave unpredictably. To treat these four tasks as Four Noble Truths risks converting a creative strategy of responsiveness into a predictable body of doctrines and techniques. This, I believe, is what happened when Gotama's "clearly visible, immediate, inviting, effective, and universal" dharma mutated into the orthodoxies, orthopraxies, and power structures of the Buddhist religion. The Parable of the Snake shows that Gotama was well aware of the dangers that could befall his teaching. Perhaps he could already see these tendencies at work in the behavior of some of those closest to him, such as his former attendant Sunakkhatta, his cousin Devadatta, and the stern ascetic Kassapa.

If the dharma is to serve as the matrix for a culture of awakening in the twenty-first century, capable of addressing the global issues of our time, it needs to be systemically reimagined and reconfigured. Simply offering psychological reinterpretations of classical doctrines is unlikely to be adequate to this task. As a living current of ideas, values, and practices, throughout its history the dharma has demonstrated a capacity to reinvent itself. This process has involved both a return to forgotten sources within the tradition as well as an engagement with fresh currents of thought, culture, and practice that lie outside the tradition.

The goal of a rigorously secular dharma is the survival and flourishing of all sentient life on earth. Each one of us will die and in all likelihood disappear back into the elementary particles from which we were made, but our fleeting presence here will continue to echo through the lives of our children and our children's children until we are forgotten. Our artifacts—like this book—will outlive us for a while until they too turn to dust. Yet what matters in the end is whether we have led a life of care, compassion, and wisdom that has played a role, however slight, in inclining human life away from reactivity to creativity, from injustice to justice, from aridity to flourishing, from selfishness to love.

26
Death by Mortar and Pestle

Socrates was a living contradiction. He played the lustful satyr but remained chaste; he drank everyone under the table but remained sober; he employed vulgar speech but spoke only of the noblest virtues; he claimed to know nothing but was considered the wisest man in Greece; he insisted that he taught no one but never stopped probing people's minds to expose nuggets of truth amidst the slurry of opinion. And the democrats of Athens voted to kill him.

By chance, the execution was delayed. Every spring, the Athenians dispatched an old sailing ship associated with the mythic king Theseus to Delos where rites were performed to Apollo at his sanctuary on the otherwise uninhabited island. From the moment of the ship's departure until its return, law decreed that the city remain "pure" and no executions take place. Since Delos was a hundred miles by sea from Athens and the journey subject to unfavorable winds, after his trial Socrates remained imprisoned, with one leg shackled, for at least a month before the ship returned.

The delay meant that Socrates's closest friends were able to visit him during the last weeks of his life. They would meet at daybreak outside the courthouse, where the trial had been held, then wait for the nearby prison to open later in the morning. For the rest of the day they would keep him company, conversing, eating, and drinking. And it was here, in a prison cell awaiting death, that the man who had hitherto never written anything began to write poetry.

Socrates explained that his decision to compose verse was prompted by recurrent dreams that had occurred over the years in different forms but always with the same underlying message: "Socrates, practice and cultivate the arts (*mousikē*)."[1] Until he found himself incarcerated, he had interpreted this to mean that he should continue his daily practice of philosophy, which he considered to be the highest kind of art. Now, since he has been prevented from debating with people in public, he wonders whether the dream might have been encouraging him to practice a more conventional art, such as poetry. In obedience to the dream, he first composed a hymn to Apollo, the god whose festival in Delos had granted him this reprieve, and then began to versify some of the fables of Aesop. None of these poems has survived.

One morning at dawn, Socrates awoke from a night of peaceful sleep to find his old friend Crito already seated in the prison cell, looking distraught. Crito had known Socrates since they were children in Alopeke, enabled him to receive an education, and remained close to him ever since. Socrates knew that there could only be one reason for Crito to have bribed his way into the prison to see him at this hour: the ship had finally returned from Delos. While Crito found the prospect of Socrates's immanent death unbearable, it did not seem to trouble Socrates at all.

Crito has come to make a last, desperate appeal for Socrates to escape from jail and flee into exile. Whatever the consequences for himself and his family, Crito is willing to pay off the necessary officials and potential informers to smuggle

Socrates out of Athens to safety. But Socrates has no intention to evade his sentence. Crito finally appeals to Socrates's principled commitment to virtue. Not only is Socrates renouncing his life when he could save it, he is giving in to the desires of his enemies to destroy him and failing his three sons by leaving them as orphans instead of raising and educating them. "You seem to me," says Crito firmly, "to choose the easiest path, whereas you should choose the path a good and courageous man would choose."[2]

By showing concern for saving one's life at all costs and raising children, Socrates accuses Crito of ignoring all the discussions they have had about the primacy of virtue over all else and reverting to the unthinking morality of the crowd. Socrates invites Crito to examine more carefully whether the course of action he proposes would be just or unjust, right or wrong. Should they conclude that it is just, then he will do it, but if not, they will abandon the idea. Crito concedes that, irrespective of what the majority believes, injustice is in all respects harmful and shameful for the perpetrator. Therefore, even if one has been wronged and unjustly harmed by others, as Socrates has been by the Athenian court, one should, insists the philosopher, "never do wrong in return, nor do any man harm, no matter what he may have done to you."[3]

The most important thing, for Socrates, "is not life, but the good life—and the good life, the beautiful life and the just life are the same." As he declared to the jurors in his defense speech, "An unexamined life is not worth living for men."[4] To give in to Crito's entreaty to save his neck by bribing officials, then sneaking out of the city in disguise to spend the rest of his days as a stranger in a foreign land would, for Socrates, be neither good, beautiful, nor just. Such a deed would dishonor his long-standing commitment to the laws of his beloved city, which, he maintains, had cared for him more than his parents and for which he had risked his life as a soldier. To flee at the last moment would be shameful and deceitful in face of the principled stand he took at his trial to choose death over exile. It would be absurd for him to flee abroad to continue exploring with others the importance of virtue and justice, when he himself had just disregarded the laws of his own city out of fear and selfishness.

While Crito is driven by a deeply human love for his old friend, Socrates is at peace with the knowledge that nothing that has happened to him since he was summoned to the magistrate's office has been resisted by the inner voice of his conscience, his *daimonion*. He accepts his fate as "the way the god is leading us."[5] On leaving the prison that evening, Crito learns that Socrates will be executed by drinking hemlock at sundown the following day.

Crito and a dozen or so other friends and acquaintances gathered in the condemned philosopher's cell the next morning. Plato was ill that day and unable to be present. Xanthippe, Socrates's wife, was already there, holding their youngest child in her arms. As the others entered, she cried out in grief that this would be Socrates's last chance to converse with his friends. Indifferent to his wife's distress, Socrates said, "Crito, have someone take her home." So the poor woman was taken away from her husband by some of Crito's servants, "lamenting and beating her breast."[6]

Once Xanthippe and the infant were gone, Socrates sat up on the bed and began to rub the leg that had been shackled. "What a strange thing that which men call pleasure seems to be," he observed calmly. "And how astonishing the relation it has with what is thought to be its opposite, namely pain!"[7] He may have had only a few hours left to live, but his attention was focused on the conundrum of what he was experiencing at that moment. Acknowledging that you cannot feel both pain and pleasure at the same time, he was struck by how the pain of bondage and the pleasure of freedom were inextricable from each other.

As sunset approached, Socrates decided to have a bath, which would save others the trouble of washing his corpse. Crito asked whether Socrates had any final instructions for his friends before he died. "Nothing that I have not told you already," he replied. Once he had washed, his three children were brought to him for the last time by the women of his household. He gave the boys his final advice, then sent them away before returning to his distressed companions. While the sun was still shining on the hilltops around Athens, he told Crito to summon the man who would administer the poison. When the man appeared with a cup filled with hemlock, Socrates asked him what to do. The man told him just to drink it, walk around the cell until his legs felt heavy, then lie down on his bed and let the hemlock take effect. Socrates took the cup, made a prayer to the gods, then drained it.

As his legs grew heavy, Socrates laid down as instructed, covered his head with a cloth, and felt his limbs grow cold as the poison advanced towards his vital organs and heart. As his belly grew cold, Socrates uncovered his head and uttered what would be his final words: "Crito, we owe a cock to Asclepius; do not forget to make this offering to him."[8] Crito promised that he would. Asclepius was the god of healing and medicine. This is sometimes interpreted to mean that Socrates wanted to offer thanks to Asclepius for having cured him of the sickness called "life." However, these final words of the philosopher may just have reflected what was passing through his otherwise untroubled mind at that moment. He simply remembered something he had forgotten to do for reasons now unknown.

27
Contemplative Life

Over time, in both the Buddhist traditions of Asia and the Greek philosophical traditions of the West, a contemplative life of quiet, thoughtful reflection came to be considered intrinsically superior to a life of labor, work, and action in the world. Yet with the rise of radical political and social movements throughout the eighteenth and nineteenth centuries in Europe and America, this traditional hierarchy was reversed. By turning philosophical thought on its head, figures like Karl Marx and John Stuart Mill sought to revolutionize how we lived on earth. An active life of worldly engagement came to be regarded as innately superior to one dedicated to contemplation, which was increasingly perceived as a rejection of earthly existence; a failure to appreciate the role of social, economic, and political forces in forming human experience; and an abnegation of responsibility for our fellow creatures.

For Hannah Arendt, the devaluing of the contemplative life has led humanity to inhabit a consumer society, managed by governments that function as little more than "gigantic, nation-wide administration[s] of housekeeping."[1] Her solution to this manmade crisis of rampant production and consumption was not to restore contemplation to its privileged position over action, but to imagine how these two dimensions of human life could be harmonized and integrated with one another. Her vision of the active life, which she analyzed in *The Human Condition*, consisted of labor, work, and action, while the contemplative life, which she considered in *The Life of the Mind*, involved thinking, willing, and judging.

Harmonizing the contemplative and active life is likewise my starting point for imagining a worldly eightfold path. In this secular iteration of the path the contemplative life breaks down into (1) mindfulness, (2) collectedness, (3) perspective, and (4) imagination, while the active life entails (5) application, (6) survival, (7) work, and (8) voice.[2] As we embark on a path that strives to integrate our philosophical and spiritual concerns with our engagement in the public affairs of the world, the eightfold path in its entirety becomes an ethical practice. Such an eightfold path leads not to the transcendent peace of Nirvana but to the building of a metaphorical city (*polis*) of awakening, a culture where human beings can dwell together in equality, tolerance, freedom, and peace on earth.

1. Mindfulness (*sati*)

In the ethical ecosystem of the thirty-two virtues, the virtue of mindfulness appears four times, correlated to the role it plays in each of the four tasks (see table 1, p. 194). This highlights both the centrality and flexibility of mindfulness in the process of waking up. No other virtue has such a complex function. Rather than being a single mental state, mindfulness assumes a different complexion according to which of the four tasks is being performed. We can thus speak of *existential* mindfulness, *therapeutic* mindfulness, *contemplative* mindfulness, and *ethical* mindfulness.

In the first task of embracing life mindfulness provides the existential orientation for one's practice. By learning to pay close attention to one's physical, affective, emotional, and mental experience, one becomes more attuned to the pulse of moment-to-moment existence as a mortal, suffering being embedded in a world of impersonal processes, on one hand, and interpersonal relationships, on the other. By slowing down and becoming grounded in immediate experience, one becomes more alert to the first stirrings of reactivity triggered by contact with external and internal stimuli. Such existential mindfulness thus secures the foundations for another way of being in the world that is not driven by fear and desire, habit and conditioning alone.

The second task of letting reactivity be requires mindfulness that recognizes the flaring up of, say, jealousy but does not let one get sucked into its emotional force field. While fully aware of the jealousy, one does not succumb to its narrative. Instead, one simply observes the jealousy as it plays itself out, contemplating its conditional, ephemeral, and impersonal nature. Even when it persists and becomes more intense, one seeks to remain equanimous. In enabling one to slowly disentangle oneself from the turbulence and anxiety of such reactive mind states, such mindfulness is therapeutic. It leads to greater calm and resilience. By accepting rather than reinforcing them, even deeply entrenched neuroses may, over time, be healed.

As reactivity dies down, one comes to experience longer stretches of equanimity and stillness before the next surge of reactivity takes over. At this point one embarks on the third task of consciously attending to and valorizing the stopping of reactivity. To dwell in such stillness requires the presence of contemplative mindfulness, which recollects, senses, and rejoices in the absence of reactivity. Such sustained awareness slowly opens up an inner space of clarity and calm to serve as a foundation for making judgments less determined by reactive impulses and tendencies.

The fourth task is that of cultivating the eightfold path itself. If we treat this path as a way of life focused on becoming the kind of person we aspire to be and creating the kind of society and world we aspire to live in, this will require an ethical mindfulness that bears in mind the virtues we seek to live by, the commitments we have made to ourselves and others, and the goals we seek to creatively realize.

2. Collectedness (*samādhi*)

Just as we can train our bodies to remain fit and healthy by daily exercise, so can we train our minds to become more focused and collected by regular contemplative practice. All you need for this is a mat and cushion, a bench or chair on which to sit quietly for thirty or so minutes a day. No matter whether you practice a religious or secular form of meditation, the underlying principles are much the same. Meditation is an opportunity to stop. It interrupts the constant rush of thoughts and emotions that accompany us throughout the day, opening up a space of relative stillness and quiet within our minds. At the same time it offers a welcome pause to take stock of ourselves between periods of work and interactions with others.

Meditation is simple but not easy. Anyone can sit on a cushion and mindfully observe their breath for a few minutes, but it requires training and dedication to sustain and prolong this kind of attention. Given a chance, the mind will race off to indulge a fantasy or worry, reminisce about the past, or speculate about the future. As one trains oneself to become more inwardly focused, one becomes more collected and less reactive. Over time such collectedness begins to infuse one's life rather than being something one primarily associates with formal meditation practice.

No matter what he or she is doing, the contemplative remains peripherally conscious of this collectedness pervading their body-mind. The intimate, nonreactive space opened up by meditation is one of freedom, where intentions can be formed with greater care, clarity, and understanding. Collectedness sustains an ethical environment where one may be able to make more appropriate judgments about what to think, say, and do in response to the unpredictable life situations that impact your experience both as a contemplative being and a citizen of the world.

3. Perspective (*diṭṭhi*)

Your perspective is the invisible lens through which you see the world, the stance you intuitively assume in your encounters with other people. Formed of a matrix of mutually supportive norms, intuitions, beliefs, values, and practices, it configures how the world appears to you. Such a perspective emerges over time as a natural part of human socialization, acculturation, and education. As such it may remain largely unconscious until it finds itself confronted by another perspective that conflicts with the norms one had naïvely assumed to be self-evident and universal.

By adopting a religion or a culture other than your own—such as Buddhism in my case—we are invited to learn and adopt another perspective within which to frame our life. Consciously adopting a new perspective has the side effect of throwing into sharper relief the preexistent perspective of our own upbringing—in my case, post-Christian, secular humanism. Thus the stage is set for an intercultural dialogue between our former and present self that is not of mere sociological interest but weighted with existential urgency. As we move into an increasingly globalized and multicultural world, we need a perspective on life that is able to tolerate and celebrate human diversity rather than one that retreats into a closed world of certainties and prejudices.

In order to configure a worldly eightfold path, we need a robust understanding of the worldly self who treads that path. We return to Socrates's insight into the dialogical nature of the self, which serves as the foundation both for how we think in solitude and act in the world. For, in practice, *logic and ethics are one*. Both are ways of living with oneself without contradiction, of leading a life that offends neither reason nor conscience. The contemplative life of logical thought and the active life of ethical behavior are not two separate, unrelated spheres. They are united by the principle of noncontradiction.

We can visualize the relation between the contemplative life and the active life in the famous Gestalt image, which, from one moment to the next, can switch from appearing as a vase against a plain background to the profiles of two faces looking into each other's eyes. This image suggests how logical thought tends to dwell on a single object of contemplation (the vase) while ethical behavior entails an active relationship with other beings (the two faces). Yet both are contained in a single image that, for the viewer, can flip effortlessly from one modality into the other.

As a middle way, the eightfold path adheres to a nonbinary logic that is wary of polarization and absolutization. Instead of succumbing to the temptation to divide the world into polar opposites, nonbinary logic gives as much significance to what lies *between* these poles. Such logic acknowledges the uncertainty, provisionality, fluidity, and ambiguity inherent in most life situations and seeks to steer a course that honors these realities without falling into a relativism that impairs our ability to make consistent ethical judgments.

4. Imagination (*saṅkappa*)

Your perspective provides you with an orientation but does not tell you what to do. It only gives you a frame, which your imagination then has to fill in and flesh out. A perspective consists of a set of abstract, unchanging norms, while imagination deals with concrete, unstable situations on earth. To cultivate a perspective helps to refine your capacity to make appropriate judgments. Confronted with highly specific problems, you need to imagine solutions that both accord with the underlying values of your perspective and serve as effective responses to the issues at hand.

Imagination is the human capacity to picture to ourselves situations, things, and people who are not physically present—or don't even exist, such as characters in a play or novel. In responding to an ethical dilemma, we may spend days and weeks agonizing over a response as we imagine the consequences that could result from what we say and do. Without imagination, we would be unable to picture how other persons might feel about the same dilemma and how they may be impacted by what we say and do. Imagination is essential for empathy, our ability to sense what it is like to be in another's shoes, to experience a conflict from their perspective rather than our own.

Imagination is also essential for creativity. The creative urge arises as we imagine hypothetical solutions to the quandaries we encounter, be they at home, in the workplace, or in the artist's studio. Such quandaries are often practical—how to fix a broken piece of machinery, manage a political campaign, find a satisfying conclusion to a piece of music—rather than ethical. We are concerned with figuring out how to solve a problem rather developing our character. Imagination is the medium within which creativity stirs and soars just as air is the medium in which birds take flight.

Imagining easily blurs into thinking. For in thinking about something we also represent to ourselves a physically absent person, topic, or dilemma to understand them better. Our ideas and concepts serve as inaudible words that enable us to talk silently to ourselves, debating and arguing with our counter-self until we reach, or fail to reach, a conclusion. Thinking, coupled with observation, may lead us closer to the truth of a person's dilemma, but it requires imagination to picture an appropriate ethical response to their plight.

In the context of the eightfold path, thinking becomes a contemplative practice. This has nothing to do with the unintended, anxious, and distracted chatter in our head. Contemplative thinking is intentional, focused, and often arduous. It might adhere to a preestablished sequence of ideas as a way to meditate reflectively on a theme, or simply wrestle unaided with a philosophical or moral conundrum to gain greater clarity and insight. Such thinking keeps returning to the ideas and values that inform our perspective in order to build a more inclusive and coherent picture of how they might work together as a harmonious whole. Contemplation slows down the thought processes, allowing time to dwell quietly on a single idea, to ponder and reflect for the pure joy of thinking itself.

Imagination allows us to engage with the myths, archetypes, and symbols that constitute the great narratives of human culture. Without imagination we would be incapable of relating to the dramas of Euripides, Shakespeare, or Beckett, which reveal what humans have been, what they are, and what they could be, not only as individuals but as communities and societies over generations. Without imagination we would be unable to shape our lives in the light of what is preserved in the imaginaries of our families, our tribes, our nations, our religions, our world. Without imagination we would be unable to envisage a future.

Saṅkappa—the Pali word translated here as "imagination"—comes from the verb *kappeti,* which the dictionary defines as "to create, build, construct, arrange, prepare, order."[3] Imagination is crucial to the ways in which we configure ourselves and our world. It allows us to conceive of the kind of person we aspire to be and the kind of world we wish to share with others and leave to future generations once we are gone.

Imagining and thinking help us nurture and form intentions to act: to commit ourselves to say or do something that will have consequences we cannot foresee in an uncertain world that does not yet exist. Our intentions may be founded on noble principles and values, but they need to be realized in our messy, volatile, and ambiguous life on earth. Imagination can lead us to the threshold of action but cannot cross it. It leaves us suspended, waiting for us to take the risk of initiating something new.

28
Active Life

The contemplative virtues of mindfulness, collectedness, perspective, and imagination do not appear in the world but remain concealed. We might infer their presence from the way a person comports herself in public, but we cannot be sure whether she is simply performing a well-rehearsed role. Without witnessing how someone responds to serious pain or adversity, it can be hard to judge their inner state of mind. Only when we come to know them intimately can we tell from a glance in their eyes or a quiver in their voice whether or not they are being sincere. The same, of course, applies to us. To what extent do we too hide behind a mask as we perform our role in the world?

Yet as soon as we cross the threshold from contemplative silence to action, we allow ourselves to be seen and judged through the impact of our words and deeds on others. Once the syllables have left our mouth or a bodily act has been executed, they are irrevocable. No longer ours, they become part of the weave of our world.

5. Application (*vāyāma*)

When asked to define action (*kamma/karma*), Gotama replied: "action is intention (*cetana*)."[1] This response acknowledges how words and deeds are outward manifestations of choices and decisions made in the hidden interior of our soul—the word *cetana* (intention, volition, will) being closely related to *citta* (soul, psyche, anima). Intention is understood as a conscious *movement* towards an inanimate object or a sentient being in order to perform an act or utter words. Buddhist ethics recognizes how the intention to act is not equivalent to the act itself (the intention to rob a bank is not the same as actually robbing a bank), but that the two are connected as part of a single, dynamic continuum that starts in the soul and ends in the world. In this sense, since contemplation moves seamlessly into action, there is no real threshold to "cross," no decisive moment at which contemplation ends and action begins.

Action is anything that is thought, said, or done intentionally. Contemplative thinking is an intentional act that we choose to undertake, just as we would a spoken or bodily act. Like acts of body and speech, such thinking has consequences. Regular performance of a meditative exercise, for example, can have the effect of stilling the mind's chatter, sustaining focus on a chosen object, establishing mindful attention, and heightening awareness of our psychological dynamics. In intentionally deciding to remain with an object of meditation rather than let ourselves be swept away by a fantasy, we make an *ethical* choice to improve the quality of our affective ecosystem. Ethics, as the formation of character, begins with our own subjective decisions. Contemplative acts create a supportive environment for thinking more carefully and empathetically about what to say or do in response to a dilemma in the world. Such "mind training" strengthens the resolve to initiate an intentional movement towards words and deeds.

Just as recollection is concerned with our past, intention is concerned with our future. In contrast to the past, which is certain and fixed, the future is uncertain and lies open for the actualization of our projects to change both ourselves and our world. The future is the domain of possibility to which we apply ourselves with resolution and perseverance to work toward the ethical goals enshrined in our perspective on life. Such application recognizes how lasting change needs to be nurtured over time through creating the conditions for another way of personal and collective life on earth to evolve. This entails applying oneself to creating the inner and outer conditions for reactivity not to determine our lives and for enabling liberative skills and virtues to play a greater role.

To enter the stream of the eightfold path requires setting in motion the sequence of conditions that allows pathing to happen. This sequence is a positive feedback loop that operates according to the logic of awakening: embracing life allows us to let reactivity be; letting reactivity be allows us to see reactivity stop; and seeing reactivity stop allows us to *path*—to proceed to a destination without impediment in community with others. This feedback loop describes a spiral that moves forward into the future with each turn of the loop. This is similar to how the natural hormone oxytocin triggers birth contractions, which in turn trigger the release of oxytocin, which triggers further contractions until finally a child is born into the world.

6. Survival (*ājīva*)

No matter how much you aspire to cultivate a life of the mind, you will be unable to do so if you lack the necessary material conditions. Without adequate shelter, food, and clothing, you will be obliged to spend most of your waking life acquiring and maintaining these basic necessities simply for your own survival. Like millions of people the world over, you will have little choice but to labor from dawn to dusk to get enough food on the table to feed yourself and your family so you will have sufficient energy to return to your labor the next day. As a woman, your life will be taken up with bearing, raising, and caring for children, who are needed to provide for you and your spouse in old age. This relentless cycle of labor, reproduction, consumption, and rest keeps you tied to routines that allow few periods of respite for contemplation, creativity, and participation in civic life.

Greek men overcame these obstacles by confining women to the home to raise children, weave cloth, and supervise the servants and slaves who performed the household tasks and tilled the soil. Male citizens were thereby freed to engage in political life and pursue their interests in the arts and philosophy. Gotama overcame the same obstacles by instituting celibate communities of men and women, who renounced family life, subsisted on alms, and reduced their needs to a bare minimum. In both cases, a privileged minority were able to free themselves from daily toil and dedicate themselves to a life of the mind. Yet they were only able to enjoy this freedom on the condition that others remained unfree to provide for the nonlaboring male citizens or monastics.

This relationship has now become global. Those of us who have the education and leisure to study the works of Plato and Nāgārjuna are able to do so because of the labor of myriad unknown other men and women, who grow our food, make our clothes, and provide the raw materials to build our houses. Slavery may have been abolished in law, but people continue to live under conditions of grinding necessity that give them little if any freedom to enjoy the pursuits we take for granted. We may aspire to "human flourishing," but our flourishing is often achieved at the cost of others barely flourishing at all. Labor and consumption are simply different phases of the same repetitive biological cycle.

Yet there can be dignity to labor. Immigrants leave the familiarity of a beloved homeland to labor long hours in poorly paid menial jobs in a foreign country to provide a good education for their children. They sacrifice their own welfare, comfort, and advancement to care for others. Despite suffering discrimination and maltreatment, they live with the hope of a better future for the next generation, who will be able to enter a trade or profession and find fulfilling work rather than be condemned to a life of repetitive labor.

Since Gotama regarded contentment with shelter, food, and clothing as a prerequisite for cultivating the eightfold path, it would follow that a society founded on these principles would be one that sought to ensure these necessities for its members. The duty of the state would be to secure the basic conditions under which all men and women could realize their full potential as human beings. A modern welfare state aspires to such goals but would find it difficult to determine what would be sufficient for its citizens to achieve *contentment*. There are no objective standards for judging what is "enough." A nun may be content with a thatched hut, one bowl of rice a day, and a threadbare robe, but a mother of five would not be content unless adequate education, healthcare, transport, and entertainment were provided for her children. In a world of diminishing resources and growing populations, the question of what is enough to lead a fully human life becomes all the more pressing.

We may lead a privileged urban existence, engaged in creative and fulfilling professional work, with enough disposable income to enjoy holidays and luxuries, but we are still subject to the unavoidable pressures of survival. How much of our attention is taken up with the generalized, low-level hassle of simply getting through the day? How many hours are spent performing necessary but unrewarding chores? How much time do we consider to be "wasted" in shopping, housework, childcare, traffic jams, upgrading software, filing tax returns, and so on? Despite being facilitated by "labor saving" devices and involving no back-breaking toil, these often-resented activities are necessary for survival. In addition, we need to spend about a third of each day fast asleep just to be able to function at all.

7. Work (*kammanta*)

To distinguish between "labor" and "work," terms which today are often used interchangeably, Arendt differentiated the *animal laborans*—laboring animals, whose sole asset is their body, from *homo faber*—human beings who fabricate things with their hands. While Gotama's monastic followers renounced both labor and work to join his order, his lay followers tended to be artisans, merchants, physicians, and bureaucrats who had renounced lives of labor to become skilled workers in a town or city. Gotama frequently cited the example of artisans to illustrate how to practice the dharma, thereby implicitly honoring specialist know-how gained through training. Over time, Buddhist tradition likewise came to blur the difference between labor and work, but it seems that Gotama saw them as sufficiently different to make both *ājīva* (survival) and *kammanta* (work) separate elements of the eightfold path.

It is through work, not labor alone, that human beings construct a world of durable buildings, roads, institutions, technologies, and cities that are able to withstand the entropy of the natural world. Unskilled labor that is employed in the service of achieving these goals ensures not just the survival of the laborer from day to day but the endurance of a world over generations. Our treasuring of ancient artifacts is rooted in our admiration of the human capacity to conceive of and erect edifices that resist the impermanence inherent in all natural processes. The Parthenon and the great stupa at Sanchi are instances of the past persisting in the present. Even Buddhists, with their repeated insistence on the transience of all conditioned things, go to great lengths to build institutions and structures that will endure. Without such dedicated work, undertaken by individuals and communities over centuries, there would be no world for human beings to inhabit. In the end, of course, even the most magnificent temple will collapse and be subsumed by the earth from which it came. But this is no reason not to build it in the first place.

"The most important part of the human artifice," observed Arendt, "is to offer mortals a dwelling place more permanent and stable than themselves."[2] It was only in such an enduring world that Gotama was able to emerge as an exemplar of what a human life could be. The language he used to articulate the dharma likewise reflected a world fabricated by the skills of artisans more than a world of fields and villages where the laborer toiled. In presenting the practice of dharma as a set of tasks to be performed and its goal of "awakening" as mastery of these tasks, Gotama employed the metaphors of work. Not only did he speak of the eightfold path as leading to the construction of a city, he compared the "taming" of the self to the work of skilled artisans. The practitioner was urged to gain self-mastery in the same way as a farmer develops an irrigation system, a fletcher fashions an arrow, and a carpenter shapes a piece of wood.[3]

In understanding the self as raw material to be configured with the "hands" of your mind, Gotama extended the notion of work from an external, world-creating activity to an internal, self-creating activity. Thus you were able to transcend the natural, instinctive, and cyclical patterns of reactivity to embark on a path of creativity that could lead to the birth of something new. It is no accident that meditation instructors and psychotherapists alike speak of the need to "work" on yourself as though you were a project, a work-in-progress, rather than a stubborn, immutable fact.

A practitioner living in a domestic setting rather than a monastery would aim to find meaningful work that enabled her to flourish as a person in the world as well as generate sufficient income for her day-to-day survival. Such practitioners would not consider their "practice" in terms of contemplative exercises alone. Instead of privileging meditation or chanting, it would extend to everything they do. The fourth task involves cultivating the eightfold path *in its entirety,* thereby making the active life of application, survival, work, and voice just as necessary and important as the contemplative life of mindfulness, collectedness, perspective, and imagination.

Yet the construction of an enduring home in the world for featherless bipeds inevitably entails acts of violence against nature: ore is smelted for iron, trees are felled for wood, oil is burned for heat and electricity. Today *homo faber* has evolved from being the artisan who turns clay pots on a wheel into the architect who constructs schools and hospitals, the technician who launches satellites into space, the manufacturer who builds container ships, airplanes, computers, robots, guns, and missiles. With the advent of industrial technology and the mechanization of the labor process, the peasant farmer becomes a cog in the mass production of consumer goods in factories, while the artisan becomes the engineer who designs and maintains the machinery to which the laborer is tied.

The relentless construction of a world that has enabled accelerating numbers of humans to spread across the earth threatens the very survival of the nonhuman species with whom they share the planet. It is estimated that thirty-seven thousand species are currently at direct risk of extinction as a result of human activity, ten thousand times more than would result from natural extinction rates. Writing in 1958 Arendt already feared that within a century humans would come to exchange the natural world for something entirely manmade and artificial. She considered the question as to what kind of future humankind wishes to create on earth to be "a political question of the first order," which "can hardly be left to the decision of professional scientists or professional politicians."[4] Now, sixty-five years later, the rapidity and extent of the devastation being visited on the earth by human beings would appear to vindicate her concerns.

8. Voice (*vācā*)

To become fully human entails finding your own voice. In both Greek and Buddhist traditions, speech came to be understood as what defines us. For Aristotle the human being was "the thinking-speaking animal"[5] and for Tibetan Buddhists "one who knows how to speak and understand meanings."[6] Yet we are able to think, speak, and understand meanings perfectly well without ever finding our own voice. We can pass our entire lives in uncritical or grudging obedience to the actual and internalized voices of our political, cultural, and religious leaders, our parents, spouses, and bosses. In this sense, our lives are not truly our own. To own our lives requires taking the risk to speak out, to make statements through words and deeds in the public space that lies between human beings.

When, on December 1, 1955, Rosa Parks refused a bus driver's order to vacate her seat to allow white passengers to occupy it, her simple act of disobedience became a key moment in the civil rights movement in the United States. She said very little—"I don't think I should stand up"—but she found her voice. She didn't do anything; she just sat there. Her largely silent act was a statement of principle for which she was prepared to suffer. Rosa Parks's action was neither labor nor work. She was fired from her job as a seamstress, received death threats, and was obliged to move from Montgomery to Detroit to find employment. She was not a professional politician but her act was quintessentially political. In our own time, comparable acts by Malala Yousafzai and Greta Thunberg have had a similar impact in challenging a status quo and initiating an empowering wave of change in how to think and live on this earth.

By taking a public stand, each of these women distinguished themselves in a way that enabled their lives to be told as stories. For *what* they did revealed *who* they were. Their lives became their practice. No longer reducible to labor and fabrication alone, their actions became elements of a biography against which others could consciously or unconsciously measure themselves. To find your voice, therefore, is to become a practicing human, whose life can be read as a story that inspires and challenges others long after your death. The care and compassion that drive such people is implied by the oft-stated aspiration to be "a voice for those who have no voice."

In the public realm, you appear as a unique self among myriad other unique selves. You are no longer the two-in-one dialogical self of your subjective consciousness. Through finding your voice, you speak to others in the same way you would speak to yourself in the privacy of your thoughts. In public dialogue, other people replace the self to whom you inwardly speak. This conversation occurs in the space between us, which is the sphere of the *bios politikos,* the active rather than the contemplative life, where you encounter the bodies, voices, desires, fears, and opinions of others. Here and only here can we explore the question of how to live together on earth, how to communicate and associate with one another in building the world we share. This is where strangers become friends—a friend, for Aristotle, being our "other self."

Finding our voice requires paying as much attention to how we listen to others as how we speak to them. Just as we cultivate a voice which is truthful, direct, kind, and trustworthy, so we cultivate a listening that is nonreactive, unprejudiced, empathetic, and caring. For Emmanuel Lévinas, as soon as we encounter another person the look in their eyes confronts us with a silent injunction: *Do not kill me!* This "first word of the face," as Lévinas calls it, is both the primary ethical command not to hurt or cause harm as well as the primary revelation of the tragic vulnerability of others.[7] From here springs a sense of responsibility to respond to their suffering and a longing to care for them. This call serves as the source both for the first commandment in Judaism and the first precept in Buddhism: *Thou shalt not kill.*

Finding your own voice is also achieved through making and understanding art. To become a writer, you need to differentiate your own voice from the voices of other writers who have inspired you. Painters, sculptors, and architects too need to free themselves from the influence of the masters of the past to find their own visual "language." Only in this way can a poem or painting become more than just an accomplished piece of craftwork and be recognized as a work of art that has broken free from the intentions of the artist who made it and the patron who commissioned it. It is able to "speak" to the human condition of readers and viewers across generations and cultures. Instead of repeating what has been said and done before, such works enable you to see the world from another perspective.

While fabricated by human hands, a work of art transcends the utility of objects that constitute the human artifice. For art is work at play. Art is useless. Unlike a bicycle or a computer, there is nothing you can do with it. Art's sole justification is itself; it invites mute contemplation alone. Works of art *say* something of the greatest importance to us, but it is often hard to say exactly what. Wherever there are human beings, such works are treasured; they are cared for and endure more than any other objects in the world.

The qualities of durability and permanence are far less evident in the performing arts of music, dance, and theater. Unlike a book, a painting, or a sculpture, all that survive of them are scores and scripts, which need to be interpreted and performed anew. These works allow for endless variations in interpretation yet vanish as soon as each performance is over. In contrast to the painting or statue that remains the same, they reflect and embody the transience of life itself. A drama portrays the words and deeds that constitute the characters' *stories*. Through imitating the *acts* of Oedipus, the actor on stage thereby reveals who Oedipus *is*.

Once your voice becomes a practice, you begin to tell your own story. Your life becomes a performance, however humble and modest, on the stage of the world. Cultivation of a worldly eightfold path becomes a political act as soon as you engage in dialogue with others about how best to live and flourish on earth together. You no longer passively follow the received opinion of those in power nor do you necessarily align yourself with a political party. You strive to emulate through your words and deeds the kind of person you aspire to be. You strive to participate in building the kind of world you long for all beings to inhabit. You strive to be a good ancestor for those who are not yet born.

VIII
Entering the Stream

29
Lucid Confidence

The cover art of the *Jewel Ornament of Liberation* that caught my eye in Watkins bookshop in 1971 consisted of a single large yellow Tibetan letter *A* (ཨ) set inside a plain brown circle. The image had been designed by a thirty-one-year-old lama from Gampopa's Kagyu tradition called Chögyam Trungpa. In his foreword, Trungpa explains how he chose the letter *A* (pronounced *AH*) since this is the sound that symbolizes "all pervading speech" as well as being the "seed syllable" of emptiness. It thereby captures well how nonreactivity is the precondition for finding one's own voice.

Like Geshe Rabten, Chögyam Trungpa was a native of Kham, the vast border region between Central Tibet and China, inhabited by fiercely independent nomads and farmers. I first heard stories about Chögyam Trungpa while studying at the Library of Tibetan Works and Archives. Unlike the Gelug monks I knew, here was a Tibetan lama who spoke fluent English, dressed in a suit and tie, practiced Japanese flower arrangement, and taught the dharma with a bottle of sake on the table in front of him. In 1973 he published *Cutting Through Spiritual Materialism,* a book that had a seismic effect on how Buddhism could be communicated in English.

Idiomatic, witty, psychologically astute, occasionally irreverent, yet rooted in the tradition of Gampopa, Trungpa's book was devoured by Western dharma students in Dharamsala. I had not read anything like it before.

I never met Chögyam Trungpa, but he became a lodestar for my journey through Tibetan Buddhism. He was a figure against whom I tacitly measured myself. More than just a scholar or teacher, Trungpa was an artist who valued imagination and considered the path to awakening as a creative process. He composed poems, practiced calligraphy, and took photographs. Trungpa treated the whole of his life as an extended performance. He taught his students through the unconventional and provocative ways in which he displayed himself. In addition to founding urban communities, retreat centers, a contemplative system of psychotherapy, an abbey, and a university, he established a quasi-royal court around himself and his consorts, appointed a regent to succeed him, and was protected by a uniformed militia called the Vajra Guard. Partially paralyzed after a car accident in Scotland, Trungpa was also a tragic and polarizing figure. He slept with his students, smoked, drank heavily, used cocaine, and died from alcohol-related illnesses at the age of forty-eight.

Among the *Connected Discourses on Stream Entry* found in the Pali Canon we learn of a man called Sarakani the Sakiyan. On being told that Sarakani had died, Gotama declared him to have been a stream entrant, someone who had overcome doubt, acquired lucid confidence, and was no longer bound by egoism or attachment to moral rules. He acknowledged Sarakani to be one who was engaged in the process of awakening and had become autonomous in his practice. This praise of Sarakani scandalized his fellow Sakiyans. They called a meeting, then sent a delegation to Gotama to deplore the very notion that Sarakani could have entered the stream of the eightfold path. "Sarakani was too weak for the training," they insisted. "He drank intoxicating drink!"[1]

Rather than caricature Sarakani as a hopeless drunk, let's imagine him as a creative artist, a quick-witted, playful personality involved in all kinds of projects, who, for whatever reasons, also had a penchant for palm toddy and Sakiyan ganja. By praising Sarakani, Gotama is pointing out how stream entry has nothing to do with outward moral improvement. It has to do with an existential shift in one's core values. This shift leads to lucid confidence in what your life is ultimately for, in the philosophy and disciplines that guide you along the way, and in the friends who support you in your task. That you are practicing such a path might be evident to no one except yourself.

A similar account is given of Śāntideva, author of *A Guide to the Bodhisattva's Way of Life*. As a monk in Nalanda Monastery, Śāntideva—so the legend goes—had the reputation of being a freeloader and layabout. In order to expel him, a public examination was held to test the insight and integrity of the monks. When Śāntideva's turn came, rather than being exposed as a good-for-nothing, he recited from memory his now famous *Guide* in metered Sanskrit verses. Then he abruptly left the monastery and disappeared.

Śāntideva cherished anonymity. He had no wish to stand out and make a display of himself in the foremost center of Buddhist learning of his day. He thus embodied the ideal of the Chinese philosopher Zhuangzi, who understood how a sage "will not harm others, but makes no show of benevolence or charity."

> He will not wrangle for goods or wealth, but he makes no show of refusing or relinquishing them.... His actions differ from those of the mob,

but he makes no show of uniqueness or eccentricity. . . . All the titles and stipends of the age are not enough to stir him to exertion; all its penalties and censures are not enough to make him feel shame.[2]

Śāntideva expresses a similar sentiment in his *Guide*. "Even when I have done things for the sake of others," he reflects, "no sense of amazement or conceit arises. It is just like feeding myself; I hope for nothing in return."[3]

As Buddhism evolved into a patriarchal religion committed to moral purity and doctrinal orthodoxy, it served to widen the gap between a supposed spiritual elite in the monasteries and the benighted people of the world. Before he became a revered Zen Patriarch, Deshan was a textual scholar who specialized in the *Diamond Sutra*. On hearing of the Zen teaching of sudden awakening, which rejected the need to study the scriptures, Deshan was furious. He set off to the far south of China to refute the proponents of such heretical ideas. On the way he came across an old woman selling dumplings by the roadside and stopped to eat. Noticing the books he was carrying on his back, she said: "I have a question for you. The *Diamond Sutra* says: 'The past mind can't be found, the present mind can't be found, and the future mind can't be found.' So what mind are you displaying now?" Deshan was speechless. His certainties shaken, he was directed by the old woman to a nearby Zen teacher called Longtan.

When he arrived at the monastery late that evening, Longtan handed Deshan a lamp only to immediately blow out its flame. At that moment, Deshan experienced a sudden awakening. "All these mysterious doctrines," he admitted, "are but a speck of dust in a vast emptiness."[4] Then he set fire to his books.

Here is a man who has retreated from life into a world

of abstract ideas and opinions. Snared in the binaries of right and wrong, Deshan had come to justify his existence in terms of doctrinal correctness. He would meet any threat to his convictions with anger and violence. Only when hungry and weary did he let down his defenses, allowing the opening for an old woman to expose the shallowness of his views.

The same thing happened to the learned Indian Buddhist scholar and abbot Nāropa two centuries later. As he was poring over his texts one day in Nalanda Monastery, a terrifying shadow fell over him. He swung round to see an old woman with "thirty-two hideous bodily features" standing in the doorway. "You understand what those books mean?" she asked. "Yes," he answered. The hag broke down in tears and shouted, "Liar!" Rattled by her words, Nāropa asked her who did understand their meaning. She told him to go and see her brother Tilopa. When Nāropa finally tracked down the elusive Tilopa, he turned out to be "a dark man dressed in cotton trousers, his hair knotted in a tuft, with protruding bloodshot eyes"—another Socrates/Diogenes lookalike. Nāropa prostrated before him and became his disciple.[5]

In both these cases, the monastic suppression of the feminine creates the conditions for its disruptive return. Once again we find a man who had secluded himself in a monastery until the appearance of an old woman forced him to recognize that he was stuck in the dead end of intellectuality. To be fully alive, Nāropa had to resuscitate those atrophied parts of himself from which he had become alienated. Human flourishing is achieved through integrating reason with feeling, imagination, creativity, and intuition, not by denying them. The ugly hag casting her shadow and the wild, unkempt Tilopa serve as counterimages to the serene, cerebral monk with shaven head and downcast eyes.

Nāropa went on to develop yogic disciplines that integrated the energies of the body, dream experiences, and in-between states (*bardo*) into the practice of dharma. One of his disciples was the Tibetan translator Marpa, who taught these practices to the yogi Milarepa, who in turn passed them on to his student Gampopa, author of the *Jewel Ornament of Liberation*.

Fifty years after Gampopa's death, in thirteenth-century Japan, a similar pattern repeated itself as the different Buddhist schools—Shingon, Tendai, Pure Land, Zen—were vying for ascendency over each other in the turbulent process of establishing the dharma in the Land of the Rising Sun.

Shinran was ordained as a novice monk at the age of nine. For the next twenty years he lived in a Tendai monastery on the forested hilltops of Mount Hiei outside Kyoto and devoted himself to observing the precepts, performing rituals, studying texts, and practicing meditation until one day he realized the futility of it all. Nothing he had personally experienced or witnessed in others indicated that such rigorous practices made any significant difference to the quality of a person's life. No matter how many hours you sat on a cushion, how many sutras and commentaries you pored over, how strictly you kept your vows, how eloquently and subtly you explained Buddhist philosophy, in the end you remained—like him—"a foolish being filled with blind passion." Having abandoned what he saw as the bombast and pretense of organized religion, he insisted that all one needed to practice the dharma was lucid confidence in it. "When beings just turn about at heart," he wrote, "and say the name of the Buddha (*nembutsu*), it is as if bits of rubble were turned into gold."[6]

As he reflected further, Shinran realized there was no difference at all between aristocrats and peasants, monks and lay people, men and women, young and old. It didn't matter how much evil one had committed or how many good deeds one had performed. Lucid confidence (*shinjin*), he insisted, was "the medicine that destroys the poisons of our wisdom and foolishness, the dharma by which . . . the lowly such as butchers and wine dealers in an instant transcend birth-and-death and attain Buddhahood."[7]

Shinran adopted the name "Stubble Head," a pejorative term for disgraced monks, and described himself as "neither a priest nor a layman." He married a woman called Eshinni, with whom he had at least four children. He confessed that he was incapable of religious practices, that as a teacher he was still motivated by the desire for profit and fame, that he couldn't distinguish between good and evil and was, like most people, duplicitous and insincere. He continued to hold informal gatherings for those who showed interest in his ideas, but he insisted that he had not a single disciple and called his followers "equal companions." He said that he had no wish to be the founder of a new Buddhist tradition and should not be given any special honors at death: his ashes should just be thrown into a river to feed the fish.

In revealing himself with such devastating honesty, Shinran offered a vivid, personal account of how to practice the first of the four tasks: embracing life. Gotama defined this embrace as comprehending oneself and one's world without reactivity. Since Gotama also defined nirvana as the absence of reactivity, then such an embrace or comprehension was *already* nirvanic. In this way, Shinran showed how a foolish person blinded by passion can also be one who is fully awake to his foolishness and blindness. Nirvana is not, therefore, a distant goal to be attained through years of dedicated practice until every last trace of ignorance has been uprooted, but a perspective on life that is available to everyone here and now. For as a dialogical self, one can be both a fool and a sage at the same time.

Shinran's key concept of *shinjin* is comparable to the Pali term *pasāda*, both of which I have rendered as "lucid confidence." The original sense of *pasāda* is "clearness, brightness, purity," which, for early Buddhists, were defining qualities of faith, confidence, and trust. For many today faith has become synonymous with mere belief. For Gotama, though, a person who enters the stream of the eightfold path is one who has acquired *pasāda*—lucid confidence—in the buddha, dharma, and sangha. This shift in one's primary existential commitments has little to do with belief. Shinran likewise understands *shinjin*—lucid confidence—as an ecstatic "turning about at heart" that radically and suddenly alters the orientation of one's life. Shinran's *shinjin* is, therefore, equivalent to Gotama's stream entry.

Such a radical change of heart leads one to relinquish a life of egotistic calculation and moral superiority and opens oneself to the light of life itself, personified in the figures of Amitābha ("Immeasurable Light") and Amitāyus ("Immeasurable Life"). Shinran believed that Amitābha was a buddha who presided over a Pure Land in the west where those who faithfully recited his name would be reborn after death. He also maintained that the very act of lucid confidence granted immediate access to the Pure Land here and now. From a secular Buddhist perspective, you are "born" in a Pure Land whenever you dwell, however briefly, in a nonreactive state of mind. This very world we inhabit now, with all its suffering and anguish, reveals itself as a Pure Land as soon as we embrace it with a consciousness uninflected by the "impurities" of greed, hatred, and opinionatedness. The Pure Land is this world as seen through the eyes of the artist, the poet, the mystic.

Since the source of all light is the sun, the immeasurable light of Amitābha recalls Gotama's description of himself as belonging to the Lineage of the Sun (*ādiccagotta*) and being a Kinsman of the Sun (*ādiccabandhu*). There is something solar about the dharma.[8] As our primal source of both heat and light, the sun has made the emergence and flourishing of complex forms of life on earth possible. In this way, it symbolizes both the warmth of love and the luminosity of wisdom. The sun is also a symbol of selfless generosity. For in consuming itself as it gives itself away, it dies in the very act of granting life to others. And we too can live like the sun, burning up as we deliver ourselves to the world for which we care, expressing ourselves without inhibition, giving this life the best possible shot until we are finally extinguished at death.

Such solar living needs to steer a middle way between caution and rigidity, on one hand, and abandon and recklessness, on the other. It requires structure and logic just as much as creativity and imagination. Today the physical basis of this underlying polarity in human life, found throughout human cultures, would be understood to lie in the different functions of the two hemispheres of the brain.[9] Nietzsche conceived of this polarity as the cultural tension between an Apollonian and Dionysian stance towards the world. Deshan, Nāropa, and Shinran alike became trapped in an Apollonian (left hemisphere) dead end of dogmatic rigidity, from which they broke free into a Dionysian (right hemisphere) release of imaginative creativity. In my own journey through Buddhism, I needed the structure, rules, and logic drilled into me by Geshe Rabten but also admired—from a safe distance—the "crazy wisdom" of Chögyam Trungpa.

30
An Ethics of Uncertainty

We pass each moment of our lives suspended between the certainty of our own death and the uncertainty of its time. Everything we long for or dread in the future has no certainty of happening simply because we may not survive long enough to experience it. The only certainty the future holds is that at some point, which we cannot predict, we will die. To consider our lives from this perspective, either as a contemplative practice or a philosophical reflection, can induce a sense of profound ethical urgency. If death is certain and its time uncertain, *then what should we do?*

Gotama's first discourse, *Turning the Wheel,* answers this existential question by declaring the aim of human life to be the recognition, performance, and mastery of four tasks. Having thus established the logic of awakening, his second discourse, *On Not-Self,* distinguishes between what a dialogical self can achieve (such as letting anxiety be), and what it cannot (such as dispelling anxiety by telling oneself not to worry).

Having identified the template of an ethical life and the kind of self who can pursue it, Gotama's third discourse, *On Fire,* presents the site of one's ethical practice as a world consumed by reactivity. For Gotama, the reactivity that drives so many human endeavors is like fire. "Everything," he declares, "is burning with the fires of greed, the fires of hate, and the fires of opinionatedness."[1] He describes a world ablaze with these fires to be barren, arid, a wasteland where nothing can grow or flourish.[2] On reading these words today it is hard not to think of the steady warming of the delicate atmosphere that envelops this planet. Although Gotama lived in an era when the planetary consequences of unrestrained craving would have been hard to imagine, he identified some of their root causes and employed the disquietingly prophetic imagery of fire and wastelands to illustrate them.

A contemporary meditation on death needs to extend beyond our own personal mortality to contemplate the death of Homo sapiens as a species. This meditation could be framed as a kōan:

Extinction is certain;
The time of extinction is uncertain;
How should we live now?

Extinction is certain. Either the human species will evolve into a form of life that we cannot now even imagine or, if we manage to survive in a more or less humanoid form, we will be wiped out when the sun becomes too hot to sustain life on earth in around a billion years' time. Yet neither of these scenarios is certain. A massive meteor impact, a highly virulent disease, volcanic eruptions, nuclear devastation, the runaway dominance of artificial intelligence, or the looming threat of climate change could terminate human existence much sooner.

Just as death focuses attention on what matters most for you as an individual, extinction focuses attention on what matters most for us as a species. In embracing extinction, we become intensely conscious that we are complex thinking, feeling, sensing, caring creatures, who emerged from millions of years of evolution by natural selection. For self-aware animals like you and me to contemplate extinction can open up an astonished, quasi-religious wonder at the grandeur of being alive at all.

In building and maintaining civilizations that can withstand the entropic power of the natural world to provide a sense of permanence and safety, human beings have engaged in a relentless war against nature. Until the advent of modern industrial technologies, the destructive impact of human work and labor was relatively localized. In the struggle among species for survival and dominance, the fires of reactivity contributed to the extinction of other species, but it did not yet threaten the biosphere as a whole. That started to change with the industrial revolution. Human craving and fear were now able to employ increasingly efficient and powerful technologies to achieve their goals. Coupled with colonialism, legitimated by the biblical injunction to "subdue" the earth and "have dominion over every living thing," their impact became global. Today "everything is burning" is no longer a metaphor but a reality.

It is easy to be dazzled by space probes that photograph the rings of Saturn or computers that perform two hundred quadrillion calculations per second. These technological feats, however, can blind us to the nature of technology itself. Heidegger was less concerned with the destructive capacity of modern technologies than with the way technology has to come to serve as an internalized framework (*Gestell*) for our relationship with the natural world itself.[3] This technological frame is a *perspective,* an invisible lens through which we see and give shape to the world. It configures not only how the world appears to us but how we feel about and react to it. Such a technological perspective disconnects us from and numbs us to the natural world in which we are embedded. It presents the world either as a resource for the gratification of human longings or as a set of problems to be solved for the alleviation of human discontents. Technology provides the tools to achieve these goals with maximum speed and efficiency, while neoliberal capitalism provides the economic environment to optimize their impact. Yet we live in a technological age not only because of the widespread availability of these tools but because our minds have been taken over by a technological way of thinking and feeling to which we remain largely oblivious.

So familiar are we with framing our lives within a technological mindset that it seems self-evident today to present dharma practice as "inner engineering," a "science of the mind," or a "contemplative technology"—to take just three current examples. Human suffering is thus conceived as a problem to be solved through the skilled application of effective spiritual techniques.

The Burmese Buddhist reformers who developed the techniques of Vipassanā meditation at the beginning of the twentieth century would have found such a way of thinking well adapted to their own understanding of the path to enlightenment. For the technological mindset is not, as Heidegger assumed, a unique feature of the Western philosophical tradition that started with Plato. It has long dominated the Buddhist tradition as well. The doctrine of the Four Noble Truths provides a perfect example of this. It likewise presents suffering as a problem that can be solved by understanding its causes and then applying the right techniques to eliminate those causes.

Buddhism may ring true for many today because it seems so well adapted to a technological perspective. It can thereby also serve to blind us further to the nature of technology and its hold over us. We should not be surprised by the commodification and instrumentalization of mindfulness. A technological approach to life has proved so successful in everything from building skyscrapers to eliminating polio that many today regard it as simply the most reasonable basis on which to conduct their lives. As a result, we find ourselves treating our own lives as problems to be solved by application of the right techniques. We thus risking losing what is most essentially human about us: that we are contemplative beings who can ponder the mystery of being here at all.

To think in a more contemplative way means to slow down and recover our rootedness on earth, which allows us to question who we are and how best to live in this world. For the self-declared "neo-Socratic" philosopher and playwright Gabriel Marcel, our existential condition of having been born and being subject to death is not a problem to be eradicated but a mystery to be embraced. A problem, for Marcel, always stands apart from the one confronting it, whereas a mystery is inseparable from the one who embraces it. As the person who falls sick, ages, and is destined to die, I cannot stand outside these processes to treat them as problems to be solved. Instead, I can open myself to the mystery of being here and embrace it in wordless astonishment. Unlike a problem, which vanishes as soon as it is solved, as we embrace a mystery the more mysterious it becomes.

The more we come to view life through the lens of technology, the more we risk losing a sense of our unfathomable poignancy and strangeness. In order to manipulate technically the physical and mental elements of our world, they need to appear to us as discrete, definable, readily graspable objects. Only then can we confidently embark on bending them to our will.

An Ethics of Uncertainty

Not only do we need to break free from the technological mindset that keeps us in thrall to the hope of achieving a techno-utopia on earth, we also need to leave behind consolatory religious beliefs that promise a postmortem salvation. Both political and religious leaders bear responsibility for preserving the unsustainable status quo. The challenge is to embrace life in all its complexity, tragedy, and beauty, to immunize ourselves against the viruses of complacency within our own minds, and, crucially, to imagine how human communities might best survive and flourish in the radically changing world in which we find ourselves. It calls for the recovery of our nature as contemplative beings, acutely aware of our inseparability from the biosphere that sustains us and all other life forms. And it requires an ethics that can translate our core values into forms of action that can respond to the potential crises that threaten sentient life on earth.

In his book *This Life*, the Swedish philosopher Martin Hägglund makes a distinction between "religious faith" and "secular faith." These represent two radically different conceptions of what constitutes our ultimate concern in life. "The most fundamental form of secular faith," writes Hägglund, "is the faith that life is worth living, which is intrinsic to all forms of care."[4] To embrace such faith entails recognizing that what we most care about might be lost, thereby causing us grief and pain. The religious conception of faith is the opposite of this. It requires that the object of faith be something that can never fail you or let you down, such as God or Nirvana. Were one to attain such salvation or liberation, then nothing would matter anymore for either the Christian saint or Buddhist arahant. In 1989, when asked whether a Buddhist would be concerned about environmental destruction, the Dalai Lama replied, "A Buddhist would say it doesn't matter."[5] Since then he has become a vociferous advocate of climate action, but there is no indication that he has changed or modified his underlying religious beliefs.

For even if the world were to become uninhabitable and mass extinction ensued, traditional Buddhists believe that each sentient being who perished would be reborn according to his or her karma in another realm in this or some other world. Buddhists may well feel deep compassion for those who suffer the consequences of climate change and do their best to alleviate that suffering, but in the end they believe that some form of consciousness will survive death to be reborn elsewhere and continue its journey to enlightenment. The ultimate goal of Buddhism remains the same: to free oneself from the cycle of rebirth and attain the ineffable peace of Nirvana, which is no longer troubled by the suffering of life on earth. His analysis leads Hägglund to conclude that the climate crisis can only be addressed effectively from the perspective of a secular faith committed to the survival of sentient life on earth as an end in itself.

A secular faith calls upon us to embrace unequivocally the suffering of humans and animals alike and respond to it with situation-specific compassion. In eighth-century India, Śāntideva realized that if a sage, such as Gotama, truly cared for others out of compassion, then he would suffer as a result:

> Just as one whose body is on fire
> Finds no pleasure in sensual objects,
> The compassionate ones feel no joy
> When a sentient being is in pain.[6]

Buddhism maintains that an awakened sage no longer suffers, but for Śāntideva this would be impossible as long as that sage continued to care. This follows from his conviction that an awakened person empathetically identifies with other beings as though they were himself. "Then why," he asks himself, "do I not revere these buddhas who appear in the form of ordinary creatures?"[7] From this perspective, a buddha is not an aloof quasi-god, serenely contemplating the suffering of the world, but could just as well appear on the streets of a modern city as an otherwise unremarkable person.

Gotama and Socrates embodied and enacted an ethics of uncertainty. Although they came from different cultures separated by thousands of miles, they both advocated a life of questioning and self-examination. Any situation in life that presents us with a significant dilemma and calls for an appropriate response, is, by its very nature, a site of uncertainty. We may be traumatized by the breakdown of a relationship or the potential impact of climate change on our grandchildren, but we find ourselves fraught with uncertainty about what to do. Not only is our understanding of the diverse factors that contributed to the dilemma incomplete, but we can never be sure whether our response to the dilemma will not make matters worse. Yet if all such ethical situations are uncertain, and any choice we make a risk, then to speak of an "ethics of uncertainty" might seem redundant. The phrase simply states the obvious.

In ethical contexts uncertainty is often considered a *weakness*, something of which to be ashamed. Our moral heroes tend to be those who exhibit certainty in their ethical choices, who stick to their decisions in the face of opposition, who stand resolutely behind what they have said and done. Afraid of appearing weak, we may tend to project, to ourselves as well as others, a level of conviction in our decisions that deep down we know is lacking. Such a stance is prone to making choices that are driven more by our need to appear sure of what we are doing than by the complex and ambiguous demands of the situation to which we are responding.

Both Socrates and Gotama transformed uncertainty from a weakness into a source of ethical strength. Socrates's repeated confession of ignorance did not make him indecisive and timid. On the contrary, it drove him to test himself and his interlocutors ever more probingly. It enabled him to confront his accusers during his trial with steadfastness, calm, and honesty. Gotama's resolve to avoid the binary of "is" and "is not" by dwelling in a nonreactive emptiness did not weaken him either. Rather than render him immune to the vicissitudes of the world, it empowered him to engage with the world more directly, truthfully, and compassionately.

Acknowledging ethical uncertainty creates more space and time to ponder and reflect on what needs to be done, to listen to the quiet voice of intuition, to find the courage to risk speaking or acting in ways that might meet with outrage and condemnation. Being mindful of the intrinsic uncertainty of ethical situations can foster humility, patience, and tolerance. It makes me notice how, even on a trivial point in an argument with a friend, I am driven by a silent insistence to be right and an irrepressible urge to prove her wrong. I want *my* certainties to replace *her* mistakes. At such moments I experience for myself how invested I am in the rightness of my cherished opinions.

By itself, uncertainty is an inadequate basis for leading an ethical life. Uncertainty and certainty are poles of a spectrum. You cannot have one without the other. The necessary tension between certainty and uncertainty underscores, for example, the distinction between the values of justice and care. Whereas an ethics of justice emphasizes the importance of adhering to unchanging laws and rules, an ethics of care is concerned with responding with empathy and love to the uniqueness of each moral situation. In the case of abortion, an ethics of justice would emphasize respecting a society's religious or moral principles, while an ethics of care would emphasize the unprecedented and unrepeatable needs of a particular woman and her unborn child.

For Buddhists the same ethical tension between justice and care is found between respecting the impersonal laws of karma and heeding the call of compassion. Justice treasures certainty, while care honors uncertainty. But in practice neither justice nor care is an absolute. At times the pendulum may swing more towards one pole than the other, but in the end ethics is an ongoing struggle to find a response that is both compassionate and fair.

An ethics of uncertainty allows us a nonreactive space in which to reflect on how moral values shift and change through history and within different human societies. While broad and enduring agreements may be reached on what counts as good or evil at any given epoch, such consensus rests neither on Platonic moral absolutes nor the immutable laws of karma. An adequate definition of virtue will perhaps forever elude us, but this does not mean that we are incapable of leading a good and ethical life. For we intuitively know the virtues through the way they are enacted in our own and other's behavior. We recognize wisdom, courage, and justice as soon as we witness them embodied in the words and deeds of a real or fictional person.

In the final section of his *Conversations of Socrates,* Xenophon reports a dialogue between Socrates and the Sophist Hippias of Elis. Hippias complains that Socrates constantly makes fools of others by his relentless questioning but refuses to state his own view or position on anything. Socrates seems surprised. "Aren't you aware," he replies, "that I never stop revealing what I think is right?" Hippias asks him to elaborate. "If I don't reveal my views in a formal account," replies Socrates, "I do so by my conduct. Don't you think that actions are more reliable evidence than words?"[8]

Socrates's Zen-like distinction between "telling" and

"showing" points unequivocally to virtues being embodied acts rather than mere qualities of the soul. His claim that virtues are revealed through being enacted rather than defined further supports his supposed collaboration with Euripides. For where better to enact virtues for the edification and instruction of the public than on a stage? In this way, the comic and tragic dramas performed at the Dionysian festivals provided an ethical education. Like Socrates, Euripides did not present his audience with definitions of the virtues. He revealed what justice, courage, moderation, and wisdom were through the words and deeds of the protagonists alone. By contemplating the moral struggle played out on stage, spectators were able to contemplate how their own lives too were forged by their choices and acts, and how what they say and do now will have consequences in the future.

In addition to providing spectators with a mirror in which to contemplate their own individual and collective struggles, theatrical performances implicitly reveal how each spectator's life is also a performance. As social animals we are looked at, listened to, and judged by others in terms of how we perform our role on the stage of the world, whether that be in the privacy of our family or in public as an elected politician. Our sense of self is not innate: it emerges over time through how we repeatedly present ourselves to and perform for other people. This idea was foreshadowed by Gotama's insights that you *create* yourself through your thoughts, words, and deeds and *become* the kind of person you are through the actions you perform in the world.[9] In all these cases, a sense of self is understood to grow out of the social relations in which we are embedded rather than any essential individuality concealed within us. Our dialogical self is only conceivable because we are thinking beings grounded in a language shared with other language users.

As we confront together the uncertain, troubling, and bewildering future into which we are hurtling as a community crowded into the fragile biosphere enveloping the earth, we may reach a point where our historical religions, philosophies, political systems, and cultures are no longer fit for purpose in this global village. As populations in developing countries continue to grow, vital resources such as water become more scarce, and the gap between rich and poor widens, it seems increasingly possible that this will lead to ever more violence and injustice in the struggle for survival. The disadvantaged will doubtless suffer most from this, while the privileged will have the means to retreat into nation-sized gated communities designed to keep the wretched of the earth at bay.

Alan Watts used to say that materialists are not those who love matter but those who hate it. Their goal is to overcome the constraints and limits of the physical world that impede the fulfilment of their desires. The materialist is forever seeking quicker and more efficient ways of defeating the matter that stands in his way. Only when people have subjugated nature by transforming it into parks and reserves do they begin to speak lyrically of its beauty. But nature is terrifying in her ruthless fecundity that will inevitably overwhelm whatever human artifice, no matter how carbon neutral, is placed in her way. The deep-seated longing for a God or Nirvana uncorrupted by the ways of the world is perhaps no more than a despairing symptom of our tragic human condition.

The climate crisis we face is the latest and perhaps most fatal consequence of forcing our desires onto nature in our attempts to bring it under our control. Although this process was accelerated by burning industrial levels of coal, oil, and gas, it started as soon as men and women laid the foundations of their first houses and plowed their first fields. In retrospect, it now seems self-evident that to ceaselessly pump tons of carbon dioxide into the finite atmosphere of a medium-sized planet would have consequences. Yet even with a sound scientific understanding of what those consequences will be and international protocols in place to decrease emissions, each year we still release ever more quantities of greenhouse gases into the atmosphere. The International Energy Agency predicts that consumption of fossil fuels will reach its peak at some point before 2030, then begin to decline once climate policies take effect. They warn, however, that the rate of decline may simply not be steep enough to prevent temperatures rising to levels that would cause potentially catastrophic consequences.

Are we not like those deer who stray onto a road at night then stare and squint in bewilderment at the headlights of an approaching vehicle? Such animals have not evolved to understand that two tons of metal are heading their way at seventy miles an hour and a collision is imminent. Had it detected the scent of an approaching mountain lion, the deer would have immediately fled. Confronted by an approaching car, it just keeps squinting myopically as the headlights get bigger and brighter. Human beings have likewise not evolved an instinct to recognize an existential threat that will impact their descendants in the decades to come. Conceptually we might know all about the dangers of a heating planet, but many of us remain emotionally numb and experience no inner prompt to respond. We assuage our denial of what is happening by making token gestures, like recycling plastic bottles, but otherwise, like squinting deer, keep on behaving much in the same way as we have always done.

In a world with as many conflicting opinions and multiple viewpoints as our own, it may no longer be feasible to remain immured within the certainties of the ancestral traditions into which one was born. Raised in Britain as a post-

Christian secular humanist and trained in Asia as a Tibetan and Zen Buddhist monk, I find that I can no longer identify exclusively with either a Western or an Eastern tradition. I am more at home in the gaps and abysses that open up between them. I enjoy the freedom of creating and navigating new pathways that are no longer predetermined by a priori conceptions of their destination. Although at times unsettling and disorienting, these spaces of uncertainty seem far richer in creative possibilities, more open to leading a life of wonder, imagination, and action.

Afterword

Kenneth McLeish, to whom this book is dedicated, was my first-year class teacher at grammar school in Watford. He also taught us Latin, which I had been studying with zero enthusiasm since the age of eight, and was a leader of the Boy Scout troop. When I was twelve or thirteen, I spent a week in a scout camp on a muddy, mist-covered hillside in the Yorkshire Dales. It rained incessantly. Confined to the sick tent, I spent much of the time sobbing uncontrollably. This was explained away as a severe case of homesickness, which I knew not to be the case. Today it would likely be described it as a panic or anxiety attack. I had no idea what was happening or why.

The only person who seemed genuinely concerned about my plight was Ken—as everyone called him. He would visit regularly to chat and keep me company. He also lent me detective thrillers by John Creasey, popular books written for adults rather than adolescents, which both distracted me from my despair and allowed me to think myself more mature than I was. Ken was the first adult outside my immediate family to take me seriously. He showed unconditional kindness and care yet always with a sense of bonhomie and humor. I think of him as my first mentor.

After this traumatic summer, I have few recollections of

Ken and none whatsoever of his Latin lessons. In the years that followed, I picked up occasional pieces of information about him. Ken stopped teaching and began working in theater and television. Exactly what he did I wasn't sure, but I was chuffed to have known someone whose name appeared in the entertainment sections of magazines and newspapers. I learned from my brother David, who was also taught by Ken, that he died in 1997, at the relatively young age of fifty-eight. But it was only two decades later, as I began working on *Buddha, Socrates, and Us,* that I rediscovered him via the footnotes and bibliographies of books I was reading on ancient Greek drama.

Ken grew up in a working-class family in the north of England, excelled in ancient and modern languages at the local grammar school, then went up to Worcester College in Oxford, where he studied classics and music. The obituary by his colleague Stephen Unwin in *The Independent* declared him to be "the most widely respected and prolific translator of drama in Britain."[1] In addition to translating all forty-seven surviving plays of Aeschylus, Sophocles, Euripides, and Aristophanes, he also produced translations of most of Ibsen's plays—from Norwegian—and Feydeau's—from French. His translations were performed at the Royal Shakespeare Company and other major theater companies. In addition to writing plays and TV scripts of his own, he also published *The Theatre of Aristophanes* (1980), described by Unwin as "a milestone in the understanding and appreciation of Greek comedy."

Stephen Unwin's obituary concludes with an assessment of Ken that echoes my own adolescent experience of him. "He was a kind, modest man, big-hearted with a rough and ready sense of humour." And it also confirms my own views about how best to translate classical texts, albeit from Tibetan and

Pali rather than Latin or Greek. "His strength," writes Unwin, "was that he passionately believed that the great works of the past should be communicated to the present in ways that neither patronised the reader nor compromised the original. In times when those ideals are too often ignored, Ken McLeish's was a brave and brilliant voice."

I knew nothing about Ken's musical training, linguistic gifts, or theatrical passions as I struggled with my anxieties in the Yorkshire Dales nearly sixty years ago. Ken would have been fully aware of the gulf between the pedagogic values of the 1960s in Britain and those of Greek antiquity. Rather than an impersonal exercise in conveying the information needed to pass exams, the teacher-student relationship in classical Greece could be both personal and passionate. Socrates sought to engage the young men who sought him out existentially, to challenge them to wake up and think for themselves. Ken was the first teacher I met who seemed to embody and enact his deepest concerns. Perhaps his openhearted care for a young teenager suffering alone on a hillside introduced me to the sort of existential education I subsequently came to value in the Buddhist monasteries of Asia.

Dramatis Personae

Adrastus	Legendary king of Argos, who appears as a character in Euripides's play *Suppliant Women*. See Chapter 6.
Aeschylus	(c. 525/524–c. 456/455 BCE): The eldest of the three great Attic tragedians. Author of *Persians*, the *Oresteia Trilogy*. See Chapter 10.
Ajātasattu	[Sanskrit: Ajātaśatru] (fl. 5th century BCE): King of Magadha during the last seven years of Gotama's life. He murdered his father Bimbisara to gain the throne; a supporter of Gotama's cousin Devadatta.
Āḷāra Kālāma	(fl. 5th century BCE): A teacher of Gotama, who taught him formless meditation, about whom nothing else is known.
Alcibiades	(c. 450–404 BCE): A charismatic but controversial Athenian statesman and military leader, a prominent student of Socrates, who offers praise of his teacher in Plato's *Drinking Party* (*Symposium*). See Chapter 2.
Alexander the Great	(356–323 BCE): Tutored by Aristotle, crowned king of Macedon at the age of twenty, a brilliant military leader who spent most of his life establishing an empire that extended from Greece to modern Pakistan and Egypt.
Ameipsias	(fl. 5th century BCE): A comic playwright, contemporary of Aristophanes, none of whose plays survive. See Chapter 2.
Ānanda	(fl. 5th century BCE): Gotama's nephew and attendant for the last twenty-five years of his life. See Batchelor, *After Buddhism*, Chapter 10.

Anaxagoras	(c. 500–c. 428): A naturalistic philosopher active in Athens at the time of Socrates.
Anaxarchus	(c. 380–c. 320 BCE): A Greek philosopher of the school of Democritus, who, with his student Pyrrho, accompanied Alexander the Great to India.
Antisthenes	(c. 466–c. 366 BCE): A devoted student of Socrates, who developed the ascetic and ethical side of his teacher's philosophy, which later led to the founding of Cynicism and Stoicism. See Chapter 16.
Arcesilaus	(316–241 BCE): A skeptical philosopher of the Hellenistic period, who succeeded Crates as the head of Plato's Academy.
Archelaus	(fl. 5th century BCE): A student of Anaxagoras, believed to have been the teacher and lover of the young Socrates.
Arendt, Hannah	(1906–1975): German-American political theorist, philosopher, and public intellectual, a student of Martin Heidegger and Karl Jaspers, author of *The Human Condition* and *The Life of the Mind*. See Chapters 24, 27, 28.
Aristophanes	(c. 446–c. 386 BCE): Athenian comic playwright, author of *Clouds, The Acharnians, Law and Order Women, Frogs*. See Chapters 2, 14, 18.
Aristotle	(384–322 BCE): Foremost student of Plato, tutor to Alexander the Great, founder of the Lyceum in Athens, philosopher, and all-round genius.
Aśoka	(c. 304–232 BCE): Third and final emperor of the Mauryan dynasty, who succeeded in unifying most the Indian subcontinent before converting to Buddhism.
Aspasia	(c. 470–after 428 BCE): Common-law wife of Pericles, teacher of Socrates, rare example of a woman who achieved prominence in ancient Athens.
Atossa	(550–475 BCE): Daughter of Cyrus the Great, wife of Darius the Great, and mother of Xerxes the Great, a central character in Aeschylus's *Persians*.
Auden, W. H.	(1907–1953): British-American poet, critic, essayist, and teacher.
Bimbisara	(fl. 5th century BCE): King of Magadha, first patron of Gotama, murdered by his son Ajātasattu.

Blücher, Heinrich	(1899–1970): German-American political activist, poet, and philosopher, second husband of Hannah Arendt (m. 1940).
Bodhidharma	(fl. 5th/6th centuries CE): Enigmatic Indian or Central Asian Buddhist teacher, who is believed to have introduced Chan (Zen) Buddhism to China. See Chapter 19.
Brecht, Bertolt	(1898–1956): German playwright, poet, and theater director.
Bruegel, Pieter the Elder	(c. 1525–1569): Painter and printmaker of the Flemish/Dutch Renaissance.
Chaerophon	(c. 470/460–c. 403/399 BCE): Loyal companion of Socrates, an ardent democrat.
Cioran, Emil	(1911–1995): Romanian philosopher and essayist, who lived in exile in Paris, noted for his pessimistic outlook on life.
Confucius	(c. 551–c. 479 BCE): Preeminent Chinese sage, moral and social philosopher, author of *The Analects*.
Crates of Thebes	(c. 365–c. 285 BCE): Greek philosopher of the Cynic school, disciple of Diogenes of Sinope. See Chapter 16.
Critias	(c. 460–403 BCE): Athenian aristocrat and writer, student of Socrates, who became one of the Thirty Tyrants at the end of the Peloponnesian War.
Crito	(c. 469–fourth century BCE): Athenian nobleman, who was a lifelong friend of Socrates. Plato's *Crito* recounts his final meeting with Socrates. See Chapter 26.
Cyrus the Great	(c. 600–530 BCE): Founder of the Persian Achaemenid Empire.
Darius the Great	(c. 550–486 BCE): Third ruler of the Persian Achaemenid Empire.
Democritus	(c. 460–c. 370 BCE): One of the first Greek philosophers to propose a materialist view of the universe. A native of the city of Abdera.
Deshan	[Japanese: Tokusan] (819–865): Renowned Chinese Chan (Zen) teacher of the Tang dynasty.

Devadatta	(fl. 5th century BCE): Cousin and follower of Gotama, who tried but failed to gain control of the monastic community towards the end of Gotama's life.
Dhargyey, Geshe Ngawang	(1921–1995): Lama of the Gelug school of Tibetan Buddhism, teacher at the Library of Tibetan Works and Archives, Dharamsala, from 1972 to 1985.
Diogenes Laertius	(fl. 3rd century CE): Author of *Lives of the Eminent Philosophers,* one of the primary sources about classical Greek philosophy about whom nothing is known. He was probably an Epicurean. Often criticized by modern scholars for not having written the book they would have liked him to have written.
Diogenes of Sinope	(412 or 404–323 BCE): Greek philosopher, student of Antisthenes, and teacher of Crates of Thebes, founder of the Cynic school. See Chapter 16.
Diotima	(fl. 5th century BCE): A priestess from Mantinea with whom Socrates studied. When invited in Plato's *Drinking Party (Symposium)* to offer his thoughts on love *(eros),* Socrates presents what he learned from Diotima. See Chapter 4.
Epicurus	(341–270 BCE): Greek philosopher who established the eponymous school of Epicureanism. A prolific author, most of whose work has been lost. See Chapter 15.
Epictetus	(c. 50–c. 135 CE): Greek former slave who became a prominent Stoic philosopher and teacher in the Roman Empire.
Euthyphro	(fl. 5th century BCE): Athenian priest who appears in Plato's dialogue of the same name. See Chapter 22.
Gampopa	(1079–1153): Tibetan monk, writer, doctor, and teacher ordained in the Kadampa tradition founded by the Bengali abbot Atiśa, student of the renowned yogi Milarepa, considered the "father" of the Kagyu school of Tibetan Buddhism, author of the *Jewel Ornament of Liberation.*
Goenka, Satya Narayan	(1924–2013). One of the foremost teachers of Vipassanā meditation in the twentieth century. Trained in Burma by Sayagyi U Ba Khin, he went on to establish meditation centers worldwide.

Gotama	[Sanskrit: Gautama] (c. 480–c. 400 BCE): Teacher from the kingdom of Kosala in northeast India, known as the Buddha. His memorized teachings constitute the core of the early Buddhist canon and served as the basis for the later doctrines and philosophies of Buddhism. The personal name "Siddhattha" (Siddhartha) does not appear in the Pali texts.
Hadot, Pierre	(1922–2010): French philosopher who specialized in the Hellenistic schools, which inspired him to advocate philosophy as a way of life rather than an academic discipline.
Hägglund, Martin	(b. 1976): Swedish philosopher, professor of humanities at Yale, author of *This Life: Secular Faith and Spiritual Freedom*.
Hakuin	(1686–1769): Japanese Rinzai Zen teacher, artist, and reformer.
Hamilton, Edith	(1867–1963): American classicist and author.
Heidegger, Martin	(1889–1976): Seminal twentieth-century German philosopher, student of Edmund Husserl, author of *Being and Time*, teacher of Hannah Arendt. See Chapter 23.
Herodotus	(c. 484–c. 425 BCE): Greek historian, who, with Thucydides, founded the discipline of history. Author of *Histories*, a wide-ranging account of the ancient world, culminating in the Graeco-Persian war launched by Xerxes the Great.
Huairang	[Japanese: Ejō] (677–744): Chinese Chan (Zen) monk and teacher, who is believed to have studied with Huineng. He is sometimes regarded as his successor.
Huineng	[Japanese: Enō] (638–713): The influential sixth patriarch of Chinese Chan (Zen). His teachings are collected together as the *Platform Sutra*.
Jaspers, Karl	(1883–1969): German psychiatrist and philosopher, who coined the term "axial age," teacher and lifelong mentor of Hannah Arendt.

Jīvaka	(fl. 5th century BCE): Renowned physician at the court of Magadha, who studied medicine in Taxila, follower of Gotama. See Batchelor, *After Buddhism*, Chapter 8.
Kaccāna	[Sanskrit: Kātyāyana] (fl. 5th century BCE): Also known as Kaccānagotta and Mahākaccāna, a disciple of Gotama from Avantī, possible author of the *Chapter of Eights*. See Chapter 5.
Kassapa	[usually Mahākassapa; Sanskrit: Mahākāśyapa] (fl. 5th century BCE): Prominent follower of Gotama, who believed himself to be his heir, convenor of the First Council.
Kennedy, Robert F.	(1925–1968): American Democratic politician, attorney general and senator, supporter of the civil rights movement.
King, Martin Luther	(1929–1968): American Baptist minister, civil rights activist, political thinker, Nobel Peace Laureate.
Koṭṭhita	[usually Mahākoṭṭhita] (fl. 5th century BCE): A senior disciple of Gotama, an intellectual. See Chapter 17.
Kuki Shūzō	(1888–1941): Japanese philosopher, student of Bergson, Sartre, Husserl, and Heidegger.
Kusan Sunim	[also romanized as Gusan] (1909–1983): Prominent Korean Buddhist reformer and Son (Zen) master of Songgwang Sa Monastery. Teacher of the author.
Laozi	[previously romanized as Lao Tzu] (either 6th or 4th century BCE): Author of the *Tao Te Ching*, together with Zhuangzi revered as a founding figure of philosophical Daoism. See Chapter 19.
Lévinas, Emmanuel	(1906–1995): Lithuanian-French Jewish philosopher, student of Husserl and Heidegger, known for his contributions to ethics.
Linji	[also romanized as Linchi; Japanese: Rinzai; Korean: Imje] (d. 866 CE): Chinese Chan (Zen) monk, founder of the Linji [Rinzai/Imje] school, the Zen lineage found in Korea.
Lucretius	(c. 99–c. 55 BCE): Roman poet and Epicurean philosopher, author of *On the Nature of Things* (*De rerum natura*).

Dramatis Personae

MacLeish, Kenneth	(1940–1997): Author's school teacher, translator of the works of Aeschylus, Sophocles, Euripides, and Aristophanes. See Afterword.
Mahānāma	(fl. 5th century BCE): Gotama's cousin, ruler of Sakiya after Gotama left home, follower and supporter of Gotama. See Batchelor, *After Buddhism,* Chapter 2.
Márai, Sándor	(1900–1989): Hungarian novelist and journalist.
Marcel, Gabriel	(1889–1973): French philosopher, playwright, and composer, a leading Christian exponent of Existentialism.
Marcus Aurelius	(121–180 CE): Emperor of the Roman Empire, Stoic philosopher, author of *Meditations.*
Marpa	(1012–1097): Tibetan translator, student of Nāropa, teacher of Milarepa.
Metrodorus of Chios	(fl. 4th century BCE): Hellenistic philosopher in the tradition of Democritus, an atomist and skeptic.
Milarepa	(1028/40–1111/23): Tibetan yogi and ascetic, known for his songs of enlightenment, student of Marpa, teacher of Gampopa.
Milinda	[Greek: Menander Soter] (c. 165/155–130 BCE): Indo-Greek king who ruled over an area extending from Afghanistan to the Punjab, known for the questions he posed to the Buddhist monk Nāgasena in the *Milindapañhā.* See Chapter 12.
Montaigne, Michel de	(1533–1592): Philosopher, essayist, diplomat, former mayor of Bordeaux. See Batchelor, *The Art of Solitude,* Chapters 2, 5, 10, 13, 18, 24, 27, 29.
Nāgārjuna	(dates uncertain: c. 150–c. 250 CE): Indian Buddhist philosopher regarded as the founding father of Centrist thought, author of *Verses from the Center* (*Mūlamadhyamakakārikā*). See Chapter 12.
Nāgasena	(fl. 2nd century CE): Indian Buddhist monk, probably of the Sarvāstavāda school, known for answering King Milinda's questions in the *Milindapañhā.* See Chapter 12.
Nāropa	(1016–1100): Indian scholar and yogi, known for his tantric doctrine of the Six Yogas, student of Tilopa and teacher of Marpa. See Chapter 29.

Nietzsche, Friedrich	(1844–1900): German philologist, philosopher, and author, who declared the death of God and sought a revaluation of all values. See Chapter 23.
Nishitani, Keiji	(1900–1990): Leading Japanese philosopher of the Kyoto school, student of Heidegger, Zen Buddhist, author of *Religion and Nothingness*. See Chapter 19.
Parks, Rosa	(1913–2005): American civil rights activist.
Pajjota	(fl. 5th century BCE): Known as Caṇḍapajjota, "Pajjota the Terrible." King of Avantī at the time of Gotama.
Pasenadi	[Sanskrit: Prasenajit] (fl. 5th century BCE): King of Kosala during much of Gotama's lifetime. The dialogues recorded between the two men suggest they were friends. See Batchelor, *After Buddhism*, Chapter 4.
Pentheus	Mythical ruler of Thebes, character in Euripides's play *Ecstatic Women* (*Bacchae*). See Chapter 18.
Pericles	(c. 495–429 BCE): Athenian statesman and orator, who encouraged philosophy and the arts during the golden age of Athens.
Philip II	(382–336 BCE): King of Macedon, father of Alexander the Great.
Plato	(c. 427–348 BCE): Athenian nobleman and writer, founding father of Western philosophy, student of Socrates, teacher of Aristotle.
Plutarch	(c. 46–119 CE): Greek Platonist philosopher, essayist, and biographer.
Pukkhusāti	(fl. 5th century BCE): A wandering ascetic, possibly from Taxila, to whom Gotama delivered a discourse. See Chapter 13.
Purana	(fl. 5th century BCE): Buddhist monk, who refused to accept the canon established by Kassapa after Gotama's death.
Pyrrho	(c. 360–c. 270 BCE): Greek philosopher from Elis, who traveled to India with Alexander the Great and is considered the founder of philosophical Skepticism. See Chapter 15.
Rabten, Geshe Tamdrin	(1921–1986): Tibetan Buddhist lama of the Gelug school, philosophical advisor to the Dalai Lama, the author's principal teacher. See Chapter 9.

Dramatis Personae

Ram Dass	(1931–2019): Born Richard Alpert, colleague of Timothy Leary at Harvard, advocate of psychedelics turned spiritual teacher who popularized Indian philosophy and religious practice in America.
Śākyamuni	[Sanskrit] (c. 480–c. 400 BCE): The "Sage of the Sakiyans," an epithet for Gotama used widely in Mahayana Buddhism.
Śāntideva	(fl. 8th century CE): Mahayana Buddhist monk-poet, author of *A Guide to the Bodhisattva's Way of Life*.
Sarakani	(fl. 5th century BCE): Lay follower of Gotama from Sakiya. See Chapter 29.
Sāriputta	[Sanskrit: Śāriputra] (fl. 5th century BCE): Senior disciple of Gotama. See Chapter 17.
Schopenhauer, Arthur	(1788–1860): German philosopher, whose atheistic and pessimistic work shared and affirmed aspects of Buddhist thought.
Scylax of Caryanda	(fl. late 6th–early 5th century BCE): Greek explorer and writer, employed by Darius the Great to trace the course of the Indus River.
Seneca	(c. 4 CE–65 CE): Roman statesman; tutor to the emperor Nero; Stoic philosopher, writer, dramatist.
Sengai	(1750–1837): Japanese Rinzai Zen monk, renowned for his brush paintings.
Shinran	(1173–1263): Radical Japanese Pure Land Buddhist priest and teacher, whose descendants founded the Jōdo Shinshū school of Buddhism. See Chapter 29.
Socrates	(c. 470–399 BCE): Athenian ethical philosopher, who inspired Plato, Xenophon, and others to lead an examined life, lampooned in Aristophanes's *Clouds*.
Soṇa	(fl. 5th century BCE): A disciple of Kaccāna from Avantī. See Chapter 5.
Sophocles	(497/6–406/5 BCE): One of the great tragedians of Attic theater of whom seven plays have survived, including *Oedipus the Tyrant* and *Antigone*.
Soreyya (m.) / Soreyyā (f.)	(fl. 5th century BCE): A person whose story is recounted in the *Dhammapada Commentary*. See Chapter 5.
Strepsiades	The protagonist of Aristophanes's *Clouds*. See Chapter 2.

Sunakkhatta	(fl. 5th century BCE): A nobleman from Vajjī who served as Gotama's attendant but eventually denounced him. See Batchelor, *After Buddhism,* Chapter 6.
Suzuki, D. T.	(1870–1966): Japanese Buddhist scholar, translator, and writer, whose books introduced Zen and Mahayana Buddhism to the English-speaking world.
Tanabe Hajime	(1885–1962): Japanese philosopher of the Kyoto school, who studied with Edmund Husserl and Martin Heidegger in the 1920s.
Telecleides	(fl. 5th century BCE): Athenian comic playwright, none of whose plays have survived.
Thales	(626/3–548/545 BCE): Greek naturalistic thinker, mathematician, and astronomer from Ionia, often considered the first philosopher in the Greek tradition.
Theseus	Mythic king of Athens, featured in Euripides's play *Suppliant Women.* See Chapter 6.
Thucydides	(c. 460–c. 400 BCE): Athenian general and historian, whose *History of the Peloponnesian War* is considered a foundational work of evidence-based historical writing.
Thunberg, Greta	(b. 2003): Swedish environmental activist.
Tilopa	(988–1069 CE): Bengali tantric adept, who became the teacher of Nāropa.
Timon	(c. 320 BCE–c. 235 BCE): Greek student of Pyrrho, best known as the author of *Silloi,* a collection of satirical caricatures of philosophers.
Tiresias	Mythical blind prophet from Thebes, a character in Euripides's *Ecstatic Women* (*Bacchae*).
Trungpa, Chögyam	(1939–1987): Reincarnate lama of the Kagyu school, teacher, writer, and artist, key figure in the introduction of Tibetan Buddhism to the West. See Chapter 29.
Tsongkhapa	(1357–1419): Founder of the Gelug school of Tibetan Buddhism, author of *The Great Treatise on the Stages of the Path to Enlightenment* (*Lamrim Chenmo*).
Udaka Ramaputta	(fl. 5th century BCE): A teacher of Gotama, who taught him formless meditation, about whom nothing else is known.

Dramatis Personae

Vaccha	[usually known as Vacchagotta] (fl. 5th century BCE): A wandering ascetic at the time of Gotama with whom a number of dialogues are recorded. See Chapter 5.
Viḍūḍabha	[Sanskrit: Virūḍhaka] (fl. 5th century BCE): Son of King Pasenedi of Kosala, who overthrew his father to become king and invaded Sakiya towards the end of Gotama's life.
Wagner, Richard	(1813–1883): German composer and theater director, best known for his Ring Cycle of operas, mentor to the young Friedrich Nietzsche.
Watts, Alan	(1915–1973): British-born author and philosopher, who played a seminal role in introducing Buddhist, Daoist, and Hindu ideas to Western readers.
Wu Weishan	(b. 1962): Chinese sculptor and curator. See Prologue.
Xanthippe	(fl. 5th century BCE): Wife of Socrates.
Xenophon	(c. 430–355/354 BCE): Athenian nobleman, military strategist, and writer; follower of Socrates; and author of *Conversations of Socrates*.
Xerxes the Great	(c. 518–465 BCE): Fourth ruler of the Achaemenid Empire, son of Darius the Great and his queen Atossa, invaded Greece in 480 BCE, sacked Athens but was defeated at the battle of Salamis. See Chapter 10.
Yousafzai, Malala	(b. 1997): Pakistani human rights activist and advocate of education for women, winner of the Nobel Peace Prize.
Yunmen	[Japanese: Ummon] (864–949 CE): Chinese Chan (Zen) master famous for his "one word" answers to questions.
Zeno of Citium	(c. 334–c. 262 BCE): Greek Hellenistic philosopher, founder of Stoicism. See Chapter 16.
Zhuangzi	[also known as Zhuang Zhou, previously romanized as Chuang Tzu] (fl. 4th century BCE): Chinese philosopher known as the author of the eponymous book *Zhuangzi*. Together with Laozi, regarded as one of the founding fathers of philosophical Daoism. See Chapter 19.

Notes

All the discourses of the Pali Canon can be found in both Pali and English at http://suttacentral.net/.

The complete works of Plato, translated by Benjamin Jowett, are available at https://www.holybooks.com/wp-content/uploads/plato-complete-works.pdf.

All the plays of Aeschylus, Sophocles, Euripides, and Aristophanes, translated by George Theodoridis, are available at https://bacchicstage.wordpress.com/.

Abbreviations

A.	*Anguttara Nikāya*. Bodhi, trans., *The Numerical Discourses of the Buddha*.
Ap.	*Apology [Defense Speech]*. Plato, *Complete Works*.
BCA.	*Bodhicaryāvatāra*. Śāntideva, *Bodhicaryāvatāra*.
Cri.	*Crito*. Plato, *Complete Works*.
D.	*Dīgha Nikāya*. Walshe, trans., *Long Discourses of the Buddha*.
Dhp.	*Dhammapada*. Fronsdal, trans., *Dhammapada*.
DL.	Diogenes Laertius. *Lives of the Eminent Philosophers*.
Euthphr.	*Euthyphro*. Plato, *Complete Works*.
Grg.	*Gorgias*. Plato, *Complete Works*.
M.	*Majjhima Nikāya*. Ñāṇamoli and Bodhi, trans., *The Middle Length Discourses of the Buddha*.
Mil.	*Milindapañhā*. Horner, trans., *Milinda's Questions*.
MMK.	*Mūlamadhyamakakārika*. Garfield, trans., *Fundamental Wisdom of the Middle Way*. Batchelor, *Verses from the Center*.
Mx.	*Menexenus*. Plato, *Complete Works*.
Phd.	*Phaedo*. Plato, *Complete Works*.
Phdr.	*Phaedrus*. Plato, *Complete Works*.

R.	*Republic*. Plato, *Complete Works*.
S.	*Samyutta Nikāya*. Bodhi, trans., *Connected Discourses of the Buddha*.
Smp.	*Symposium* [*Drinking Party*]. Plato, *Complete Works*.
Sn.	*Sutta Nipāta*. Bodhi, trans., *Suttanipāta*. Fronsdal, *Buddha before Buddhism*.
Tht.	*Theaetetus*. Plato, *Complete Works*.
Xen.	Xenophon. *Conversations of Socrates*.

Prologue

1. Duncan Howitt-Marshall, "Statues of Socrates and Confucius unveiled at the Ancient Agora," https://www.ekathimerini.com/culture/1168500/statues-of-socrates-and-confucius-unveiled-at-the-ancient-agora/.

2. Tasos Kokkinidis, "Confucius and Socrates Statues Mark Greece-China Year of Culture," https://greekreporter.com/2021/09/17/confucius-socrates-statues-mark-greece-china-year-culture/.

3. In particular, I refer to the work of Heinz Bechert and Richard Gombrich. See Bechert, *When Did the Buddha Live?* The Buddha is still often dated from c. 563–c. 483 BCE.

4. See Armstrong, *Great Transformation*.

5. A Stoic reading of *On Not-Self* is found in Chapter 16; a secular iteration of the eightfold path is presented in Chapters 27 and 28.

1.
Life as Practice

1. Gampopa, *Jewel Ornament of Liberation*, p. 208.

2. The Parable of the Raft is in M. 22. The Parable of the Arrow is in M. 63.

2.
The Wisest Man in Greece

1. Ap. 21b.

2. DL. 2:20–21.

3. The Battle of Delium is described by Thucydides in *History of the Peloponnesian War*, ed. Finlay, trans. Warner, 4:14.

4. DL. 2:28.

5. The presence of Socrates in the audience at the premiere of *Clouds* is reported by the third century CE Roman author Aelian in his *Varia Historia*. See Dover, ed., *Aristophanes: Clouds*, p. xxxiii.

6. Alcibiades's encomium to Socrates is from Smp. 215b–222c.

7. Aristophanes, *Clouds* 362.
8. Smp. 216b.
9. Smp. 216c.
10. DL. 2:25.
11. Smp. 216e.
12. R. 1.354c.

3.
Fraternal Twins

1. M. 12.
2. D. 16.
3. A. 3:65.
4. M. 4; M. 38.
5. Ap. 40c–d.
6. Phd. 65a.
7. Elsewhere, Gotama states that consciousness cannot exist independently of the physical world and other mental states (*namarūpa*) and thus cannot be reborn. See S. 22:55, and Batchelor, *After Buddhism*, Chapter 7.

4.
Diotima's Middle Way

1. Mx. 249d.
2. Smp. 201e.
3. Smp. 201e–202a.
4. Smp. 202a.
5. Smp. 202e.

5.
An Unbearable Silence

1. See Ellis, *Buddha's Middle Way*, for an in-depth examination of the dharma from a middle way perspective.
2. S. 44:10.
3. This is the *Discourse to Kaccānagotta* (S. 12:15). I consider the person Kaccānagotta in this discourse to be identical to the monk Mahākaccāna. Both are called Kaccāna. The former has the suffix *gotta* ("clan" or "lineage") added, implying that initially he was known simply by his clan name. The latter has the honorific prefix *mahā* ("great") added, which acknowledges the eminent status Kaccāna achieved in the community later in his life. For details on the life of Kaccāna, see Nyanaponika and Hecker, *Great Disciples of the Buddha*, pp. 213–244.

4. S. 12:15.
5. S. 12:15.
6. S. 22:86.
7. Two accounts of this story are found in the canon, a longer version in the *Mahāvagga* of the *Vinaya* (see Horner, *Book of the Discipline*, vol. 4, pp. 260–267) and a shorter one in the *Udāna* [5.6] (see Ireland, trans., *Udāna*, pp. 75–78).
8. Sn. 772. This and all following quotations from *The Chapter of Eights* are from my own translation. See Batchelor, *Art of Solitude*, pp. 157–162. Cf. Fronsdal, *Buddha before Buddhism*, Chapters 2–5.
9. Sn. 791.
10. Sn. 794.
11. Sn. 796.
12. M. 9.
13. Dhp. 183.
14. See Burlingame, *Buddhist Legends*, vol. 2, pp. 23–28.

6.
The Socrates Show

1. Ax. 366d. This dialogue, *Axiochus*, is no longer regarded by scholars as a work of Plato.
2. Scholia to Aristophanes, *Clouds* 144, and Plato, *Ap.* 21a. Scholia are textual comments made to classical works in antiquity, which have subsequently been collected and compiled by scholars. See Dickey, *Ancient Greek Scholarship*.
3. DL. 2:18.
4. Telecleides, Fragments 41 and 42.
5. Aristophanes, *Frogs* 1490–1499.
6. Aristophanes, *Acharnians* 390.
7. Aristophanes, *Law and Order Women* 380.
8. Aristotle, *Poetics* 11.2.
9. Euripides, *Suppliant Women* 239, trans. John Peacock (unpublished).
10. Euripides, *Suppliant Women* 199, trans. John Peacock (unpublished).
11. Tht. 150c–d.

7.
Whose Buddha? Whose Socrates?

1. DL. 2:48.
2. Xen. 1.4.1.
3. Xen. 1.2.
4. Xen. 2.1.

5. Xen. 1.4.
6. Xen. 2.2.
7. Xen. 1.2.
8. Xen. 1.2.
9. *Culavagga* XI. See Horner, *Book of the Discipline*, vol. 5, pp. 401–2, and Batchelor, *Confession of a Buddhist Atheist*, p. 233.
10. *Theragāthā* 1036. See Caroline Rhys Davids, *Psalms of the Early Buddhists*.
11. D. 31.
12. See Graeber and Wengrow, *Dawn of Everything,* for further examples of this phenomenon.

8.
Convenient Fictions

1. Herodotus, *The Histories*, 7:152.
2. See Attwood, "Possible Iranian Origins for the Śākyas and Aspects of Buddhism."
3. S. 4:20. See Batchelor, *Living with the Devil,* for a study of Buddha and Mara.
4. M. 93.
5. M. 28.
6. M. 79.

9.
The Quest for Certainty

1. This oft-cited Tibetan verse is not found in the Pali Canon, though it is entirely in keeping with the early discourses. In the *Numerical Discourses* Sāriputta compares having his understanding tested by Gotama in the same way a goldsmith tests gold. See A. 7:70.

10.
The Tragedy of Being Human

1. Aeschylus, *Agamemnon* 175–180. Sarah Ruden's translation is in Mary Lefkowitz and James Romm, eds., *The Greek Plays*, p. 58.
2. The text of this speech is available at Wikisource: https://en.wikisource.org/wiki/Speech_on_the_Assassination_of_Martin_Luther_King,_Jr.
3. Aeschylus, *Agamemnon* 790.
4. Thucydides, *History of the Peloponnesian War,* 5:89.

11.
A Religion Is Born

1. Phdr. 275a–b.
2. Phdr. 276a, my italics.
3. A. 3:119–139.
4. For Mahānāma, see Batchelor, *After Buddhism*, Chapter 2; for Jīvaka, Batchelor, *After Buddhism*, Chapter 8.

12.
Nāgasena or Nāgārjuna?

1. Plutarch, *Moralia* 28.6; cf. D. 16.
2. Mil. I.6, II.6.
3. Mil. VI.
4. M. 28. See Batchelor, *After Buddhism*, Chapter 3, Section 1.
5. MMK. 24:11.
6. MMK. 13:8.
7. MMK. 15:7. See Chapter 5.
8. MMK. 24:40.
9. The four plays of Euripides which conclude with a version of this refrain are *Medea, Alcestis, Helen,* and *Ecstatic Women (Bacchae)*.

13.
Refining Gold

1. The story of Pukkhusāti is found in the *Dhātuvibhanga Sutta* (M. 140).
2. M. 140.
3. A. 3:101.
4. A. 5:23.
5. A. 3:102.
6. D. 2.
7. From the novel *Casanova in Bolzano*. See Sándor Márai, *Casanova in Bolzano*, trans. George Szirtes.
8. A stock passage cited widely in the canon to describe creativity (*iddhi*). See, for example, D. 2.
9. D. 11.
10. These four steps of creativity (*iddhipada*) outlined by Gotama are similar to the four stages of creativity proposed by the British social psychologist Graham Wallas in the 1920s. Wallas's four stages are preparation, incubation, illumination, and verification. Preparation, like Gotama's aspiration, describes the phase when one identifies and investigates the na-

ture of the problem one desires to solve. Incubation is the period when one no longer consciously thinks about finding a solution but lets it gestate in the unconscious. Gotama likewise compared the process of cultivating virtues to how a hen incubates her eggs by maintaining the right conditions for them to be able to hatch in their own time. Wallas's third stage, illumination, refers to those moments of intuitive insight in which a solution to the problem suddenly dawns, which corresponds neatly to Gotama's "intuition" (*citta*). The fourth stage in Wallas's model, verification, refers to the phase of putting one's intuitions to the test by realizing them as concrete forms in the world. Gotama calls this final step "experimentation," which likewise has to do with testing and figuring out how to make the intuitive solution work.

11. S. 12:65. Cf. Batchelor, *After Buddhism*, pp. 87–89.
12. S. 22:94.
13. See the dialogue with Sīvaka: S. 36:21.

14.
The Truth of Comedy

1. Long and Sedley, *Hellenistic Philosophers*, pp. 14–15. This passage is analyzed in Chapter 15.
2. Aristophanes, *Law and Order Women* 390.
3. See Auden's 1940 poem "Musée des Beaux Arts."
4. Aristotle, *Poetics* 4.1.
5. Quoted in Young-Bruehl (1982), p. 331.

15.
Ataraxia

1. DL. 9:35.
2. DL. 9:38.
3. DL. 9:36.
4. DL. 9:72.
5. DL. 9:40.
6. Sextus Empiricus, *Against the Professors*, 7.87–88.
7. Aetius, *Placita Philosophorum*, i.5.4.
8. DL. 9:61.
9. Long and Sedley, *Hellenistic Philosophers*, pp. 14–15.
10. S. 35:23.
11. DL. 9:76.
12. Sn. 786, 800.
13. DL. 10:12.
14. DL. 10:4.

15. Lucretius, *Nature of Things* 3.1043–49.
16. Lucretius, *Nature of Things* 2.1–33.

16.
A Dialogical Self

1. DL. 6:3.
2. D. 16.
3. *Mahavagga* I.11. See Horner, trans. *Book of the Discipline*, vol. 4, p. 28.
4. Xen. 8.2.
5. DL. 6:6.
6. DL. 6:21.
7. DL. 6:24.
8. D. 24.
9. DL. 6:31.
10. DL. 6:74–75.
11. DL. 7:3.
12. S. 22:59.
13. Dhp. 80.
14. DL. 10:2.

17.
The Foolish and the Wise

1. See Sacks, *Anthropologist in Mars*, Chapter 4.
2. M. 43.
3. M. 43.

18.
Only Tragedy Can Save the City

1. Aristophanes, *Frogs* 65.
2. Aristophanes, *Frogs* 950.
3. Aristophanes, *Frogs* 1020, 1040.
4. Aristophanes, *Frogs* 1490.
5. Xen. *Apology*, 8.

19.
The Great Matter of Birth and Death

1. Nishitani, *Religion and Nothingness*, p. 16.
2. Nishitani, *Religion and Nothingness*, p. 20.

3. *Mahāpadāna Sutta* D. 14.
4. Nishitani, *Religion and Nothingness,* p. 18.
5. Ferguson, *Zen's Chinese Heritage,* p. 199.
6. Ferguson, *Zen's Chinese Heritage,* p. 199.
7. This is the first case in the *Blue Cliff Record.* See Cleary and Cleary, *Blue Cliff Record,* p. 1.
8. A. 7:70.
9. Case 86 of the *Blue Cliff Record.* See Cleary and Cleary, *Blue Cliff Record,* p. 554.
10. Hakuin, *Wild Ivy,* p. 79.

20.
What Is This Thing?

1. Waley, *The Way and Its Power,* Chapter 8.
2. Waley, *The Way and Its Power,* Chapter 8.
3. See Awakawa, *Zen Painting,* for all these paintings.
4. Watson, trans., *Chuang Tzu,* Chapter 3.
5. Watson, trans., *Chuang Tzu,* Chapter 4.
6. M. 10.
7. Watson, trans., *Chuang Tzu,* Chapter 2.
8. Montaigne, *Complete Essays,* 3:12, *On Physiognomy.*
9. Montaigne, *Complete Essays,* 3:12, *On Physiognomy.*
10. Cited in Buswell, *Korean Approach to Zen,* p. 335.

21.
A Cartography of Care

1. D. 16.
2. D. 16.
3. A. 7:71.
4. A. 7:71.

22.
Silencing Socrates

1. Plato's *Euthyphro* is the first dialogue in his *Complete Works.*
2. Euthphr. 3c.
3. See Wilson, *Death of Socrates,* p. 93.
4. Ap. 33b.
5. Ap. 29b–c.
6. Ap. 42a.

23.
A Revaluation of All Values

1. Nietzsche, *Birth of Tragedy*, p. 9.
2. Nietzsche, *Birth of Tragedy*, pp. 54–55.
3. Nietzsche, *Twilight of the Idols and the Anti-Christ*, cited in Emily Wilson, *The Death of Socrates*, p. 198. I have modified the translation following the German text available online.
4. Nietzsche, *Birth of Tragedy*, p. 60.
5. Nietzsche, *The Wanderer and His Shadow*, p. 86.
6. Cited in Mistry, *Nietzsche and Buddhism*, p. 1.
7. Nietzsche, *Thus Spoke Zarathustra*, p. 72.
8. See Mistry, *Nietzsche and Buddhism*, p. 140.
9. See Mistry, *Nietzsche and Buddhism*, p. 17.
10. See Mistry, *Nietzsche and Buddhism*, p. 117.
11. Parkes, *Heidegger and Asian Thought*, p. 94. In 1989, Reinhard May published a book, which later appeared in English under the title *Heidegger's Hidden Sources*. May does not dispute that the major sources of Heidegger's work are to found in his close reading of texts within the Western philosophical and theological traditions, but he convincingly demonstrates how East Asian thought played a major role in inspiring and shaping his ideas. He accuses Heidegger of "unparalleled . . . clandestine textual appropriation of non-Western spirituality," which could have "far reaching implications for our future interpretation of Heidegger's work." May, *Heidegger's Hidden Sources*, p. xviii.
12. Arendt, *Life of the Mind*, p. 174. See footnote on pp. 236–237.
13. Arendt, *Life of the Mind*, p. 175.
14. "Only a God Can Save Us": The *Spiegel* Interview (1966), *Der Spiegel*, Nr. 23 (1976), pp. 193–219. For an English translation: https://www.ditext.com/heidegger/interview.html.
15. Graham Parkes, in May, *Heidegger's Hidden Sources*, p. 106.

24.
For Love of the World

1. See Batchelor, *Confession of a Buddhist Atheist*, p. 53.
2. Arendt, *Human Condition*, pp. 1–3.
3. Young-Bruel, *Hannah Arendt*, p. 49.
4. Grg. 482c.
5. Arendt, *Promise of Politics*, p. 18.
6. MMK. 18:1.
7. Arendt, *Promise of Politics*, pp. xxv, 20–21.

8. A. 4:23.
9. Grg. 482c.
10. A. 6:55.
11. Arendt, *Promise of Politics*, p. 32.
12. Arendt, *Promise of Politics*, p. 33.
13. Arendt, *Promise of Politics*, pp. 33–34.
14. Heisig, *Philosophers of Nothingness*, p. 184.
15. Arendt, *Life of the Mind*, pp. 1, 167.
16. Arendt, *Life of the Mind*, p. 169.
17. Arendt, *Life of the Mind*, p. 198.
18. Arendt's refusal to engage with non-European traditions of thought is all the more surprising given that two of the most influential people in her life, her husband Heinrich Blücher and her lifelong teacher, mentor, and father figure Karl Jaspers, *did* engage with them. At Bard College, Blücher taught a "Common Course" on philosophy, designed to introduce students to the "arch-fathers of the free personality." In addition to Abraham, Jesus, and Socrates, Blücher included Zarathustra, Gotama, and Laozi. Arendt took this course at her home in New York, but it did not lead to sharing her husband's interest in Asian thought. Towards the end of his life, Karl Jaspers had devoted himself to developing a "World Philosophy," which would likewise give equal weight to key thinkers from Asia as well as Europe. As part of this project, he published in 1957 a short book entitled *Buddha, Socrates, Confucius, Jesus: The Paradigmatic Individuals*. The English translation of this book was edited by none other than Hannah Arendt, yet, as far as I can tell, nothing in her subsequent writings suggests that she was influenced by her teacher's vision of a philosophical practice unconstrained by geographic and cultural boundaries.

25.
The Parable of the Snake

1. Cf. *On Cultivation* (A. 7:71).
2. M. 43.
3. This is found in the *Alagaddūpama Sutta*, M. 22.

26.
Death by Mortar and Pestle

1. Phd. 60e.
2. Cri. 44e–45d.
3. Cri. 52a.
4. Ap. 38a.

5. Cri. 54e.
6. Phd. 60a.
7. Phd. 60b.
8. Phd. 118a.

27.
Contemplative Life

1. Arendt, *Human Condition*, p. 28.
2. The traditional sequence found in all Buddhist traditions is: perspective (*diṭṭhi*), imagination (*saṅkappa*), voice (*vācā*), work (*kammanta*), survival (*ājīva*), application (*vāyāma*), mindfulness (*sati*), collectedness (*samādhi*).
3. Rhys Davids and Stele, *Pali Text Society's Pali-English Dictionary*, p. 188.

28.
Active Life

1. A. 6:63.
2. Arendt, *Human Condition*, p. 152.
3. Dhp. 80.
4. Arendt, *Human Condition*, p. 3.
5. Aristotle's definition *zōon logon echon* is found in the *Nicomachean Ethics*, 1098a3–5.
6. Tib: *smra shes don go*. I memorized this definition as a Tibetan Buddhist monk.
7. See Lévinas, *Ethics and Infinity*.

29.
Lucid Confidence

1. S. 55:24.
2. See Watson (1964), p. 100.
3. BCA 8:116.
4. Ferguson, *Zen's Chinese Heritage*, p. 197.
5. Guenther, *Life and Teaching of Nāropa*, pp. 24–25, 37.
6. On Shinran, see Dobbins, *Jōdo Shinshū*, Chapter 3. This citation is from Shinran's *Essentials of Faith Alone*.
7. Shinran, *Collected Works of Shinran*, Chapter on *Shinjin*, 51 and 55.
8. I am indebted to Don Cupitt for his concept of "solar ethics." See Cupitt, *Solar Ethics*.
9. See McGilchrist, *Master and His Emissary*.

30.
An Ethics of Uncertainty

1. S. 35:28.
2. *Cetokhila Sutta*, M. 16.
3. See *The Question Concerning Technology* in Heidegger, *Basic Writings*, pp. 283ff.
4. Hägglund, *This Life*, Chapter 1, Section III.
5. Cited in Hägglund, *This Life* (Introduction). The interview with the Dalai Lama was made by Peter Berglund and broadcast on Swedish Television (SVT), April 10, 1989.
6. BCA 6:123.
7. BCA 6:126.
8. Xen. 4.4.
9. Dhp. 80; Sn. 651–53.

Afterword

1. Obituary: Kenneth McLeish, *The Independent* (London), December 11, 1997, https://www.independent.co.uk/news/obituaries/obituary-kenneth-mcleish-1288109.html.

Bibliography

Aetius. *Placita*. Edited and translated by Jaap Mansfeld and David T. Runia. Cambridge: Harvard University Press, 2023.
Arendt, Hannah. *Eichmann in Jerusalem: A Report on the Banality of Evil*. New York: Viking, 1963.
———. *The Human Condition*. Chicago: University of Chicago Press, 1958/1998.
———. *The Life of the Mind*. New York: Harcourt, 1971/1978.
———. *The Promise of Politics*. Edited by Jerome Kohn. New York: Schocken, 2005.
Aristophanes. *The Complete Plays*. Translated by Paul Roche. New York: New American Library, 2005.
Aristotle. *Poetics*. Translated by Malcolm Heath. London: Penguin, 1996.
Armstrong, Karen. *The Great Transformation: The Beginning of Our Religious Traditions*. New York: Knopf/Doubleday, 2007.
Attwood, Jayarava. "Possible Iranian Origins for the Śākyas and Aspects of Buddhism." *Journal of the Oxford Centre for Buddhist Studies* 3 (2012): 47–69.
Awakawa, Yasuichi. *Zen Painting*. Translated by John Bester. Tokyo: Kodansha International, 1970.
Banks, Jennifer. *Natality: Toward a Philosophy of Birth*. New York: W. W. Norton, 2023.
Batchelor, Stephen. *After Buddhism: Rethinking the Dharma for a Secular Age*. New Haven: Yale University Press, 2015.
———. *Alone with Others: An Existential Approach to Buddhism*. New York: Grove, 1983.
———. *The Art of Solitude*. New Haven: Yale University Press, 2020.
———. *Buddhism without Beliefs: A Contemporary Guide to Awakening*. New York: Riverhead, 1997.

———. *Confession of a Buddhist Atheist*. New York: Spiegel & Grau, 2010.
———. *The Faith to Doubt: Glimpses of Buddhist Uncertainty*. Berkeley: Counterpoint, 2015. First published 1990.
———. "Greek Buddha: Pyrrho's Encounter with Early Buddhism in Central Asia." Review Article. *Contemporary Buddhism* 17, no. 1 (2016).
———. *Living with the Devil: A Meditation on Good and Evil*. New York: Riverhead, 2004.
———. *Secular Buddhism: Imagining the Dharma in an Uncertain World*. New Haven: Yale University Press, 2017.
———. *Verses from the Center: A Buddhist Vision of the Sublime*. New York: Riverhead, 2000.
———, and Martine Batchelor. *What Is This? Ancient Questions for Modern Minds*. Wellington, New Zealand: Tuwhiri, 2019.
Bechert, Heinz, ed. *When Did the Buddha Live? The Controversy on the Dating of the Historical Buddha*. Delhi: Sri Satguru Publications, 1995.
Beckwith, Christopher I. *Greek Buddha: Pyrrho's Encounter with Early Buddhism in Central Asia*. Princeton: Princeton University Press, 2015.
Billings, Joshua. *The Philosophical Stage: Drama and Dialectic in Classical Athens*. Princeton: Princeton University Press, 2021.
Bodhi, Bhikkhu, trans. *The Connected Discourses of the Buddha: A New Translation of the* Saṃyutta Nikāya. Somerville: Wisdom Publications, 2000.
———, trans. *The Numerical Discourses of the Buddha: A Translation of the* Aṅguttara Nikāya. Somerville: Wisdom Publications, 2012.
———, trans. *The Suttanipāta: An Ancient Collection of the Buddha's Discourses together with Its Commentaries*. Somerville: Wisdom Publications, 2017.
Bronkhorst, Johannes. *Buddhism in the Shadow of Brahmanism*. Leiden: Brill, 2011.
Burlingame, Eugene Watson, trans. *Buddhist Legends (Dhammapada Commentary)*. 3 Vols. Oxford: Pali Text Society, 1995. First published 1921.
Buswell, Robert E. *The Korean Approach to Zen: The Collected Works of Chinul*. Honolulu: University of Hawaii Press, 1983.
Cioran, Emil. *The Trouble with Being Born*. Translated by Richard Howard. London: Quartet, 1993.
Cleary, Thomas, and J. C. Cleary, trans. *The Blue Cliff Record*. Boulder: Shambhala, 1977.
Conche, Marcel. *Nietzsche et le bouddhisme*. Encre marine, 2009.
Cooper, John M. *Pursuits of Wisdom: Six Ways of Life in Ancient Philosophy from Socrates to Plotinus*. Princeton: Princeton University Press, 2012.

Bibliography

Critchley, Simon. *Tragedy, the Greeks, and Us.* London: Profile Books, 2019.

Cupitt, Don. *Solar Ethics.* London: SCM Press, 1995.

Dalai Lama. *The Universe in a Single Atom: The Convergence of Science and Spirituality.* New York: Morgan Road Books, 2005.

D'Angour, Armand. *Socrates in Love: The Making of a Philosopher.* London: Bloomsbury, 2019.

Dickey, Eleanor. *Ancient Greek Scholarship: A Guide to Finding, Reading and Understanding Scholia, Commentaries, Lexica, and Grammatical Treatises, from Their Beginnings to the Byzantine Period.* Oxford: Oxford University Press, 2007.

Dobbins, James C. *Jōdo Shinshū: Shin Buddhism in Medieval Japan.* Honolulu: University of Hawaii Press, 2002.

Dover, K. J., ed. *Aristophanes: Clouds.* With introduction and commentary. Oxford: Oxford University Press, 1968.

Dreyfus, Georges B. J. *Recognizing Reality: Dharmakirti's Philosophy and Its Tibetan Interpretations.* Albany: State University of New York Press, 1997.

———. *The Sound of Two Hands Clapping: The Education of a Tibetan Buddhist Monk.* Berkeley: University of California Press, 2003.

Ellis, Robert M. *The Buddha's Middle Way: Experiential Judgement in His Life and Teaching.* Sheffield: Equinox, 2019.

Farnsworth, Ward. *The Socratic Method: A Practitioner's Handbook.* Boston: Godine, 2021.

Ferguson, Andy. *Zen's Chinese Heritage: The Masters and Their Teachings.* Boston: Wisdom Publications, 2000.

Fronsdal, Gil. *The Buddha before Buddhism: Wisdom from the Early Teachings.* Boulder: Shambhala, 2016.

———. trans. *The Dhammapada.* Boston: Shambhala, 2005.

Gampopa. *Jewel Ornament of Liberation.* Translated by Herbert V. Guenther. London: Rider, 1959; 2nd edition, with preface by Chögyam Trungpa, 1970.

Garfield, Jay L., trans. *The Fundamental Wisdom of the Middle Way: Nāgārjuna's Mūlamadhyamakakārikā.* New York: Oxford University Press, 1995.

Gethin, R. M. L. *The Buddhist Path to Awakening.* Oxford: One World, 2001.

Gombrich, Richard. *Buddhism and Pali.* London: Mud Pie Slices, 2018.

———. *How Buddhism Began: The Conditioned Genesis of the Early Teachings.* London: Athlone, 1996.

———. *What the Buddha Thought.* London/Oakville: Equinox, 2009.

Graeber, David, and David Wengrow. *The Dawn of Everything: A New History of Humanity.* London: Allen Lane, 2021

Guenther, Herbert V. *The Life and Teaching of Nāropa*. Boston: Shambhala, 1986.
Hadot, Pierre. *Philosophy as a Way of Life*. Edited by Arnold I. Davidson. Oxford: Blackwell, 1995.
Hägglund, Martin. *This Life: Secular Faith and Spiritual Freedom*. New York: Pantheon, 2019.
Hakuin. *Wild Ivy: The Spiritual Autobiography of Zen Master Hakuin*. Translated by Norman Waddell. Boulder: Shambhala, 1999.
Hall, Edith. *Facing Down the Furies: Suicide, the Ancient Greeks, and Me*. New Haven: Yale University Press, 2024.
Hamilton, Christopher. *A Philosophy of Tragedy*. London: Reaktion Books, 2016.
Hanink, Johanna. "The Great Dionysia and the End of the Peloponnesian War." *Classical Antiquity* 33, no. 2 (2014): 319–346.
Hanner, Oren, ed. *Buddhism and Scepticism: Historical, Philosophical and Comparative Perspectives*. Bochum: projektverlag, 2020.
Heidegger, Martin. *Basic Writings*. Edited by David Farrell Krell. London: Routledge & Kegan Paul, 1978.
———. *Being and Time*. Translated by John Macquarrie and Edward Robinson. Oxford: Basil Blackwell, 1962.
———. *An Introduction to Metaphysics*. Translated by Ralph Manheim. New Haven: Yale University Press, 1959.
Heisig, James W. *Philosophers of Nothingness: An Essay on the Kyoto School*. Honolulu: University of Hawaii Press, 2001.
Herodotus. *The Histories*. Translated by Aubrey de Sélincourt. London: Penguin Classics, 1954. Revised edition with notes by John Marincola, 1996.
Horner, I. B., trans. *The Book of the Discipline*. Vol. 4, *Mahāvagga*. Oxford: Pali Text Society, 1951.
———, trans. *The Book of the Discipline*. Vol. 5, *Cūlavagga*. Oxford: Pali Text Society, 1952.
———, trans. *Milinda's Questions (Milindapañhā)*. Oxford: Pali Text Society, 1963.
Hughes, Bettany. *The Hemlock Cup: Socrates, Athens and the Search for the Good Life*. London: Vintage, 2011.
Huntington, C. W., Jr. "The Nature of the Mādhyamaka Trick." *Journal of Indian Philosophy* 35 (June 2007): 103–131.
Ireland, John D., trans. *The Udāna and the Itivuttaka*. Kandy: Buddhist Publication Society, 1997.
Jaspers, Karl. *Socrates, Buddha, Confucius, Jesus: The Paradigmatic Individuals*. Translated by Ralph Mannheim. Edited by Hannah Arendt. New York: Harcourt Brace Jovanovich, 1962.

Karatani, Kōjin. *Isonomia and the Origins of Philosophy*. Durham: Duke University Press, 2017.
Krznaric, Roman. *The Good Ancestor: How to Think Long Term in a Short-Term World*. London: Penguin, 2020.
Kusan Sunim. *The Way of Korean Zen*. Boston: Weatherhill, 2009.
Kuzminski, Adrian. *Pyrrhonism: How the Ancient Greeks Reinvented Buddhism*. Lanham, MD: Lexington Books, 2008.
Laertius, Diogenes. *Lives of the Eminent Philosophers*. Translated by Pamela Mensch. Edited by James Miller. Oxford: Oxford University Press, 2018.
Lamotte, Etienne. *History of Indian Buddhism: From the Origins to the Śaka Era*. Translated by Sara Webb-Boin. Louvain: Peeters Press, 1983.
Lefkowitz, Mary, and James Romm, eds. *The Greek Plays: Sixteen Plays by Aeschylus, Sophocles, and Euripides*. New York: Modern Library, 2016.
Lévinas, Emmanuel. *Ethics and Infinity: Conversations with Philippe Nemo*. Translated by Richard A. Cohen. Pittsburgh: Duquesne University Press, 1985.
Ling, Trevor. *The Buddha: Buddhist Civilisation in India and Ceylon*. London: Temple Smith, 1973.
Long, A. A., and D. N. Sedley. *The Hellenistic Philosophers*. Vol. 1. Cambridge: Cambridge University Press, 1987.
Lucretius. *The Nature of Things*. Translated by A. E. Stalling. London: Penguin, 2007.
Macaro, Antonia. *More Than Happiness: Buddhist and Stoic Wisdom for a Sceptical Age*. London: Icon Books, 2018
Malalasekera, G. P. *Dictionary of Pali Proper Names*. 3 Vols. Oxford: Pali Text Society, 1997. First published 1938.
Márai, Sándor. *Casanova in Bolzano*. Translated by George Szirtes. New York: Knopf, 2004. First published in Hungarian, 1940.
May, Reinhard. *Heidegger's Hidden Sources: East Asian Influences on His Work*. Translated by Graham Parkes. London: Routledge, 1996.
McEvilley, Thomas. *The Shape of Ancient Thought: Comparative Studies in Greek and Indian Philosophy*. New York: Allworth, 2002.
McGilchrist, Iain. *The Master and His Emissary: The Divided Brain and the Making of the Western World*. New Haven: Yale University Press, 2010.
McLeish, Kenneth. *The Theatre of Aristophanes*. London: Thames and Hudson, 1980.
Mistry, Freny. *Nietzsche and Buddhism: Prolegomenon to a Comparative Study*. Berlin: Walter de Gruyer, 1981.
Montaigne, Michel de. *The Complete Essays*. Translated and edited by M. A. Screech. London: Penguin, 1991.
Ñāṇamoli, Bhikkhu. *The Life of the Buddha*. Kandy: Buddhist Publication Society, 1978.

Ñāṇamoli, Bhikkhu, and Bhikkhu Bodhi, trans. *The Middle Length Discourses of the Buddha (Majjhima Nikāya)*. Boston: Wisdom Publications, 1995.
Nehamas, Alexander. *The Art of Living: Socratic Reflections from Plato to Foucault*. Berkeley: University of California Press, 2000.
Nietzsche, Friedrich. *The Birth of Tragedy*. Translated by Shaun Whiteside. London: Penguin, 1993.
———. *Thus Spoke Zarathustra*. Translated by R. J. Hollingdale. London: Penguin, 1961.
———. *The Twilight of the Idols and the Anti-Christ: or How to Philosophise with a Hammer*. Translated by R. J. Hollingdale. London: Penguin, 1990.
———. *The Wanderer and His Shadow*. Translated by R. J. Hollingdale. Cambridge: Cambridge University Press, 1986.
Nishitani, Keiji. *Religion and Nothingness*. Translated by Jan Van Bragt. Berkeley: University of California Press, 1982.
Nixey, Catherine. *The Darkening Age: The Christian Destruction of the Classical World*. London: Macmillan, 2017.
Norman, K. R., trans. *The Group of Discourses (Sutta-Nipāta)*. Oxford: Pali Text Society, 2001.
Nyanaponika Thera, and Hellmuth Hecker. *Great Disciples of the Buddha: Their Lives, Their Works, Their Legacy*. Edited by Bhikkhu Bodhi. Somerville: Wisdom Publications, 2003.
Onfray, Michel. *Les sagesses antiques: Contre-histoire de la philosophie*. Vol. 1. Paris: Grasset, 2006.
Parkes, Graham, ed. *Heidegger and Asian Thought*. Honolulu: University of Hawaii Press, 1987.
Plato. *Complete Works*. Edited by John M. Cooper, with associate editor D. S. Hutchinson. Indianapolis: Hackett, 1997.
Plutarch. *Moralia*. Translated by Frank Cole Babbitt et al. Loeb Classical Library. Cambridge: Harvard University Press, 1927–2004 (16 volumes).
Rabten, Geshe. *The Life and Teaching of Geshé Rabten*. Translated and edited by B. Alan Wallace. London: George Allen and Unwin, 1980.
———. *The Mind and Its Functions: A Textbook of Buddhist Epistemology and Psychology*. Translated and edited by Stephen Batchelor. Le Mont-Pèlerin: Editions Rabten Choeling, 1992. First published 1978.
Ram Dass. *Be Here Now*. New York: Harmony, 1978. First published 1971.
Rhys Davids, Caroline A. F., trans. *Psalms of the Early Buddhists*. Oxford: Pali Text Society, 1980. Includes the *Theragāthā*, first published in 1909, and the *Therīgāthā*, first published in 1937.
Rhys Davids, T. W., and William Stede. *The Pali Text Society's Pali-English Dictionary*. London: Pali Text Society, 1979. First published 1921–25.

Sacks, Oliver. *An Anthropologist in Mars: Seven Paradoxical Tales*. London: Picador, 1995.

Śāntideva. *The Bodhicaryāvatāra*. Translated from Sanskrit by Kate Crosby and Andrew Skilton. Oxford: Oxford University Press, 1996.

———. *A Guide to the Bodhisattva's Way of Life*. Translated from Tibetan by Stephen Batchelor. Dharamsala: Library of Tibetan Works and Archives, 1979.

Schettini, Stephen. *The Novice: Why I Became a Buddhist Monk, Why I Quit and What I Learned*. Austin: Greenleaf Book Group Press, 2009.

Schumann, H. W. *The Historical Buddha: The Times, Life and Teachings of the Founder of Buddhism*. Translated by Maurice Walshe. London: Arkana, 1989.

Sextus Empiricus. *Against the Professors*. Translated by R. G. Bury. Cambridge: Harvard University Press, 1949.

———. *Outlines of Pyrrhonism*. Translated by R. G. Bury. Amherst, NY: Prometheus Books, 1990.

Shinran. *The Collected Works of Shinran*. Translated by Dennis Hirota et al. Kyoto: Jōdo Shinshū Hongwanji-ha, 1997. Online at www.shinranworks.com.

Slott, Mike. *Mindful Solidarity: A Secular Buddhist–Democratic Socialist Dialogue*. Wellington, New Zealand: Tuwhiri, 2024.

Sopa, Geshe Lhundup, and Jeffrey Hopkins. *Practice and Theory of Tibetan Buddhism*. London: Rider, 1976.

Spiegelhalter, David. *The Art of Uncertainty: How to Navigate Chance, Ignorance, Risk and Luck*. London: Pelican, 2024.

Sujato, Bhikkhu, and Bhikkhu Brahmali. "The Authenticity of Early Buddhist Texts." *Journal of the Oxford Centre for Buddhist Studies* 5 (2014): supplement.

Thucydides. *History of the Peloponnesian War*. Edited by M. I. Finlay; translated by Rex Warner. London: Penguin Classics, 1972.

Tillich, Paul. *The Courage to Be*. London: Fontana, 1962.

———. *The Dynamics of Faith*. New York: Harper and Row, 1958.

———. *Systematic Theology*. Chicago: University of Chicago Press, 1967.

Trungpa, Chögyam, as told to Esmé Cramer Roberts. *Born in Tibet*. London: George Allen and Unwin, 1966.

———. *Cutting Through Spiritual Materialism*. Boulder: Shambhala, 1973.

Tsong-kha-pa. *The Great Treatise on the Stages of the Path to Enlightenment*. 3 Vols. Translated by the Lamrim Chenmo Translation Committee. Ithaca: Snow Lion, 2000, 2002, 2004.

Villa, Dana. *Arendt*. London: Routledge, 2021.

Vlastos, Gregory. *Socrates: Ironist and Moral Philosopher*. Cambridge: Cambridge University Press, 1991.

Yamada, Kōun, trans. *The Gateless Gate: The Classic Book of Zen Koans*. Somerville: Wisdom Publications, 2004.
Yampolsky, Philip B., trans. *The Platform Sutra of the Sixth Patriarch*. New York: Columbia University Press, 1967.
Wallas, Graham. *The Art of Thought*. New York: Harcourt, Brace, 1926.
Walshe, Maurice, trans. *The Long Discourses of the Buddha: A Translation of the Dīgha Nikāya*. Boston: Wisdom Publications, 1995.
Waley, Arthur. *The Way and Its Power: A Study of the Tao Te Ching and Its Place in Chinese Thought*. New York: Grove Press, 1958.
Warder, A. K. *Indian Buddhism*. Delhi: Motilal Banarsidass, 1970.
Waterfield, Robin. *Why Socrates Died: Dispelling the Myths*. London: Faber, 2009.
Watson, Burton, trans. *Chuang Tzu: Basic Writings*. New York: Columbia University Press, 1964.
Watts, Alan. *The Way of Zen*. New York: Pantheon, 1957.
Wilson, Emily. *The Death of Socrates*. Cambridge: Harvard University Press, 2007.
Woodruff, Paul. *Living toward Virtue: Practical Ethics in the Spirit of Socrates*. New York: Oxford University Press, 2023.
Xenophon. *Conversations of Socrates*. Translated by Hugh Tredennick and Robin Waterfield. London: Penguin, 1990.
Young-Bruel, Elisabeth. *Hannah Arendt: For Love of the World*. New Haven: Yale University Press, 1982.

Acknowledgments

Buddha, Socrates, and Us is the result of half a century of study, reflection, conversation, and debate with numerous people, both living and dead, from Asia and the West, who have inspired and embodied the ideas that animate this book.

I am grateful to His Holiness the Fourteenth Dalai Lama for having established the Library of Tibetan Works and Archives in Dharamsala, India, and served as a lifelong beacon in my engagement with Buddhism. For my training in Buddhist thought and practice, I am indebted to my teachers Geshe Ngawang Dhargyey, Geshe Tamdrin Rabten, and Ven. Kusan Sunim.

Among the contemporary Western thinkers who have influenced my work, I need to acknowledge the philosophers Hannah Arendt, Robert Ellis, Martin Hägglund, Martin Heidegger, Gabriel Marcel, and Richard Rorty; the theologians Don Cupitt, John Macquarrie, and Paul Tillich; and the Buddhist scholars Bhikkhu Bodhi, Johannes Bronkhorst, Richard Gombrich, Trevor Ling, Ñāṇamoli Thera (Osbert Moore), and Ñāṇavīra Thera (Harold Musson).

The title of the book was inspired by Simon Critchley's *Tragedy, the Greeks, and Us*.

Without the long-standing support and encouragement

of Helen Tworkov, James Shaheen, and others at *Tricycle: The Buddhist Review*, I doubt whether my career as a writer would have developed as it has. Some of the material in the final chapter of this book first appeared in the Fall 2020 issue of *Tricycle*.

I am particularly grateful to John Peacock, whose extensive knowledge of both Buddhist and Western philosophical thought has helped me find my way through the abundance of textual material on these subjects, and whose language skills have provided me access to ancient Greek sources.

Special thanks to Konrad Mohrmann and Dale S. Wright for their insightful comments on and unstinting support for the project, as well as the two anonymous reviewers of the manuscript for Yale University Press. All of you played a crucial role in helping me to see the book as a whole rather than as a collection of disparate parts.

Also thanks to everyone who read and commented on various drafts of this book while it was still a work-in-progress: Leigh Brasington, Anne-Laure Brousseau, Winton Higgins, Cathryn Jacob, Michael Santi Keezing, Wibo Koole, Ramiro Ortega, Mike Slott, Ronn Smith, Pam Spritzer, Michael Vermeulen, Robert Walsh, Gay Watson, Shannon Whitaker, and Sherry Woods.

By hosting me at the Moulin de Chaves for a personal retreat in December 2020, Martin and Gail Aylward unwittingly helped the structure of the book crystallize in its present form. *Merci beaucoup*.

Deep bows to Shoukei Matsumoto, Kenneth Tanaka, and Ruriko Watanabe for enabling me to consider this work from the perspective of contemporary Japanese Buddhism and introducing me to the life and teachings of Shinran Shonin.

Thanks to Roger Berkowitz for an illuminating post-dinner conversation on the work of Hannah Arendt.

Acknowledgments

I am immensely grateful to my agent Anne Edelstein, who steered this work from conception to publication with her gentle but firm advice, and to Jennifer Banks, my editor at Yale University Press, for her unwavering commitment to my work. Both of you have been instrumental in helping *Buddha, Socrates, and Us* discover its final shape. Likewise thanks to Eliza Childs for her eagle-eyed copyediting.

Regular conversations with my brother David Batchelor and my old friends Guy Claxton, Ken McLeod, and Stephen Schettini have helped keep my eye on the ball. As always, my wife Martine Batchelor has provided constant, unspoken support for everything that appears in these pages.

Index

Abhidharma literature, 34–35, 112–13, 116
absolutism/certainty: asceticism and, 174; as basis of conflict, 54; binary thinking and, 230–31; dangers of, 53; epistemological theories of, 89–90; ethical living in the absence of, 5, 33, 48; Gotama's rejection of, 33; limits of, 169; and omniscience of Gotama, 157; perspective-taking as challenge to, 242–43; quest for/comfort of, 51–52, 83–94, 221–22, 229; Socrates's rejection of, 33; Sutrist school and, 154, 157, 161; uncertainty in relation to, 278–79. *See also* binary thinking; ignorance; opinions; truth(s); uncertainty
active life: Arendt and, 223; contemplative vs., 6, 185, 238–39, 243; and a secular eightfold path, 247–58; Socrates and, 222–23
Aeschylus, 58, 97–101, 116, 165–67; *Agamemnon*, 97–99; *Oresteia* trilogy, 97–98; *Persians*, 99–100
afterlife, 35, 303n7

Ahriman, 77
Alcibiades, 26–28, 31, 106, 198
Alexander the Great, 109, 132–34
Allegory of the Cave, 16–18, 37–38
Ameipsias, *Beard*, 24, 62
Amitābha, 268
Amitāyus, 268
Ānanda, 66, 70–71
Anaxagoras, 32
Anaxarchus, 132
Antisthenes, 140–42, 144, 147
Anurādha, 52
apatheia (dispassion), 145, 147–49. See also *ataraxia*; equanimity
Apollo, 112
aporia, 29, 34. *See also* uncertainty
application, 247–49
*arahant*s (enlightened individuals), 71, 106, 110–11, 113
Arcesilaus, 137
Archelaus, 1, 32, 38, 137
Arendt, Hannah, 6, 214, 216–19, 221–23, 238–39, 252–53, 255, 311n18; *The Human Condition*, 216–17, 239; *The Life of the Mind*, 222–23, 239; *The Promise of Politics*, 218
Aristippus, 137, 140–41

Aristophanes, 5, 32, 64, 127–31, 163–67, 185, 199; *The Acharnians*, 59; *Clouds*, 24–27, 57, 62, 64, 128–29, 131, 199–200; *Frogs*, 59, 164–67, 170; *Law and Order Women (Thesmophoriazusae)*, 59, 128; *Lysistrata*, 128, 166; *Peace*, 127, 166
Aristotle, 6, 22, 49, 131–33, 199, 255, 257
art, 123, 257–58
artisans, 122, 182–85, 252–54
asceticism, 35–36, 70, 71, 119, 133, 136, 142–43, 173, 174
Aśoka, 64, 111
Aspasia, 39–40
Assalāyana, 78–79
ataraxia (untroubledness), 135, 137–39, 148–49, 215. See also *apatheia*; equanimity
Athens: Aristophanes's comic portrayals of, 127–31; author's experiences of, 21–22; and the Melian massacre, 100–101; sociopolitical conditions in, 3, 5, 30–32, 61–62, 163–70; Socrates in, 3, 5, 30–32, 61–62, 196–203. See also Dionysia, in Athens
atoms, 10, 112, 133, 138–39. See also materialism
attachment: as basis of conflict, 54; contingency as hindrance to, 79–80; letting go of, 51; to self, 50. See also opinions
autonomy: as essential to ethical living, 3, 5, 6, 15, 33, 51, 124–25; Socrates's and Gotama's encouragement of, 141. See also solitude
awareness: bodily, 184; of contingency, 80, 221; of fixed opinions/beliefs, 115; of life cycle, 175; of mind and thought, 87, 92, 240–41, 248; nonreactive, 121–22, 137, 147, 149, 150, 175, 240–41; of our place in the world, 275; self-, 202, 272

Batchelor, David, 286
Batchelor, Stephen, *Alone with Others*, 211
Beatles, 10
bhāvanā (cultivation/meditation), 190–92. See also cultivation
Bildung, 92
Bimbisara, 32
binary thinking: concept of existence subject to, 33, 48–51, 54, 59, 154, 176; concept of uncertainty subject to, 230; Diotima's critique of, 40–42; gender fluidity and, 55; language's reinforcement of, 22, 33, 49, 159, 230; letting go of, 33, 40–42, 49–51, 56, 114, 176, 265, 269; logic and, 59, 243–44; moralism attached to, 54; questioning and uncertainty resulting from letting go of, 50, 176; Sutrist school and, 154; Zoroastrianism and, 76–77. See also absolutism/certainty; excluded middle
birth/rebirth: Buddhist conception of, 210; cycle of, 12–13, 107–8, 110–11, 143, 276; escape from cycle of, 13, 107, 173–74, 276; Gotama and, 173–75; no-self and, 110–11; past lives' influence on, 143; uncertainty concerning, 172–73, 175
Blücher, Heinrich, 311n18
Bodhidharma, 176–78, 206
bodhisattvas, 13, 84, 93, 112
body: awareness of, 184; self distinguished from, 145–46
brahmins, 78, 107, 136

Brecht, Bertolt, 131
Bruegel, Pieter, 129–30
Buddha. *See* Gotama
Buddhism: analytical practice of, 34–35, 110, 112–13; Arendt's lack of interest in, 223; author's early encounters with, 9–15, 19–20, 47–48, 83–94; and contingency, 14–15, 79–80; critiques of traditional, 79–80, 93, 102–8, 112–16, 141, 154, 161–62, 175–77, 179–80, 189–90, 192, 195, 210, 229, 231–32, 264–65, 273–74; in diverse contexts, 5–6; early years of, following Gotama's death, 102–7; first precept of, 257; goal of, 107; Greek perspective on, 3–4, 109–13, 134–36, 145–46, 148, 219–20; Heidegger and, 211; in the Hellenistic period, 109–11; Hinayana, 13–14, 19–20, 87, 89, 93; Kyoto school and, 172; Mahayana, 13–14, 19; monastic vs. non-monastic, 71; Nietzsche on, 208–9, 216; non-monastic practice of, 71, 106–7; Persian influences on, 76–77; source material on, 64–66; technological perspective in, 273–74; transformation of Gotama into God in, 157; in Western context, 6. *See also* Centrist (Madhyamaka) school; dharma; Mind-Only (Cittamatra) school; Sutrist school; Theravada Buddhism; Tibetan Buddhism; Zen Buddhism
butchers, 182–84

care: cartography of, 193–94; as essential to ethical living, 20, 42, 52, 105, 115, 160, 191, 232; justice vs., 278–79; openness as foundation of, 160; secular faith and, 275; virtues encompassed by, 193. *See also* love
caste system, 78
catharsis, 131
Centrist (Madhyamaka) school, 86–87, 93, 115, 156–57, 179
certainty. *See* absolutism/certainty; uncertainty
Chapter of Eights, 53, 136–37
character: cultivation of, 120–21, 148; as essence of ethical living, 13. *See also* self; virtue(s)
Christianity, 10–11, 16, 205, 208–9, 211, 216
Cioran, Emil, 108
climate crisis, 5, 167, 271, 275–77, 281–82. *See also* nature/earth
collectedness, 121, 241–42
comedy, 127–31, 165–67
conceptual knowing, 154–57
confidence. *See* lucid confidence
Confucius, 1, 181
Connected Discourses on Stream Entry, 262–63
Connected Discourses on the Undeclared, 48
consciousness, 107, 138, 158, 160, 276, 303n7
consequential reasoning, 218–19
contemplative life/practice: active vs., 6, 185, 238–39, 243; Arendt and, 223; Buddhist, 148–49; embrace of suffering through, 222; Hellenistic philosophers and, 135, 148–49; as human nature, 274–75; and a secular eightfold path, 238–46; Socrates and, 27, 149, 221–23; Sutrist, 86, 90–94; Zen Buddhist, 222. *See also* meditation

contingency: Buddhism and, 14–15, 79–80, 113, 115–16; dharma linked to, 79–80, 113, 116; ethical living in the context of, 4, 80; of history/historiography, 79–80; of life events, 47–48, 116; obstacles to recognizing, 53; of personhood, 147; recognition of, as path to Buddhist practice, 115–16. *See also* uncertainty
courage, 121
Crates of Thebes, 144
creativity, 119–25, 147, 178, 244–45, 306n10
Critias, 31, 106, 170, 198
Crito, 106, 234–37
cultivation, path of, 92–93, 190–92
Cunda the Smith, 31
Cynicism, 141, 143–44
Cyrenaic school, 141
Cyrus the Great, 75, 78

Dalai Lama, 11, 83–84, 154, 275–76
D'Angour, Armand, 197
Daoism, 181–83
Darius the Great, 75
death: Epicurean view of, 138; Gotama and, 2, 31–32, 173–74; of the human species, 271–72; Socrates and, 2, 36, 202, 233–37; uncertainty concerning, 172–73
Delphic Oracle. *See* Oracle of Apollo at Delphi
democracy: in Athens, 61, 163–67, 202; in India, 31; in the present day, 163–64
Democritus, 133–38, 149
Descartes, René, 42
Deshan, 175–76, 264–65
Devadatta, 231
Dhammapada, 54–55

Dhammapada Commentary, 55, 136
Dhargyey, Geshe Ngawang, 11–14, 19
dharma: city governed by principles of, 3, 124; contingency linked to, 79–80, 113, 116; eightfold path and, 227; embodiment of, 51–52, 84, 121; as ethical practice, 5, 15, 18–20, 54, 104–6; existential motivations for having an interest in, 12, 79–80; four paths and, 91–93; four tasks and, 227; Gotama on the practice of, 119–24, 189–90, 229, 231; Gotama's followers' approach to, 104, 107, 110–13; key principles of, 113; metaphysics as obstacle to practice of, 18–20; middle way and, 51–52, 107–8; present-day practice of, 107, 195, 232; secular, 6, 107, 193, 210, 229, 232; as sole teacher of Buddhist practice, 189–90; virtues associated with, 104–6
Dharmarakshita, 111
dialogue: ethical living based on, 5; self understood through perspective of, 6, 146, 207, 218–20, 243, 267, 270, 280; written word vs., 103
Diamond Sutra, 264
Diogenes Laertius, *Lives of the Eminent Philosophers*, 58, 149
Diogenes of Sinope, 142–44
Dionysia, in Athens, 24–25, 57, 60, 62, 64, 96–97, 100–101, 131, 142–43, 170
Dionysus, 24, 96, 165–69, 206–7
Diotima, 39–43
doubt: as component of ethical living, 5; Descartes and, 42; re-

ligion vs. philosophy concerning, 175; Sutrist epistemology and, 90–91; Zen Buddhism and, 173. *See also* skepticism/Skepticism; uncertainty

earth. *See* nature/earth

eightfold path: active limbs of, 247–58; balancing of active and contemplative lives in, 239; contemplative limbs of, 49, 239–46; context for, 192–93; entering and experiencing, 51, 181, 183, 190–93, 249, 262–63, 268; as essential aspect of Gotama's dharma, 190; as ethical living, 190, 239–58; as foundational doctrine, 14; middle way equated with, 49; purpose of, 227; secular, 239–58; traditional sequence of, 312n2. *See also* middle way

Elis, 126–27

Ellis, Robert, 48

embracing life, 267

empathy, 13, 100, 276–77

emptiness: anxiety about, 35; contemplation and, 184; emptiness of, 93–94; Heidegger's "clearing" and, 215; as letting go, 114; meditation and, 12, 84, 86, 114; of mind/judgment, 113–16; Nāgārjuna and, 113–16; possibility associated with, 63, 115; of the self, 86–88; solitude associated with, 53; Sutrist vs. Centrist conceptions of, 87–88, 93–94; *wu-wei* equated with, 183

enlightenment: of the Buddha, 19, 35, 86–87; Mahayana Buddhism and, 13; mindfulness as crucial to, 228; nature of, 93; paths to, 11, 90–93, 154–57; Sutrist conception of, 90–93, 154–57

Epictetus, *Enchiridion (Handbook)*, 149

Epicurus/Epicureanism, 2, 137–38, 148–50; *Chief Maxims*, 149

epistemology, 89–91, 153–57. *See also* ignorance; logic

equanimity, 119–21, 135. See also *apatheia; ataraxia*

ethical living: action/response as constitutive of, 17, 20, 42–43, 48, 50–51, 76, 279–80; autonomy as essential to, 3, 5, 6, 15, 33, 51, 124–25; character as essence of, 13; contingency of contexts for, 4, 80; Daoism and, 181, 183; dialogical basis for, 5; dialogical self and, 146–47; eightfold path as, 190, 239–58; emptiness associated with, 113–16; goals of, 33; Gotama's focus on, 2–3, 33, 43, 48–51, 227, 277–78; logic and, 219–20, 222, 243; love and care as essential to, 20, 42, 52, 105, 115, 160, 232; meditation and, 149–50; metaphysics unnecessary for, 4, 18–20, 33, 43, 158–60; middle way required for, 41; morality and religion distinguished from, 13, 51, 275; recognition of suffering as starting point of, 51; reflection on existential condition as basis for, 12; self-harmony and, 142, 218, 220–21, 228; skepticism compatible with, 230; Socrates's focus on, 2–3, 23, 27–29, 33–34, 41–43, 68, 197–98, 220, 235–36, 277–80; tragedy as the context for, 20, 42, 58; uncertainty as the context for, 4–5, 17, 29, 33–

ethical living (*continued*) 34, 42–43, 48, 51, 55, 277–83; Zoroastrianism and, 76–77
Euripides, 5, 58–64, 97, 116, 128, 163, 165–67, 206–7, 280; *Ecstatic Women (Bacchae)*, 167–70, 207; *Suppliant Women*, 60–63, 69, 163, 169, 202; *Trojan Women*, 100–101, 163
Euthyphro, 196–99
excluded middle, 22, 49, 55–56, 59. *See also* binary thinking
existence: binary thinking about, 33, 48–51, 54, 59, 154; concern with defining/comprehending, 49, 159; of the self, 48–50, 110–11
extinction of species, 271–72

faith, secular vs. religious, 275–76
First Council at Rājagaha, 107
flourishing: in contingent and uncertain circumstances, 20; Democritean philosophy and, 133; as essence/goal of ethical living, 5, 33, 119, 159; as essence of ethical living, 183; labor of others required for, 250; middle way required for, 42; obstacles to, 18, 20, 53–54
formation, path of, 91–92
Forms. *See* Theory of Forms
Four Noble Truths, 14, 161, 176, 191, 209, 229, 231, 273
four paths, 91–93, 191–93, 228
four tasks, 105, 145, 158–62, 191–93, 210, 227–28, 231, 239, 267, 270
freedom: Buddhist conception of, 13, 19, 33, 52, 54, 80, 107, 147; for ethical judgment and living, 33, 54, 80, 107, 113, 122, 137–38, 147; Stoic conception of, 145
free will, 18, 43

Gampopa, *Jewel Ornament of Liberation*, 9–12, 91, 261–62, 266
Gelug tradition, 86
gender fluidity, 55–56
Gestalt image, 243
Goenka, S. N., 88
gold, 120–22
Gotama (Buddha): and the afterlife, 35, 303n7; asceticism criticized by, 143; and creativity, 119–25, 306n10; death of, 2, 31–32; dialogical practice of, 103; discourses of, 6, 35, 43, 65–66, 68, 70–72, 77–79, 89, 102–7, 110, 112–13, 145–47, 218, 229, 270–71 (*see also* Gotama (Buddha): teachings of); on embracing life, 267; encounter with suffering and death, 173–74; enlightened nature of, 19–20; Epicurus compared to, 138; ethical living as the focus of, 2–3, 33, 43, 48–51, 227, 277–78; followers' treatment of the teachings of, 34–35, 70–72, 102–7, 112–13, 141, 161–62, 191, 231; and karma, 76, 157, 247–48; on labor and work, 252–53; life and portrayals of, 32, 64–66, 70–73, 75–77, 120; metaphysics eschewed by, 19–20, 33, 125, 209; middle way sought by, 33, 48–55, 113; Nietzsche on, 208–9; omniscience of, 20, 157; physical reminders of, 112; politics eschewed by, 32; on the practice of dharma, 119–22; public denunciation of, 30–31, 143; questioning as the path of, 33–34, 86–87; relevance of, 5; and Sarakani, 262–63; and the self, 6, 48–50, 110, 145–48, 218–19,

253–54, 280; skepticism of, 154; sociopolitical conditions experienced by, 3, 5, 30–32, 124; Socrates compared to, 2–3, 30–36, 64–65, 68–69; and the sun, 268–69; as a teacher, 13, 15, 37, 48, 125, 141; teachings of, 48–55, 107 (*see also* dharma; Gotama (Buddha): discourses of; Gotama (Buddha): followers' treatment of the teachings of); on true personhood, 220–21; and uncertainty, 33, 195, 278; visual images of, 112

Great Discussion, 158, 193

Greece, in Pali Canon, 77–79

Greek life and thought: Buddhist perspective on, 3–4, 57–58, 98, 109–13, 145–46, 148, 219–20; the gods and, 95–96; pre-Socratic, 213–14; source material on, 64–65; suffering in, 58, 62, 96–97. *See also* Athens; philosophy; tragedy

gymnosophists, 135–36

habits, 2, 50–51, 53. *See also* prejudices

Hadot, Pierre, 149

Hägglund, Martin, 275

Hajime, Tanabe, 212

Hakuin, 178

Hamilton, Edith, 98

Hare Krishna, 10

Hegel, G.W.F., 212

Heidegger, Martin, 180, 210–17, 272, 273, 310n11; *Being and Time,* 210–12, 216, 217

Hellenistic philosophies, 133–50

hemlock, 22, 31, 164, 236–37

Heraclitus, 78

Herodotus, 64, 74–75

Hinayana Buddhism, 13–14, 19–20, 87, 89, 93

Hinduism, 107

Hippias of Elis, 279–80

Hippocrates, 22, 78

history/historiography, 74–75, 79–80

Hsiao, Paul Shih-yi, 213

Huairang, 186

Huineng, 176, 186

ignorance, 90; in ordinary thinking, 19; as origin of suffering, 90; philosophical/Socratic confrontation of, 22, 221, 278; wisdom vs., 40–42. *See also* absolutism/certainty

imagination, 244–46. *See also* creativity

intention, 76, 209, 242, 246–48

International Energy Agency, 282

Ionia, 78–79

Jainism, 107, 136

Japanese thought and art, 172–73, 175, 178, 182, 211–12, 215, 261, 266–68

Jaspers, Karl, 3, 311n18

Jesus, 16, 77, 208

Jeta's Grove, 53

Jīvaka, 106

Judaism, 257

judgment(s): ethical, 20, 33, 41, 51, 54, 77, 104; and the middle way, 40–41, 48; opinions/beliefs as obstacles to, 20, 33, 54, 113; suspension of, 127, 134–37

Jung, Carl, 131

justice, vs. care, 278–79

Kaccāna, 49–50, 52–56, 114, 125, 136–37, 154, 303n3; *The Cell,* 53

Kalama, Alara, 32
karma, 76, 157, 210, 247–48, 276
Kassapa, 66, 70–71, 103, 106, 141, 231
Kennedy, Robert F., 98
killing, injunction against, 257
King, Martin Luther, 98
Korakkhattiya, 143
Koṭṭhita, 158–62, 193, 228
Kusan Sunim, 179–80, 189
Kuṭikaṇṇa, Soṇa, 53
Kyoto school of Japanese philosophy, 172

labor, 249–52. *See also* work
Lamprocles, 68
Lam-rim (Stages of the Path), 11
language: binary thinking reinforced by, 22, 33, 49, 159, 230; conceptual knowing and, 156; Heidegger and, 211; inadequacy/limits of, 34, 50, 182, 230, 279–80; Sutrist study of, 85–88. *See also* silence; voice; writing
Laozi, 2, 181, 183, 186, 213
Leibniz, Gottfried Wilhelm, 212
Lévinas, Emmanuel, 216, 257
Library of Tibetan Works and Archives, Dharamsala, India, 11–14, 261
Linji, 176
logic: binary, 59; Buddhist, 83, 85–87, 89–91, 154, 218; ethics in relation to, 219–20, 222, 243; nonbinary, 243–44; Sophistic, 23, 25. *See also* epistemology; excluded middle
Longtan, 264
love: absent in Heidegger's work, 216; Diotima's teaching on, as a middle way, 40–42; ethical living characterized by, 42. *See also* care
lucid confidence, 262–63, 267–68
Lucretius, 139

Mahākassapa. *See* Kassapa
Mahānāma, 106
Mahayana Buddhism, 13–14, 19, 227
Mara, 77
Márai, Sándor, 122
Marcel, Gabriel, 274
Marcus Aurelius, 144
Marpa, 266
Marx, Karl, 238
materialism, 137–38, 281. *See also* atoms
May, Reinhard, 310n11
McLeish, Kenneth, 285–87; *The Theatre of Aristophanes*, 286
meditation: *bhāvanā* as, 190–91; Buddhist practice of, 13, 32, 84, 91–93, 149–50; and conceptual thinking, 156; difficulties of, 148, 241; and emptiness, 12, 84, 86, 114; ethical living and, 149–50; Greek philosophers and, 149; mindfulness, 88–89; practice of collectedness in, 241–42; Socrates's contemplative absorption compared to, 221. *See also* contemplative life/practice
Melos, 100–101
memory, 102–6
metaphysics: ethical living in the absence of knowledge about, 4, 18–20, 33, 43, 158–60; Gotama's refusal to address, 4, 19–20, 33, 125, 209; Heidegger and, 211, 213; Socrates's refusal to address, 33, 209. *See also* truth(s)
Metrodorus of Chios, 134

middle way: binary thinking avoided by, 48–51; Daoism and, 185; Diotima and, 40–42; eightfold path equated with, 49; as an exercise of judgment, 48; Gotama's pursuit of, 33, 48–55, 113; Nāgārjuna and, 113–15; nirvana associated with, 185; Sutrist abandonment of, 154; between worldliness and unworldliness, 36, 107. *See also* eightfold path; excluded middle

Milarepa, 266

Milinda, 109–11

Mill, John Stuart, 238

mindfulness: importance of, in awakening and ethical living, 228, 239; as limb of eightfold path, 239–41; practices of, 104; technological approach to, 274; types of, 239; and the virtues, 104–5

mindfulness meditation, 88–89

Mind-Only (Cittamatra) school, 179

Mitsotakis, Kyriakos, 1–2

Montaigne, Michel de, 185–86

Monty Python, 25

Nalanda tradition, 86

Nāgārjuna, 113–16, 218–19; *Verses from the Center*, 113–15, 218

Nāgasena, 109–12, 115

Nāropa, 265–66

nature/earth: Arendt and, 216–17; human transformation of and threat to, 254–55, 272–73, 275, 281–82; power of, 96, 167–69, 281; as a source of wonder, 139. *See also* climate crisis

Nazis, 213, 216

Nehamas, Alexander, 208

Nero, 144

Nietzsche, Friedrich, 204–10, 213, 216–17, 269; *The Birth of Tragedy*, 204–5; *Thus Spoke Zarathustra*, 208; *Twilight of the Idols*, 206; *The Wanderer and His Shadow*, 208

nihilism, 51–52, 107–8, 204, 209

nirvana: characteristics of, 13, 53, 107, 135, 137; as goal of traditional Buddhist practice, 13, 20, 71, 90; gold compared to, 122; Heidegger's "clearing" and, 215; middle way associated with, 185; misconceptions of, 113; non-monastic pursuit and attainment of, 107, 111, 267; *wu-wei* equated with, 183

Nishitani, Keiji, 212–13, 222; *Religion and Nothingness*, 172–73, 175

Noble Eightfold Path. *See* eightfold path

nonreactivity: benefits of, 41, 54; gold and, 121; practices for achieving a state of, 148–49; reactivity vs., 20, 54, 92

On Cultivation, 191–92

On Fire, 167, 270–71

On Not-Self, 6, 145–47, 218, 270

On the Simile of the Elephant's Footprint, 79

opinions: confusion/inconsistency of, 38; letting go of, 20, 33, 50; as obstacles to flourishing, 20, 53–54, 221–22. *See also* absolutism/certainty; attachment; prejudices

Oracle of Apollo at Delphi, 22, 58, 96

Pajjota, 49, 52
Pali Canon, 5, 37, 39, 43, 48, 68, 71–72, 74, 77–78, 89, 106–7, 114, 125, 136, 138, 158, 191, 209, 227, 262
Parable of the Arrow, 18–20
Parable of the City, 124
Parable of the Raft, 14–15, 20
Parable of the Snake, 229, 231
parables, 15–16
Parks, Rosa, 255–56
Pasenadi, 32
Peloponnesian War, 23, 27, 30, 61, 100, 127, 163, 170
Pericles, 39
Persia, 75, 78–79, 99–100, 132
persons, concept of great, middling, and lesser, 12–13
perspective: defined, 242; of an ethics of uncertainty, 33–34, 49–51, 54–55, 114–15, 243–44; Gotama on, 33, 49–51, 54–55, 114–15; as limb of eightfold path, 49, 242–44; Socrates's, 33–34; technology as, 272–73; testing one's, 242–43
Philip II of Macedon, 132–33
philosophy: Allegory of the Cave and, 16–17; Aristophanes's comic portrayal of, 24, 27, 62, 129; benefits of, 142; questioning as the essence of, 221; Socrates's practice of, 22–23, 27, 29, 43; wonder as the origin of, 62, 134, 139, 180, 221. *See also* Greek life and thought
Plato: Academy founded by, 132, 137, 141, 142; Allegory of the Cave, 16–18, 37–38; *Defense Speech*, 67, 200–203; and Democritus, 134; dialogues composed by, 199; *Drinking Party (Symposium)*, 26–27, 40, 67, 141, 206; *Gorgias*, 218, 220; *Menexenus*, 39–40; *Phaedo*, 35; *Phaedrus*, 102–3; relevance of, 5; *Republic*, 16, 28–29, 69; Socrates as portrayed by, 34, 37, 140, 149, 199, 208, 218, 236; as source of information on Socrates, 3, 64, 66–67, 69; on suffering, 58; and the technological perspective, 273; *Theaetetus*, 63; theories of, 34, 37, 67, 112, 141, 144
pleasure, 12, 111, 137, 140, 236–37
Plutarch, 109–10, 197
politics: Gotama's renunciation of, 32; the self and, 255–58; Socrates and, 32, 36, 164, 197. *See also* society
prejudices, 50–51, 53, 129, 200, 243. *See also* habits; opinions
pre-Socratic Greek thought, 213–14
psychedelic drugs, 17
Pukkhusāti, 119–20, 125
Purana, 70, 103–4
Pure Land, 268
Pyrrho, 126–27, 132, 134–37, 148
Pythagoras, 22, 78

queerness, 55–56
questioning: absolutism challenged, 33; existential motivations for, 221; Gotama's commitment to, 33–34, 86–87; as response to binary thinking, 50; Socrates's commitment to, 22–23, 33–34. *See also* skepticism
The Questions of King Milinda, 109–13

Rabten, Geshe Tamdrin, 83–87, 93, 113, 175, 189, 212, 227, 269; *The Mind and Its Functions*, 153–54

Ramaputta, Udaka, 32
Ram Dass, *Be Here Now*, 17
reactivity: attaining freedom from, 191, 227–28; creativity vs., 119; dangers of, 18, 92, 270–72; dogmatic certainties as basis of, 54, 114; earth threatened by, 272; examples of, 20; nonreactivity vs., 20, 54, 92, 105
rebirth. *See* birth/rebirth
relativism, 244
religion: benefits and drawbacks of, 18; Buddhism institutionalized as, 102–7, 112; ethical living distinguished from, 13, 51, 275; in Greece, 96, 101; Nietzsche's death of God and, 204, 217; philosophy vs., 175; Socrates and, 196–99
revaluation of values, 204–10
rock-cut temples, 111–12
Royal Shakespeare Company, 286
Rudin, Sarah, 98

sage, characteristics of, 19, 32, 51–54, 178, 181, 185–86, 263–64, 276–77
Śāntideva, *A Guide to the Bodhisattva's Way of Life*, 86–87, 179, 263–64, 276–77
Sarakani, 262–63
Sāriputta, 158–62, 177, 193, 228; *On True Perspective*, 54
Satan, 77
Schelling, F.W.J., 212
Schopenhauer, Arthur, 209, 212
Scylax of Caryanda, 75
Scythians, 76–77
self: attachment to, 50; contingency of contexts for, 80; development of, 253–54, 280; dialogical conception of, 6, 146, 207, 218–20, 243, 267, 270, 280; emptiness of, 86–88; and ethical living, 146–47; existence/non-existence of, 48–50, 110–11; Gotama's teachings on, 6, 48–50, 110, 145–48, 218–19, 253–54, 280; harmony of, 142, 218, 220–21, 228; Nāgārjuna on, 218–19; political expression of, 255–58; tragic portrayals of, 207; and voice, 255–58. *See also* autonomy; character; solitude; virtue(s)
Seneca, 144
Sengai, painting of a rabbit, 182
Sera Monastery, 83, 85, 86, 93, 113
sex, 35–36, 38
Shin (citta, soul, mind), 179–80
Shinran, 266
Shūzō, Kuki, 212
silence, 48–49, 177. *See also* language
single-sex relationships/communities, 55–56
skepticism/Skepticism: in the Academy, 137; and *ataraxia*, 137, 148–49; defining, 134; ethical living's compatibility with, 230; Gotama and, 20, 139, 148, 154; Pyrrho and, 126–27, 133. *See also* doubt; questioning; uncertainty
society: contributions of work to, 252–55; governed by principles of dharma, 3, 124; the self in, 255–58, 280; survival requirements of members of, 251. *See also* politics
Socrates: and the afterlife, 35; Arendt and, 217–23; Bodhidharma compared to, 177–78, 206; children of, 36, 235–37; contemplative absorption of,

Socrates (*continued*)
27, 149, 221; death of, 2, 36, 202, 233–37; and Democritus, 133; dialogical practice of, 103; ethical living as the focus of, 2–3, 23, 27–29, 33–34, 41–43, 68, 197–98, 220, 235–36, 277–80; Euripides and, 58–60, 62–63, 166–67, 206, 280; followers' treatment of the example of, 34–35; Gotama compared to, 2–3, 30–36, 64–65, 68–69; Heidegger and, 213–14; life and portrayals of, 22–28, 32, 58–59, 64–69, 129, 141–42, 149, 196–203, 206, 233–37, 279–80; metaphysics eschewed by, 209; as a midwife of thought, 63, 201; Montaigne on, 185–86; natural philosophy and metaphysics eschewed by, 23, 33, 41, 43; Nietzsche on, 206, 208–9; and political engagement, 32, 36, 164, 197; in popular culture, 22; questioning as the essence of, 22–23, 33–34; relevance of, 5; and the self, 219, 243; sociopolitical conditions experienced by, 3, 5, 30–32, 61–62, 196–203; statue of, 1–2; as a teacher, 37–38, 67–69, 140–41, 196, 201, 287; thought experiment involving Buddhist encounter with, 57–58; and tragedy, 58–59; trial of, 30–32, 36, 67, 196–203; and uncertainty, 28–29, 33–34, 278; wife of, 32, 39, 68, 236; as the wisest man in Greece, 22, 58, 63
solar living, 269
solitude, 53. *See also* autonomy
Sona, 220
Songgwang Sa Monastery, 179, 186
Sophists, 23, 25, 27, 31, 200

Sophocles, 58, 59, 64, 116, 166; *Oedipus the Tyrant*, 11
Soreyya/Soreyyā, 55–56, 136
speech. *See* language; voice
Der Spiegel (magazine), 214–15
Stoicism, 141, 143–45, 148–49
Subhadda, 190
suffering: embrace of, 222; ethical living as response to, 5, 11, 13, 19–20, 43, 51; Gotama's encounter with, 173–74; Greek perspective on, 58, 62, 96–97; ignorance as cause of, 90; insensitiveness to, 20; Nietzsche on, 210; technological approach to, 273; transcendence of, 13, 107. *See also* tragedy
sun, 268–69
Sunakkhatta, 30–31, 143, 231
survival, 249–52
Sutrist school, 87–94, 113, 153–57
Sutta Nipāta, 209
Suzuki, D. T., 223; *Essays in Zen Buddhism*, 213

Takusui, 173, 174
technology, 214–15, 217, 272–75
Telecleides, 59
Thales, 78
Theory of Forms, 34, 112
Theosophy, 209
Theravada Buddhism, 227
Therigatha (Verses of the Women Elders), 39
Theseus, 60–62
thinking, contemplative, 245–46. *See also* binary thinking; logic
Thucydides, 64, 74–75, 100
Thunberg, Greta, 256
Tibetan Buddhism, 11–14, 48, 83–94, 153–54, 189, 255, 261–62
Tilopa, 265

Timon, 134–35
To Kaccāna, 114
To Sigālaka, 72
tragedy: Aristophanes's comedy about, 165–67; comedy in relation to, 129–31; contingency and uncertainty as themes in, 116; decline of, 170–71; ethical living in the face of, 20, 42, 58; Euripides and, 59–60, 206–8; of human existence, 97–101, 129–31, 207; Nietzsche on, 204–6; political value of, 165–71; virtues displayed in, 280. *See also* suffering
Trungpa, Chögyam, 261–62, 269; *Cutting Through Spiritual Materialism*, 261–62
truth: followers' (of Gotama and Socrates) devotion to, 35; Greek tragedy and comedy and, 97, 128–31; skepticism about, 127, 133–34; Socratic pursuit of, 22, 28; tragedy and comedy and, 97; ultimate, 19, 86–88, 93, 153–54; Zoroastrian conception of, 76–77. *See also* absolutism/certainty; Four Noble Truths; metaphysics
Tsongkhapa, 179
Turning the Wheel of Dharma, 145, 270

uncertainty: binary thinking and, 230–31; certainty in relation to, 278–79; ethical living in the face of, 4–5, 17, 29, 33–34, 42–43, 48, 51, 55, 277–83; Gotama and, 33, 195, 278; life cycle as a source of, 172–73, 175; as our existential condition, 270; Socrates and, 28–29, 33–34, 278; Zen Buddhism and, 172–73, 176, 178. *See also* absolutism/certainty; contingency; doubt; skepticism/Skepticism
unification, path of, 92
Unwin, Stephen, 286–87

Vaccha, 48–49, 125, 159
Verses of the Elders, 70
Vesali, India, 30–31
Vidudabha, 30
violence, 35–37
Vipassanā meditation, 273
Vipassī, 174
virāga (dispassion), 147–49
virtue(s): attempts to define, 28–29, 34–35, 279; as embodied actions, 279–80; Gotama's catalog of, 91, 105–6, 191–93; intuitive knowledge of, 34, 279; mindfulness and, 228; personal reflection on, 104–5. *See also* character; self
vision, path of, 92
voice, 255–58. *See also* language

Wagner, Richard, 205
Wallas, Graham, 306n10
Watford Grammar School, 9, 11, 16, 285
Watkins (bookshop), 9
Watts, Alan, 281; *The Way of Zen*, 9–10, 178
the Way (Dao), 181–83
Weishan, Wu, *Confucius and Socrates: An Encounter*, 1
Wilson, Emily, 169
wisdom: consciousness in relation to, 158, 160; cultivation of, 160–61; intuitive knowledge of, 34; Montaigne on peasants', 185–86; philosophy as middle way

wisdom (*continued*)
  between ignorance and, 40–42; religion vs. philosophy concerning, 175; Socrates and, 22, 58, 63, 185
women: in Athens, 39, 128, 130–31; Buddhism and, 84, 265; Gotama's teaching of, 38–39; in the India of Gotama's time, 38–39, 106; significance of, in Greek comedies and tragedies, 130–31; Socrates's philosophical practice and, 38–42
wonder: Arendt and, 221–22; *ataraxia* associated with, 135; Gotama and, 50, 173–74; life as a source of, 62, 134, 174, 180, 182, 221, 272, 274; as origin of ethical living, 178; as origin of philosophy, 62, 134, 139, 180, 221; questioning and not-knowing as means to, 169–70, 175, 283; as source of anxiety, 221–22
work, 252–55. *See also* artisans; labor
writing, 102–4, 177. *See also* language
wu-wei, 183, 215

Xanthippe, 32, 68, 236
Xeniades, 143
Xenophon, 3, 39, 64–69, 106, 140, 208; *Conversations of Socrates*, 66–67, 144, 279–80; *Defense Speech*, 67; *Drinking Party* (*Symposium*), 67, 141
Xerxes, 79, 99

Yousafzai, Malala, 256
Yunmen, 177

Zen Buddhism: anti-establishment character of, 175–77, 264; author's experiences of, 179–81, 186, 189; Bodhidharma and, 176–78; childlike innocence as model for, 173, 174; in China, 176; contemplative practice in, 222; goal of, 178; nonverbal communication in, 175, 178, 182; uncertainty and doubt as characteristic of, 172–73, 175–76, 178
Zeno of Citium, 144
Zhuangzi, 181, 182–83, 185, 213, 223, 263–64
Zoroastrianism, 76–77